UNITED FOR SEPARATION

United *for* Separation

An Analysis of
POAU Assaults
on Catholicism

by LAWRENCE P. CREEDON

and WILLIAM D. FALCON

The Bruce Publishing Company · Milwaukee

NIHIL OBSTAT:

    JOHN F. MURPHY, S.T.D.
    Censor librorum

IMPRIMATUR:

    ✠ WILLIAM E. COUSINS
    Archbishop of Milwaukee
    June 14, 1959

Library of Congress Catalog Card Number: 59–13646

INTRODUCTION

IN ALL public relations of persons or organizations it is *reputation,* not *character,* that counts. The poor reputation of the Church in this country is due to ignorance, not bigotry, and ignorance cannot be dispelled by denouncing it as bigotry. The only effective answer to ignorance is information, education, understanding. . . .

A "good example" set by a Catholic is, of course, altogether admirable, but it is never a sufficient answer to the specific distortions and plain untruths about Catholic loyalty to various vital aspects of American life. The audience that must be reached by the Catholic advocate who tries to improve the popular image of the Church will largely believe at the start that the good Catholic is not genuine, is pretending, forced into hypocrisy by the bishops and the priests. . . .

The Catholic should understand the cause and nature of the ignorance which he so frequently meets. It comes from, and is nurtured by, two sources: (*a*) ancient, familiar, well-liked prejudices reaching back into history; (*b*) the current rewards that are attached to the exploitation of this prejudice. They are, first, *cash,* and, second, *titillation of the emotions,* pleasing to people whose emotional life is narrow, and quite devoid of the thrills that can come from a "courageous" attack on the great Catholic Church. . . .

Catholics and others must give up the idea that there is anything wrong with *controversy.* Controversial discussion and debate is vital and inevitable in a free society; it is the way any free society lives and moves, and either deteriorates or improves. Catholics should stop advising other Catholics to avoid controversy, and should stop answering sincere questions by saying, "We never discuss religion." Informed and courteous controversy is not only respectable; it is the chief medium for the apostolate of the laity. The clergy cannot do this work nearly so well as the laity. They

may know the answers better than the laymen. But the laymen
know the audience better, and a sound knowledge of the audience
is absolutely vital.

                    *   *   *   *

So, as I see it, the first step is to encourage the layman never
to dodge an opportunity to answer a sincere question or an ignorant
or dishonest attack. Opportunities need not be sought; they present
themselves. The answers need not be spontaneous; they can always
be found, and presented in conversation, letter, or pamphlet. Let's
have controversy — informed, courteous, but utterly frank, with
names, dates, and accurate, documented quotations. There is no
other way to improve the image of the Church.

JAMES M. O'NEILL
in *The Commonweal* (July 4, 1958)

ACKNOWLEDGMENTS

THIS volume represents a full-length analysis of the POAU. POAU
has been maligning the Catholic Church for over ten years and
naturally it has not been possible to treat every attack on the
Church in this work. Although we could easily double the number
of case studies considered herein, to do so would be superfluous
and redundant. In its original form, UNITED FOR SEPARATION was
approximately one third again as long as it now appears, but it
was abridged in the interests of economy and readability. Nevertheless, through the assistance and encouragement of many individuals every major area of POAU animosity toward the Church
has been considered.

"Thank you" means so much but is said so quickly and so frequently that when genuine deep-felt thanks are in order the
indebted party quite often is at a loss for an adequate means of

expression. In the nearly three years this volume was in preparation the need for an adequate expression of appreciation was felt
on numerous occasions, but never fulfilled. Yet to publish this
work without public acknowledgment to some of the people who
gave of their time and talent would be a serious error of omission.

Gathering documentation is at best a tedious and time-consuming
task. The help of Mr. Lawrence D. Costello, Mr. Bernard Kelly,
and Mr. Peter Eudenbach certainly made that burden lighter.

One does not need to write a book in order to be able to appre-
ciate the skill and agility of a good typist. During the preparation
of this book we were fortunate to be able to call upon the services
of several such typists — Miss Rita M. Daigle, Mrs. Patricia
Creedon, Miss Ernestine L. Newell, and Mr. George R. Fitzgerald.
A special "thank you" is due my wife and secretary, Barbara A.
Creedon.

To ask a person to critically evaluate a manuscript is a delicate
and demanding request. To Rev. John Doherty and Mr. George
Clancy we express our sincere appreciation.

During much of the preparation of this book we were so fortunate as to have the counsel of Mr. Stanley Lichtenstein, former
research director of POAU. Mr. Lichtenstein also kindly consented
to write for this book a firsthand account of some of his experiences
with POAU.

To Professor James M. O'Neill, author and lecturer, and Rt.
Rev. Msgr. Francis J. Lally, editor of the *Boston Pilot*, we are
most deeply indebted. To Dr. O'Neill, for his faith in our endeavor
expressed through his literary contribution and his critical reading
of the manuscript. To Msgr. Lally, our first benefactor, for his
encouragement and wise counseling and for allowing us unlimited
use of the files of the *Boston Pilot*.

Owing to the nature of this work it was necessary to correspond
with many individuals and organizations in order to get firsthand
impressions of many of the incidents considered. We are therefore
grateful to the following for allowing us to quote from correspondence with them:

Our sincerest thanks to Mr. Stanley Lichtenstein, ex-POAU Re-
search Director; Mr. Claud D. Nelson, National Council of
Churches; Mr. Alan Reitman, American Civil Liberties Union; Mr.
Edgar C. Bundy, Church League of America; Mr. Verne P. Kaub,
American Council of Christian Laymen; Mr. Philip Jacobson, Amer-

ican Jewish Committee; Rev. Dr. Nathan A. Perilman, Congregation Emanu-el, New York City; Dr. R. H. Stafford, Hartford Seminary Foundation, Hartford, Connecticut; Mr. John H. Teder, Dubois County Public Schools, Jasper, Indiana; Mr. Ward L. Quaal, Station WGN, Inc., Chicago, Illinois; and Mr. Edwin J. Holman, American Medical Association.

We also acknowledge the assistance rendered by the many Catholic and government officials referred to herein.

The following newspapers and magazines have extended us the privilege of quoting from them:

The Atlantic Monthly, Time, The New York Times, The Manchester Union Leader, The Catholic World, The Commonweal, America, Our Sunday Visitor, Christianity Today, The Pilot, The Humanist, The Churchman, Christianity and Crisis, and *Commentary.*

In conclusion we would like to recognize our debt to the many publishers and authors who allowed us to quote from their works:

The New American Library of World Literature, Inc.; The Gilmary Society; The Macmillan Company; Joseph F. Wagner, Inc.; Beacon Press, Inc.; Doubleday and Company, Inc.; Farrar, Straus and Cudahy, Inc.; Liguorian Pamphlets; *Journal of the American Medical Association;* Loyola University Press; The American Council of Christian Laymen; The National Catholic Almanac; The Paulist Press; The Catholic Hospital Association; Random House, Inc.; Alfred A. Knopf, Inc.; The Church League of America; The Ave Maria Press; Henry Regnery Company; Dodd, Mead and Company, Inc.; McGraw-Hill Book Company, Inc.; Appleton-Century-Crofts, Inc.; Harper and Brothers; Harvard University Press; The Newman Press; Radio Replies Press; Rinehart and Company, Inc.; Pantheon Books, Inc.; Charles Scribner's Sons; Board of Education of the City of New York; and Rt. Rev. Msgr. Joseph H. Brady.

CONTENTS

ix

PART III — ANALYSIS OF A COMPLETE
POAU ARTICLE

PART IV — THE CHURCH AND THE STATE

UNITED FOR SEPARATION

CHAPTER 1

IMPORTANT REMARKS AND THE
IMPRIMATUR

THE decade commencing with the year 1948 has seen its share of religious controversy. Some of these debates have been fruitful; others have been needless and have caused all kinds of misconceptions. The latter are analyzed in this volume.

Foremost among the groups responsible for fanning the flames of controversy is Protestants and Other Americans United for Separation of Church and State, hereafter referred to as POAU. To some the organization is probably best known for its well-publicized questions (1958) for Catholic presidential candidates. Others are undoubtedly acquainted with it through the actions of Mr. Paul Blanshard, the group's special counsel and author of the controversial volume *American Freedom and Catholic Power* (1949; revised, 1958).

Since 1948 practically every charge ever hurled at Catholics and the Church has been repeated, refurbished, and brought up to date by POAU. Since its founding late in 1947, the organization has been the primary source of aggressive attacks on Catholicism. Although relatively small, it has received increasing publicity in recent years, and is now striving doubly hard to publicize its views on Catholic-orientated issues. It is time, therefore, to consider the validity of the arguments advanced by POAU against the Church, and that is the purpose of this volume.

In order to accomplish that purpose two things must be done. First, a factually correct view of various controversial measures must be presented. Second, the related and equally important problem of establishing a valid judgment of POAU has to be formulated.

1

That these are by no means cut and dried propositions is illustrated by the following contradictory estimates by representatives of two Protestant groups concerning POAU and the charges it presents.

In referring to POAU, the president of the American Council of Christian Laymen has stated:

> This organization is the most vicious anti-Catholic organization to operate in our country since the APA told Americans, . . . that the basement of every Catholic Church held a cache of arms and ammunition being saved for the day when the Catholics would stage a bloody revolution to change our Republic into a Papal State.[1]

An Alabama ministerial association, on the contrary, affirms that POAU:

> . . . is thoroughly American. Any charge that this organization is unpatriotic, un-American and un-Christian is directed not only against the leaders of this organization but against the rank and file of Baptists, Methodists, Presbyterians, Episcopalians, Lutherans, and others who believe firmly in this principle [of separation of Church and State].[2]

In order to clarify the issue as much as possible it is necessary to consider, at least briefly, POAU's historical setting, its history, leaders, aims, and certain internal contradictions that manifest themselves. Then random cases of POAU reporting will be examined. Among other topics, Catholic medical ethics and Catholic presidential candidates are considered. An analysis of one POAU pamphlet, *Rising Tempo of Rome's Demands,* will offer an opportunity to examine such charges as Catholic intimidation of Congress and threatened destruction of the freedom of non-Catholic churches. The last section discusses the basic POAU premises and assumptions that (1) the Church is by her very nature opposed to democracy; (2) that Catholic doctrine demands a close and formal union of Church and State with subsequent restriction of non-Catholic faiths whenever Catholics form a controlling majority; (3) that the First Amendment prohibits all government financial aid to religious groups no matter how small or equal that aid actually is.

---

[1] Verne P. Kaub, mimeographed sheet, *Bishop Oxnam Flunks His Test; Prepared Proof of Anti-Communism not Convincing.*

[2] POAU, *Church and State* (June, 1949), p. 4.

Considering the various citations of POAU statements to be found on the following pages, one may conservatively estimate that well over a hundred instances of POAU reporting are here treated. Is such a number sufficient to enable the reader to reach an accurate conclusion regarding the reliability of POAU? Obviously, it is impossible to analyze every example of POAU-endorsed information. But it is not necessary to consider every example to arrive at an accurate evaluation, just as it is not necessary to drop every chunk of iron into water to reach the conclusion that all chunks of iron sink when immersed in the liquid.

Those who are only partially informed on the issues POAU publicizes usually exhibit the standard reaction of believing POAU because it is felt that if the charges were not true, there would certainly be a detailed Catholic refutation. This volume is such a refutation. There are more worthwhile and pleasant subjects upon which to concentrate than the issues treated by POAU and, to quote an editorial of a highly respected Catholic weekly, the authors ". . . would have preferred to go along as if POAU did not exist but this would have permitted certain . . . people of good will (and innocent of POAU history) to be taken in by its claim and as a consequence ensnared into participation in its program."[3]

If POAU is really an organization that publishes such erroneous information, would not the ordinary person of good will immediately recognize the distortion and thereby render a book such as this unnecessary? The answer is no. Not every man of good will is necessarily fully informed about the subjects which POAU is able to publicize. Thus he can be deceived. The fact that a statement is false does not enable a person automatically to recognize it as such. False arguments often appear to be more convincing, at least on the surface, than true propositions. Truth of its very nature does not force the assent of man. A true statement is not always accepted as such regardless of the good will of the person to whom it is presented.

Your authors have spent two years conducting research in preparation for this book. They have listened to speeches delivered by POAU personnel, have examined every issue of POAU's monthly organ, and have read practically every pamphlet printed by POAU. For more than a year sporadic correspondence has been exchanged

---

[3] *The Pilot* (Boston), 26 October, 1957.

between the authors and the POAU national office.[4] In recognition of this, POAU launched a verbal attack upon the reputation of William Lawrence (the pen name used by your authors). Your authors have been defined by POAU as a journalist who spends much of his time doing "hatchet work" and "smear jobs on POAU." This volume is offered as evidence in vindication of the calumnies leveled at its authors by the POAU.[5]

The final remark of this chapter concerns the *nihil obstat* and *imprimatur* that appear at the beginning of the volume. *Nihil obstat* are the first two words of a formula which is translated as "Nothing stands against [this book being printed]." *Imprimatur* means "Let it be printed." These two phrases are official declarations by Catholic Church authorities that a pamphlet or book is free of doctrinal or moral error. It does *not* mean that everything written in the volume is to be considered as Catholic doctrine — simply that nothing in the book is contrary to such doctrine and morals. Since there are vast areas in which Catholic doctrine and moral teaching have no particular relevance or competence, it is possible for Catholics to disagree on a host of issues and, indeed, they do. This situation explains why the following statement often appears after an *imprimatur*: "No implication is contained . . . that those who have granted the *nihil obstat* and *imprimatur* agree with the contents, opinions, or statements expressed."[6] As a matter of fact, if a work, though written by a Catholic, has nothing to do with Church teaching, the authorities have no interest in it and it is not submitted for the *nihil obstat* and *imprimatur*.

It is hoped that the presence of the *imprimatur* will deter POAU and other groups from deceiving the uninformed of their audience. On not a few occasions POAU has implied, if not directly declared, that a book published by a Catholic without an *imprimatur* is,

---

[4] Correspondence was conducted under a pen name and under the real names of the authors because it was felt POAU would not adequately honor requests from William Lawrence. William Lawrence was the name appearing on articles relative to POAU that appeared in the Catholic press in 1957–1959. This supposition was borne out when questions included in two "Lawrence" letters were not answered. A "Lawrence" letter of 30 April, 1958, containing 86 questions was acknowledged by POAU, but none of the questions were answered for "lack of time." This, despite the fact that on 10 April, 1958, Mr. Archer had indicated in a phone conversation that the POAU Executive Committee would welcome written questions from Lawrence.

[5] For more on POAU attacks on William Lawrence see Chapter 10.

[6] Books published with an *imprimatur* in the archdiocese of New York carry this explanation.

therefore, by that fact itself a book which contains statements that Catholics cannot wholeheartedly endorse and still be good Catholics. Such an implication is not necessarily true. POAU has used such an argument to discredit Professor James M. O'Neill's well-documented volume *Catholicism and American Freedom*, written in reply to the POAU-endorsed volume *American Freedom and Catholic Power*, by Mr. Paul Blanshard. While appearing on a television show, Mr. Blanshard in substance declared that Professor O'Neill's book "was even without an *imprimatur*," thereby implying that Catholics could not in conscience accept the O'Neill rebuttal to Blanshard.[7] POAU's monthly organ also attempted to discredit the O'Neill book in the same way.[8] In another issue of its monthly, POAU attempted to discount some remarks by John Cogely, former executive editor of the Catholic weekly, *Commonweal*:

> It is significant, too, that Cogely, a layman whose writings appear with no Imprimatur or other sanction of his church, and whose views are frequently in conflict with those of Francis Cardinal Spellman and his colleagues in the church hierarchy, is nevertheless selected frequently by secular editors to present the "Catholic" point of view.[9]

It is evident that POAU's argument is at best quite inconclusive, for writings *with* an *imprimatur* may, as we have seen, embody thoughts that "are frequently in conflict with those of Francis Cardinal Spellman and his colleagues in the church hierarchy. . . ." An *imprimatur* does not mean that the book must conform to every opinion of the bishop who granted it; there is no implication ". . . that those who have granted the *nihil obstat* and *imprimatur* agree with the contents, opinions, or statements expressed."[10]

Although rudimentary, the discussion about the *imprimatur* and *nihil obstat* is important. What if someone believed that books bearing a *nihil obstat* were not approved by Catholic authorities? One would conclude that such a person is rather uninformed about the subject and that such a person would not be the best authority upon which to rely for information about things Catholic. In two letters Mr. Glenn L. Archer, POAU national executive director,

---

[7] Channel 5, WABD (New York), 11 p.m., 25 June, 1957.

[8] POAU, *Church and State* (April, 1952), p. 2. Full title prior to July, 1952: *Church and State Newsletter*.

[9] *Ibid.* (June, 1954), p. 7.

[10] See note 6.

affirms that *nihil obstat* means "not approved."[11] His letter of 2 May, 1957, informs us that "The phrase 'imprimatur' means approval." Thus, according to Mr. Archer, a book with the *nihil obstat* and *imprimatur* is one which has the unique distinction of being judged as a "not approved . . . approval."

[11] Glenn L. Archer, a letter, 17 April, 1957.

PART I

POAU: HISTORY, LEADERS,
AIMS, CONTRADICTIONS

CHAPTER 2

ORIGIN, GROWTH, LEADERSHIP
AND SUPPORT OF POAU

POAU's history actually predates the group's official founding on 20 November, 1947, when "organization was voted, officers chosen, a National Advisory Council composed of 125 members . . . authorized."[1] The best histories are derived from original documents. The late Frank H. Yost, a member of the original executive committee of POAU and recording secretary for several years, wrote a paper on the history of POAU. Unfortunately, the organization declined to honor a request for that document made in a letter of 30 April, 1958 (see note 4, Chapter 1). However, an account of the early workings of POAU, based upon Mr. Yost's paper and other documents, is found in Luke E. Ebersole's *Church Lobbying in the Nation's Capital*.[2]

A summary account of how POAU came into existence is found in a chapter called "Special Cause Lobbies."[3] Mr. Ebersole's information was derived from three major sources: (1) from the paper by Frank Yost already mentioned; (2) from POAU's original *Manifesto;* (3) from an interview with POAU's Joseph Dawson. His special section on POAU will now be briefly summarized.[4]

---

[1] POAU, *Church and State* (15 May, 1948), p. 1.

[2] Luke Eugene Ebersole, *Church Lobbying in the Nation's Capital* (New York: Macmillan Company, 1951).

[3] To term POAU a lobby is not an attempt to discredit it. Lobbies serve a useful purpose if properly regulated. Therefore, as Mr. Ebersole remarks on page viii, the function of lobbying "in the legislative process is recognized and accepted." Critics ". . . only aim at the 'selfish-interest' lobbies." Lobbying is defined on page vii of Mr. Ebersole's book as "'all activity [that] either immediately or ultimately, is to influence legislation or administrative action.'"

[4] Ebersole, *op. cit.*, pp. 67–72. Remember that this account was written in 1951.

9

Mr. Ebersole relates that many Americans were surprised when POAU publicly announced its formation on 12 January, 1948. The organization's avowed purpose was proclaimed as the defense of those portions of our Constitution which guarantee religious liberty.

According to Mr. Ebersole's account, POAU's history began in 1941 when Rufus Weaver, secretary of the Baptist Joint Conference Committee on Public Relations, promoted a conference on separation of Church and State. Motivation for Mr. Weaver's action was President Roosevelt's appointment of Myron C. Taylor as personal representative to the Vatican. However, the war interrupted Mr. Weaver's endeavor. But after the war, Mr. Weaver again occupied himself with the subject of religious freedom. In 1946, a meeting was held in the office of Senator Johnston of South Carolina.

Ultimately, Citizens United for Religious Emancipation (CURE) was organized. When Rufus Weaver died, Joseph Dawson became the leader of CURE, an organization dedicated to prevent a union of papacy and government from being included in the Italian Constitution then in preparation. At a CURE luncheon, Charl Williams, of the National Education Association, proposed the goal of doing something for religious liberty in America. On 15 May, 1947, there was a meeting of Protestant churchmen at Washington, D. C., at which Congressmen Joseph Bryson and Brooks Hays played a prominent role.

Finally, at the Methodist Temple in Chicago (20 November, 1947), POAU was officially formed. The officers: Methodist Bishop G. Bromley Oxnam, president; Reverend John A. Mackay, then president of Princeton Theological Seminary, vice-president; and Joseph Dawson, secretary. In addition to those officers, the executive committee was composed of Reverend Louie D. Newton, president of the Southern Baptist Convention; Mr. Elmer Rogers of the Masons; Charl Williams; Frank Yost of the Seventh-Day Adventists; Clyde Taylor of the National Association of Evangelicals; and Arthur Todd of the Christian Scientists.

Between November, 1947, and issuance of POAU's *Manifesto* in January, 1948, Bishop Oxnam resigned the presidency and became a vice-president. E. McNeill Poteat, then president of the Colgate-Rochester Divinity School, was named president. Charles Morrison, former editor of the *Christian Century*, became a vice-president, and E. H. DeGroot, Jr., was appointed treasurer.

Critics of POAU, reported Mr. Ebersole, point to the role played by groups referred to as "Other Americans": Southern Jurisdiction of Scottish Rite Masons (which allegedly supplied over 50 per cent of POAU's first-year budget); American Humanist Association; Ethical Society; American Liberty Association; and the American Jewish Congress.

That is a brief summary of Mr. Ebersole's special section about POAU. But in another part of his volume, Ebersole reports that POAU claims to have many friends in Congress. The names of Senator Olin D. Johnston and Representative Joseph R. Bryson are listed as members of POAU's National Advisory Council. From an interview, Mr. Ebersole learned that Joseph Dawson (vice-president emeritus of POAU) "regards Senators Walter George, Georgia; Robert Kerr, Oklahoma; Willis Robertson, Virginia; Tom Connally, Texas; and Forrest Donnell, Missouri, as legislators who, 'not because of pressure but because of their culture,' could be expected to support the causes represented by the Baptist Joint Conference Committee on Public Relations and by Protestants and Other Americans United."[5] Concerning the Baptist Joint Conference Committee Ebersole reflects: "In addition to lobbying, the primary preoccupation of the Committee has been the movement, Protestants and Other Americans United for Separation of Church and State, which it claims to have instigated and organized."[6]

Mr. Dawson also informed Mr. Ebersole that "the concern of Christian Scientists about religious liberty has been evidenced by official cooperation and support" with POAU. Arthur Todd, manager of a Christian Science Washington office, was a member of the 1948 POAU executive committee. At the death of Todd, the new Christian Science manager, James Watt, took Todd's POAU position "with the approval of the Boston office of the church."[7]

From Congressman Ralph W. Gwinn (27th District, New York) we learn that POAU "was registered as a lobby in 1948 and that year Gilbert L. Parks and E. H. DeGroot [now POAU treasurer emeritus] filed reports. In 1949, DeGroot filed a report and none has been filed since. If they are expending any monies they should send in quarterly reports."[8]

POAU declares that it was "shocked into existence" because of

---

[5] *Ibid.,* pp. 77–78.
[6] *Ibid.,* p. 67. From an interview with Joseph Dawson.
[7] *Ibid.,* p. 61.
[8] Ralph W. Gwinn, a letter to Mr. Lawrence C. Costello, 16 January, 1958.

a statement issued by the Catholic hierarchy (21 November, 1948) which "denounced Separation of Church and State. . . ."[9] But in another publication, POAU affirms that "organization was voted, officers chosen . . ." on 20 November, 1947, over a year prior to the bishops' statement.[10] POAU's *Manifesto* was publicly released on 12 January, 1948, over eleven months prior to the statement that "shocked" it into existence. In basing its existence on the 1948 declaration of the hierarchy, POAU is involved in a historical impossibility. More than this, it bases its founding on a distorted version of the bishops' statement (see Section 1, and note 12 of Chapter 14).

— 1 —

GROWTH

Since POAU started with only a borrowed typewriter, a second-hand desk, a bare room, and a national staff of three people, it is apparent that the only alternative was growth.[11] In July, 1949, POAU reported that a Washington, D. C., "zoning board abuses power" to bar POAU from a new headquarters building on Massachusetts Avenue. The reason for such action is that POAU engages "in propaganda to influence legislation." But POAU argued that other groups were located in the area, "each of which is as much interested in legislation as POAU."[12] A "milestone" in POAU history was achieved in 1950 when the board allowed POAU to reside on Massachusetts Avenue. Also, in 1950, "the federal department of internal revenue . . . determined POAU's status as a non-profit, tax-exempt corporation."[13]

"Three thousand," says the Washington group, "cheer formation of POAU local chapter in Pittsburgh,"[14] and "thousands hear Blanshard at POAU Florida meetings" in 1951.[15] POAU wins "an ever-broadening base of support among church and lay organizations";[16] Admiral H. C. Fitz, United States Navy (Ret.), was elected to POAU's board of trustees;[17] and POAU's work is considered "vital

---

[9] POAU, *Wake Up America!* (1957), p. 2.
[10] POAU, *Church and State* (15 May, 1948), p. 1.
[11] *Ibid.* (June, 1953), p. 1.
[12] *Ibid.* (July, 1949), p. 4.
[13] *Ibid.* (Sept., 1950), p. 1.
[14] *Ibid.* (February, 1951), p. 8.
[15] *Ibid.* (April, 1951), p. 1.
[16] *Ibid.* (February, 1952), p. 3.
[17] *Ibid.* (June, 1952), p. 3.

. . . in this age of . . . increased subversive action by foreign despots in the name of religion"[18] — all this in 1952.

Some of the earliest POAU-compiled statistics indicating the group's growth are reported in June, 1953.[19] "A rough index of POAU's growing influence in the life of the nation is the fact that well over 150,000 Americans received information and literature from the organization during April, a fairly typical month. . . . 24,000 Americans received copies of the April *Church and State Review* . . . 100,000 Americans received pamphlets. . . ." POAU listed thirty-nine states "having functioning chapters, committees and places where meetings have taken place and chapters are in the process of formation." Boston is included on that list. But the Boston chapter, according to its president, did not conduct organizational meetings until the spring of 1957, some four years after its listing by POAU.[20]

On 21 January, 1954, Glenn L. Archer, executive director, informed his audience at Constitution Hall that in six years of existence POAU ". . . has won the respect and confidence of Baptist, Methodist, Presbyterian, Episcopalian, Lutheran, Adventist, Christian Scientist, Assembly of God, Church of God, fraternal bodies, and many other liberty-loving denominations who look to POAU as the 'cutting edge' on the religious liberty front."[21] In 1955, POAU claimed to represent "more than 50,000 American citizens who are dedicated to the task of preserving the First Amendment's principle of church-state separation."[22]

A list of contributors published by POAU in May, 1956, indicates a preponderance of Baptist support with Presbyterians a poor second. Miscellaneous contributors include Sloane House YMCA and the American Waldensian Aid Society, both of New York City.[23] At the Southern Baptist Convention of 1956, Mr. Glenn L. Archer told his audience that POAU "has established more than 50 local chapters throughout the country . . . *Church and State* goes to about 50,000 members each month."[24]

"POAU arouses a sleeping nation" in 1957.[25] The group reports

[18] *Ibid.* (December, 1952), p. 4. Praise by new POAU member.
[19] *Ibid.* (June, 1953), pp. 4–5.
[20] M. J. Marshall (Boston Chapter president), a speech, 20 January, 1958.
[21] Glenn L. Archer, *Out of Bounds* (POAU, 1954), pp. 10–11.
[22] Archer, *Without Fear or Favor* (POAU, 1955), p. 1.
[23] POAU, *Church and State* (May, 1956), p. 7.
[24] Glenn L. Archer, *Separation and Spirituality* (POAU, 1956), p. 10.
[25] POAU, *Wake Up America!* (1957), p. 1.

various activities: "all Seminary graduates are reached in a religious liberty program that covers the nation. . . . POAU has inspired and initiated numerous litigations . . . chapters of POAU have been formed in many cities . . . POAU has reached millions by its new [sic] stories, its literature, its speakers. America is being aroused . . . Community hospitals that have fallen into Roman Catholic hands through 'give-away' deals are being restored to the public [see Chapter 7] . . . more than 250 church congregations were reached by POAU last year . . . more than 9 million pieces of literature have been distributed by POAU. The objective is . . . to show the facts."[26]

At the POAU national conference of 1958 in Atlanta, Georgia, "more than 350 Scottish Rite Masons crowded the dining room of the First Baptist Church . . . to hear Sovereign Grand Commander Luther R. Smith . . . discuss 'POAU After Ten Years.' "[27]

The Americans United, as they sometimes call themselves, noted in January, 1958, that "From nothing it has expanded rapidly until its journal now has a circulation of 60,000 [50,000 in 1956]."[28] Ironically, in May, 1957, Mr. Archer put the circulation at 80,000. If we are to assume that he reports the "facts" accurately, this shows a rapid decrease in seven months of 20,000 and not an increase.[29] Could the figures be padded?

We estimate that the 1959 circulation of POAU's "journal" is 70,000. The claim of possessing the support of "several hundred thousand in every state of the Union" is exaggerated, although it is probably accurate to say that Americans United has one or more local chapters in every state. On certain occasions, it is true that POAU reaches "millions." The group's three questions for potential Catholic candidates (see Chapter 10) were widely reported in the secular as well as the religious press early in 1958. POAU is not becoming smaller; it is growing but not at a rapid rate.

—2—

LEADERS

A brief sketch of POAU leaders will be helpful for a full understanding of the organization.

---

[26] *Ibid.*, pp. 3–6.
[27] POAU, *Church and State* (April, 1958), p. 6.
[28] POAU, *A Ten Year Balance Sheet of the Fight for Separation* (1958), pp. 5–6.
[29] Glenn L. Archer, *The Ramparts We Watch* (POAU, 1957), p. 3.

Mr. Glenn L. Archer, POAU executive director, was associate legislative director for the National Education Association. He is a lawyer and was secretary to the Governor of Kansas from 1939 to 1942.[30] He holds a Methodist preacher's license and has referred to the Catholic Church as "tyranny behind . . . the Purple Curtain of Roman clericalism";[31] has called Italy a country where "clerical tyranny rules";[32] has said parochial school children are "brainwashed";[33] and has accused Catholic hospitals of following a "medieval medical code."[34] But he courageously says that he has "never knowingly discriminated against any man or woman on account of his religious convictions."[35]

Mr. Paul Blanshard, a lawyer and an ordained Congregational minister, is POAU's special counsel. He was an official in the New York City government, but his highest post in the political field was attained while with the State Department in Washington.[36]

Mr. Blanshard, a University of Michigan graduate, considers Catholicism "a dictatorial society within America's democratic society"; the Pope a "Catholic dictator" who exercises a "system of priestly control."[37] POAU termed the 1958 revision of his *American Freedom and Catholic Power* "indispensable," "distinguished," and said it "will help our over-all effort."[38] The *New York Times* review of the original (1949) edition noted that:

> Despite occasional sorties into reality, Mr. Blanshard repeats, often in modern dress, old scandals and old wives' tales that one had assumed were forgotten. . . . Unfortunately, this reviewer can find little in these pages that is not on a very prejudiced plane.[39]

The *Times* review of the 1958 version stated:

> There are some obvious levers for criticism . . . one can find almost anything by plowing through its [Catholic Church] centuries of literature. . . . There is a kind of broad categorizing [which] constitutes its [the book] chief internal weakness. . . .

[30] Archer, *Religious Liberty Reality or Illusion?* (POAU, 1952), p. 1.
[31] Archer, *Let's Think it Through* (POAU, 1956), p. 3.
[32] Archer, *Separation and Spirituality* (POAU, 1956), p. 7.
[33] *Ibid.*, p. 4.
[34] Archer, *The Ramparts We Watch* (POAU, 1957), p. 8.
[35] Archer, *Let's Think it Through* (POAU, 1956), p. 4.
[36] POAU, *Church and State* (February, 1952), p. 4.
[37] Paul Blanshard, *American Freedom and Catholic Power* (1958) (Boston: Beacon Press, 1958), p. xii.
[38] Advertisement of POAU attached to April, 1958, issue of *Church and State*.
[39] *New York Times*, 15 May, 1949.

Mr. Blanshard casts the Roman Catholic hierarchy on one side as the villain, and opposes it to everybody and everything else on the other side as Americanism, which is the real "god" in this book.[40]

C. Stanley Lowell, associate POAU director, is outspoken regarding Catholicism: "the Roman Catholic antenuptial pact is an agreement exacted at gun point";[41] "I do not want my child in a school directed by officials who are under the control of a foreign potentate"; Catholic education "may qualify for citizenship in a totalitarian state, but it is not adequate for a citizen of a free country"; "the Roman Catholic enclave in our country is a divisive influence"; but after this patent disrespect, he can say, "I want my child to respect other faiths[!]."[42]

Mr. Lowell, a Methodist minister, served on the POAU National Advisory Council in 1950, has served on the board of trustees, and is now associate director. He graduated from Yale Divinity School, served as World War II Navy chaplain, and has been twice chosen "Preacher of the Year" at American University.[43]

Messrs. Archer, Blanshard, and Lowell are the "Big Three" of POAU. No other three individuals formulate as much of its policy.

Mr. Blanshard, who in 1959 was on a leave of absence, is considered the most influential person within the group.

A Baptist minister, Dr. Louie D. Newton, is listed as a founder of POAU and is currently its president. In 1952 *Management* magazine named him the " 'nation's outstanding minister.' "[44]

Bromley G. Oxnam, Methodist bishop and vice-president of POAU, is a well-known churchman. The Bishop is reported by POAU to have illustrated that the "political tactics used by the hierarchy . . . were indistinguishable from tactics used by the Communist Party."[45] He has declared that most Americans would be shocked "when they learn the hierarchy is responsible for denying their children higher education standards."[46] Bishop Oxnam charges that Catholic bishops are characterized by "bigotry."[47]

Dr. John A. Mackay, former president of Princeton Theological

---

[40] *Ibid.* (Book Review Section), 23 March, 1958.
[41] C. Stanley Lowell, *Truth Series No. 9* (POAU), p. 6.
[42] Lowell, *Truth Series No. 6*, pp. 2–4.
[43] POAU, *Church and State* (October, 1953; March, 1956), p. 5; p. 8.
[44] *Ibid.* (May, 1953), p. 4.
[45] *Ibid.* (September, 1949), p. 1.
[46] *Ibid.*
[47] *The Pilot,* 21 June, 1958.

Seminary, is a POAU vice-president. When Vice-President Nixon remarked that the Catholic Church was one of the major bulwarks against communism and totalitarian ideas, Dr. Mackay "sorrowfully" affirmed that "the exact opposite is true."[48]

Dr. Charles Clayton Morrison, honorary POAU president and former editor of the *Christian Century*, declared that the Catholic Church pays lip service to "good-will' and "brotherhood"; that the Catholic Church teaches "false tolerance"; has "lulled Protestants to sleep" in the face of grave perils to religious liberty; and has "scared Congress."[49] But in 1914 Morrison wrote, "Why this perennial alarm over 'a Roman Catholic menace'? . . . Much capital is made out of fears and prejudices of many Protestants by fanatical Protestant editors and lecturers . . . The surest way to consolidate the Catholic people . . . is the plan of the Protestant agitator, who . . . sends out these same groundless alarms in the blurred type of cheap, incendiary newspapers."[50]

—3—

SUPPORT AND CRITICISM

A few United States Congressmen apparently support POAU. Representative Tom Steed of Oklahoma spoke at the POAU sixth annual banquet; Representative Eugene Siler of Kentucky has been employed as a POAU attorney; and Senator W. Kerr Scott of North Carolina honored POAU's seventh annual banquet with his presence.

Several church groups have endorsed POAU. In 1950 the Universalist churches of New York State adopted a resolution endorsing the group.[51] In 1951 the Council of Bishops of the Methodist Church, after subjecting POAU's principles, leaders, and methods of work to intensive scrutiny over a period of a year, officially endorsed POAU and called for full financial support.[52] In 1952 the Southern Baptist Convention stated it was "delighted to cooperate with" POAU.[53] In 1954, the Kansas Methodist Conference

---

[48] POAU, *Church and State* (March, 1955), p. 6.
[49] *Ibid.* (November, 1949), p. 2.
[50] *Christian Century*, 23 April, 1914. Cited in *Who's Who in the POAU?* (Huntington, Ind.: Our Sunday Visitor Press, 1951), pp. 36–37.
[51] POAU, *Church and State* (December, 1950), p. 4.
[52] *Ibid.* (June, 1951), p. 1.
[53] *Ibid.* (November, 1952), p. 4.

commended "membership in the organization known as . . . POAU."[54] In November, 1956, Texas Baptists went on record as "heartily endorsing the national program" of POAU.[55] The executive vice-president of the Wisconsin Council of Churches commented in *The Churchman* of May, 1958, concerning "that indispensable organization POAU."[56] Four other pro-POAU articles, including one by Glenn L. Archer, appeared in the May issue.

Although *The Christian Century* gives blanket or invariable support to no organization, it believes POAU to be a "useful organization."[57] The American Council of Christian Churches has never taken an official position concerning POAU. However, this group, which has been criticized by Protestant author Ralph Lord Roy, in his *Apostles of Discord,* has taken one of the main planks from the POAU platform and added a few spikes of its own to it. The Council has gone on record as opposing any and all Catholic presidential candidates in 1960.[58]

The Pilot, a Catholic weekly, affirms that POAU's incessant call is, "Catholics are nice, BUT, Catholics are nice, BUT . . ." The paper declares that "most Protestants in America will have nothing to do with Blanshard bigotry and POAU mumblings. What they are presenting under the thin guise of their rhetoric is the same old anti-Catholic muck-raking which has already been effectively pinpointed by Professor Billington in his admirable study entitled *The Protestant Crusade.*"[59] *America,* the Jesuit weekly, concludes that it is "useless to look at POAU for rational debate."[60] Dr. John J. Kane, the well-known sociologist of Notre Dame, remarks that "there is no lack of literature or agencies actively attacking Catholicism. . . . Such organizations range from the Native Americans of the 1840's through the Know-Nothing Party, the American Protective Association, to Protestants and Other Americans United for Separation of Church and State."[61]

Some non-Catholics have been highly critical of POAU. The

---

[54] *Ibid.* (November, 1954), p. 1.
[55] *Ibid.* (December, 1956), p. 6.
[56] *The Churchman* (May, 1958), p. 2. Ellis H. Dana made the statement. He is on the board of trustees of POAU.
[57] Archer, form letter, May, 1959.
[58] *New York Times,* 3 May, 1959.
[59] *The Pilot,* 11 January, 1958.
[60] *America,* 15 February, 1958, p. 555.
[61] John J. Kane, *Catholic-Protestant Conflicts in America* (Chicago: Regnery, 1955), p. 23.

Church League of America, comments that it "does *not* in any way support POAU. . . . I cannot agree with their thesis and their continual attacks on the Roman Catholic Church."[62]

The *Manchester Union-Leader* of New Hampshire has severely condemned POAU. It has advised against "helping Protestants and Other Americans United for Separation of Church and State spread its doctrine . . . ," and has stated POAU "clumsily betrays its real motives by attacking Catholic beliefs. . . ."[63] Six months later, the same paper declares POAU

> . . . has attacked the beliefs and motives of others in a scurrilous manner.
> . . . If the POAU program were adopted in theory, we'd have only public schools, with all parents denied freedom of selection. . . . No tax exemptions for churches. No Army chaplains . . . moral standards by popular vote. . . . The "Catholic Plot" and its twin — the "Jewish Plot" — are two of the biggest frauds ever perpetrated on the American people.[64]

An official of the National Conference of Christians and Jews has said:

> It seems apparent that the issue of Church and State relationship is frequently exploited for purposes of bigotry, and the fact that POAU draws to itself leaders who seem more concerned with attacks upon Catholics than with the constitutional question of religious liberty has long been a concern of many of us in the National Conference of Christians and Jews.[65]

An official of the National Council of Churches refers to POAU as "a secular and political group," but the "National Council has taken no position and recorded no opinion with regard to it."[66]

The non-Catholic author, Currin Shields, refers to Paul Blanshard "as the high priest of American anti-Catholicism."[67] Another non-

---

[62] Edgar C. Bundy (general chairman), a letter, 7 April, 1958.

[63] Cited in N.C.W.C. News Service release, 13 January, 1958.

[64] *Manchester Union-Leader,* 18 June, 1958. Cited from Editor's note accompanying "Letter to Editor."

[65] Cited in an article by Virgil C. Blum, S.J., "Are Catholics Second-Class Citizens?" *Catholic World* (March, 1958), p. 423. POAU is now seeking to discredit NCCJ and similar groups by implying that they are Catholic fronts. See *Church and State* (February, 1958), p. 2.

[66] Claud D. Nelson, a letter, 12 June, 1959.

[67] Currin V. Shields, *Democracy and Catholicism in America* (New York: McGraw-Hill Book Company, Inc., 1958), p. 25.

Catholic author, Robert D. Cross, mentions several anti-Catholic groups and then in a reference to POAU (see index of his book) he affirms that "all these 'Protestants and Other Americans' have been able to 'unite' against Catholicism, as on no other issue."[68]

According to the assistant director of the American Civil Liberties Union, the "ACLU of course follows with interest much of the work of" POAU. But "with respect to 'support,' there is none."[69]

Social Action in Review, published by the Union of American Hebrew Congregations, has stated

> . . . that POAU seems to have been deflected from its intended purposes into a position of obsessive anti-Catholicism.[70]

Professor Will Herberg, who is described as a "Jewish maverick" by POAU,[71] once wrote in *Commentary:*

> For "Blanshardism" or rather the anti-Catholic animus it articulates, seems to me to constitute a much more serious threat to our democracy than any of the horrendous Romanist plots that Paul Blanshard has been so fond of conjuring up to make our flesh creep.
>
> "This kind of reasoning," says Reinhold Neibuhr, who has never hesitated to criticize Catholic teaching and practice, "is highly damaging to the mutual understanding upon which a democracy must rest. . . ."[72]

In 1957, the Protestant journal *Christianity and Crisis,* whose editorial board is headed by Dr. Reinhold Neibuhr and Dean John C. Bennett (both of Union Theological Seminary, New York), carried an article that was very critical of POAU:

---

[68] Robert D. Cross, *The Emergence of Liberal Catholicism in America* (Cambridge, Mass.: Harvard University Press, 1958), p. 208. This is a good book for those who believe Catholics have agreed or must agree on all subjects.

[69] Louis Joughlin, a letter, 16 April, 1958. Mr. Joughlin is no longer with the ACLU and at the request of the present associate director, Mr. Alan Reitman, Mr. Joughlin's statement is quoted in full:

> "The ACLU of course follows with interest much of the work of 'Protestants and Other Americans United.' From time to time we find ourselves coincidentally interested in the same situation or case. We do not, however, join in action with this group. This separation is not particularly a matter of POAU; the ACLU virtually always conducts its work apart from other organizations because of our specific and single interest in civil liberties.

> "With respect to 'support' there is none.'

[70] *Social Action in Review,* an editorial (February-March, 1959).

[71] POAU, *Church and State* (January, 1958), p. 2.

[72] *Commentary,* "The Sectarian Conflict over Church and State," by Will Herberg (November, 1952). Cited in N.C.W.C. *Bulletin,* 19 November, 1952.

... A totally inexcusable element in POAU literature is its deliberate attempt to make the Catholic position look as incompatible with democracy as possible. . . .

The common unfair tactic of POAU is to quote out of context the most disagreeable statement obtainable and present it as the universal Catholic position. . . .

One approach is to set the priest and laymen against each other and look upon the latter as integers driven by clerical machinations. . . .

It seems, then, that many POAU attitudes can only be explained as the product of an anti-Catholic animus that more sober Protestants would like to avoid.[73]

Earlier in the same year, *Christianity and Crisis* remarked editorially of POAU:

... The most recent action of POAU makes clear that it is undeserving of Protestant support and that its tactics should be repudiated. . . .

This is Protestantism reduced to anti-Catholicism. . . .

... the fact that the group gives the impression of speaking for all Protestants . . . makes it necessary for American Protestants . . . to disassociate themselves in large numbers from an organization so ill-equipped to speak in their name.[74]

Just where the proper evaluation lies is something that the reader must decide for himself. The following pages may help him to crystallize an opinion.

---

[73] Tom Sanders, "Protestantism, Catholicism, and POAU," in *Christianity and Crisis* (16 September, 1957), p. 115 ff.

[74] Editorial, "A Lamentable 'Protestant' Strategy," in *Christianity and Crisis* (1 April, 1957), p. 34.

CHAPTER 3

A VOICE FROM THE PAST?

A GLANCE backward at defunct anti-Catholic groups will afford a deeper appreciation of the true worth of the Americans United. Although the accusations hurled by POAU's predecessors are now recognized by prudent scholars as mere ignorance, POAU raises similar, if not the same, issues whenever the opportunity presents itself.

Ironically, even the name, "Americans United" is not original. In 1844 an anti-Catholic organization known as the Order of United Americans came into being. It enjoyed rapid growth, ultimately numbering some 50,000 members[1] which was POAU's estimated membership after ten years.

The Constitution of the Order of United Americans pledged opposition to all foreign political and religious groups which, it alleged, were operating against the best interests of this country. It also declared the organization to be free from affiliation with any political party.[2]

In 1948, *Church and State Newsletter* (predecessor to *Church and State*) lauded POAU's own unconcern for party politics. It stated:

> POAU abstains from approaching the platform committee of any party with an argument for including separation of Church and State, because we believe that the adoption of any plank in support of the principle should be voluntary, apart from all pressure from groups.[3]

---

[1] Ray Allen Billington, *The Protestant Crusade, 1800–1860* (New York: Rinehart and Company, Inc., 1952), pp. 336–338.
[2] *Ibid.*, p. 336.
[3] POAU, *Church and State Newsletter* (August, 1948), p. 4.

Apparently, however, the POAU hierarchy does not read what it writes, for in 1956 *Church and State* bemoaned the fact that letters to the two major political parties urging inclusion of Church-State separation planks in the party platforms were barely acknowledged. It further noted that neither party acted on this POAU request.[4] Regardless of the merits of such a plank one thing is clear, POAU stands in open contradiction of its 1948 position.

The Order of United Americans was succeeded shortly before the Civil War by the Know-Nothing Party. Members of this group had to be Protestant and had to swear they would work to bring about the defeat of any elected official who was Catholic. The Know-Nothing ritual reads in part:

> . . . Roman Catholicism has been making steady and alarming progress in our country. You cannot have failed to observe the significant transition of the foreign born and the Romanists from a character quiet, retiring or even abject, to one bold threatening, turbulent, and even despotic. . . . A sense of danger has struck the great heart of the Nation. In every city, town, and hamlet, the danger has been seen and the alarm sounded.[5]

Although a century has past since the "alarm" was sounded, the Pope still resides in the Vatican, whereas the Know-Nothings are found only in history books. Unmindful of this, POAU alleges that it was "shocked into existence" by certain actions of the hierarchy, has worked to "arouse a sleeping nation," and has "set in motion forces that may yet preserve religious liberty and the equality of churches before the law."[6] Mr. Lowell elaborates, asserting "that the hierarchy of the Roman Catholic Church is now engaged in a supreme effort to change the nature of . . . America. . . ." He continues, ". . . Catholicism with its 33 million members . . . is a divisive influence in America today."[7]

During the Civil War and for a few years thereafter the country was relatively free of organized anti-Catholic groups. Catholic soldiers, both Union and Confederate, distinguished themselves in battle. Monuments to the dead of Gettysburg and other battlegrounds attest to this. Predecessors of the nuns to whom POAU

---

[4] POAU, *Church and State* (September, 1956), p. 6.
[5] Gustavus Myers, *History of Bigotry* (New York: Random House, 1943), pp. 187–188.
[6] POAU, *Wake Up America!*, p. 1.
[7] C. Stanley Lowell, *A Summons To Americans* (POAU), p. 6.

refers as "brain-washed" and as operating hospitals on "medieval" standards also distinguished themselves. More than 600 American nursing nuns served in combat-area hospitals.

In the chronology of hate groups the Know-Nothings were replaced by the American Protective Association. Founded in 1887, the APA had a twofold purpose centered on the primary theme of anti-Catholicism. It hoped to stem the tide of Catholic immigration, and to preserve the American public schools from alleged subversion by Catholics. The president of the APA accused Catholics of carrying on "a policy of positive antagonism to the American public-school system."[8] The APA endorsed an anti-Catholic pamphlet first published in 1883 which warned of a "Romanist movement directly intended for the overthrow . . ." of the public schools. It also termed the hierarchy a "separate political government, despotic, tyrannic, absolute and anti-republican."[9]

Although it has tried, POAU has not improved on these fabrications. Mr. Lowell remarks, "the public schools . . . have become the number one enemy of the hierarchy . . . they have worked to discredit and undermine the public schools."[10] In numerous publications POAU falsely alleges that Catholics are "coerced" into going to parochial schools and are encouraged to boycott the public schools. See Chapter 8 for a complete analysis of this.

POAU has rejuvenated the "despotic," "tyrannic" cries of the APA and its predecessors. In 1949 Mr. Blanshard urged Catholics to fight "against the autocratic power of the Roman hierarchy. . . ."[11] In 1957 he lamented that "Catholic people are slaves to a dictatorial power."[12] In March, 1953, *Church and State* spoke of the "anti-democratic clerical machine that operates in virtually every community" and in April, 1958, it criticized "certain anti-democratic policies of the Catholic hierarchy."

The APA and POAU have even envisioned and warned of "Catholic control" of vital channels of government. Among other things the APA asserted that many U. S. cities had fallen under the yoke of Romanism, that leading government officials took orders

---

[8] Gustavus Myers, *op. cit.*, p. 236.

[9] *Ibid.*, p. 220.

[10] C. Stanley Lowell, *A Summons To Americans* (POAU), p. 6.

[11] POAU, *Church and State* (November, 1952), p. 5.

[12] Paul Blanshard, a speech (Boston), 24 September, 1957.

from Jesuit priests, that Washington was overrun by Catholics, and that the Army and Navy had been "Romanized."[13]

Absurd as they are, POAU repeats similar fantasies. Mr. Blanshard charged "the power of the clergy has taken Massachusetts out of the United States."[14] In 1948 POAU lamented the ". . . disproportionate number of Catholics in Washington offices."[15] Although not charging that the armed forces are controlled by Catholics, it has objected to the number of Catholic chaplains serving with the armed forces.

In 1958 it became concerned because all chiefs of chaplains in the armed forces were Catholic priests.[16] Although one priest's normal tour of duty came to a close shortly thereafter, POAU still visualized a mythical Catholic plot. In January, 1959, it charged "discrimination" in the promotion of chaplains. The Navy was in a precarious position according to POAU as "questionable" practices had placed Catholic chaplains in top posts. POAU feared that high-ranking Catholic chaplains would "use their power to promote their fellow priests and to discourage Protestant influence in the armed services."[17] The National Council of Churches did not see the grave danger portrayed by POAU. An NCC official stated that after securing the most competent information available he was satisfied that "nothing more than coincidence" was involved in the promotion of Catholic chaplains. He added that it was the same "coincidence" that had put Protestant chaplains in the majority "over and over."[18] According to the Assistant Secretary of the Navy the promotion board which recommended the chaplains for promotion was composed of seven chaplains — five Protestant and two Catholic.[19] How can discrimination be charged when a Protestant majority freely recommends more Catholics for promotion than it does fellow Protestants?

The American Protestant Defense League and the American Council of Christian Churches have been more recent predecessors of POAU. The APDL termed the Church "an exclusive power,

---

[13] Gustavus Myers, *op. cit.*, pp. 224–225, 228.
[14] Paul Blanshard, *op. cit.*
[15] POAU, *Church and State* (August, 1948), p. 3.
[16] *Ibid.* (July, 1958), p. 6.
[17] *Ibid.* (January, 1959), p. 4.
[18] Claud D. Nelson, NCC, a letter, 14 January, 1959.
[19] Richard Jackson, Assistant Secretary of the Navy, a letter, 3 February, 1959.

scheming, intransigent, domineering . . . and . . . far more dangerous than ever communism was. . . ."[20] In 1945 the Council of Christian Churches stated that the greatest enemy of freedom that faces man today is Catholicism. It concluded that between Catholicism and communism, communism was the better choice.[21]

POAU follows with its barrage. Mr. Lowell comments:

> The crude medievalism of the hierarchy, its uncritical obstructionism . . . invites Communism and encourages it. . . . Communism and Romanism are expressions of the dogmatic mind.[22]

This chapter is not an attempt to apply the invalid guilt-by-association technique to POAU, to mark it as a "hate group" or as "anti-Catholic." The purpose here is simply: (1) to indicate its historical relationship to past organizations which had at least a superficial resemblance to it; (2) to demonstrate that the charges emanating from POAU headquarters are not entirely unique in history.

That some POAU charges resemble the attacks of past anti-Catholic groups does not necessarily mean that POAU is also to be termed anti-Catholic. Perhaps those charges common to both the APA and POAU are somehow valid today although they were not valid in the past; perhaps POAU has uncovered new and valid evidence that substantiates the group's otherwise anti-Catholic conclusions. The remainder of this study will show this not to be true.

---

[20] Ralph Lord Roy, *Apostles of Discord* (Boston: Beacon Press, 1953), p. 164.
[21] *Ibid.*, pp. 165–166.
[22] C. Stanley Lowell, *Truth Series No. 4* (POAU), pp. 2–3.

CHAPTER 4

THE LEADERS—A SUBTLE
CONTRADICTION

POAU is not a communist organization, nor is it sympathetic toward communist doctrine, but it is understandable why some people invalidly conclude otherwise.

POAU continually attempts to identify communism and Catholicism; that the one is to all practical purposes the same as the other. By what standard does the Washington group arrive at such a conclusion? We are interested in discovering this standard because we shall use it, in conjunction with statements by POAU leaders, to judge POAU's own political preference. In other words, is POAU pro-communist according to POAU standards of judgment?

The primary norm whereby POAU attempts to equate Catholicism and communism is guilt by association. If communism is in a certain country and the Catholic Church is in the same country, then the Church is either communistic or else the Church's doctrine is not a bulwark against communism. If there are fascists in Italy, then the Catholic Church is fascist, etc.:

> . . . it [Catholic Church] has been Fascist in Fascist Italy, Nazi in Nazi Germany, Falangist in Falangist Spain, Hapsburg in Hapsburg Austria . . . Emperor-worshipping in Hirohito's Japan.[1]

Against Mr. Nixon, Dr. Mackay argued that Catholicism was not a major bulwark against communism; in fact, "the exact opposite is true" because "Latin countries where the Roman Catholic Church has been the predominant religious influence have been

---

[1] POAU, *Church and State* (October, 1949), p. 3.

breeding grounds for communism."[2] Mr. Archer informs us that "where the Roman Catholic Church is dominant, you regularly find Communism stronger than where the free churches are dominant."[3] Mr. Lowell states "the Roman Catholic faith is no bulwark against Communism. . . . Roman Catholic dominated lands reek with Communists."[4]

POAU also tries to associate Catholicism with fascism, nazism, etc., by drawing attention to the Vatican concordats with Mussolini, Hitler, and others:

> . . . the list of Vatican concordats or agreements with totalitarian regimes — Mussolini's, Hitler's, Franco's, Roja's, Trujillo's . . . demonstrates that the Holy See has had no real compunction about making deals with dictators, though it has naturally had greater difficulty getting along with "red" than "black" forms of totalitarianism.[5]

The implication is that Catholicism is "getting along with" red totalitarianism.

This norm of guilt by association is the POAU norm. Of course, such a standard is ridiculous. Just because event A (Catholicism) happens to be located in the same geographic area as event B, (communism), does not mean that A is B, nor that A causes B, nor that A is not a bulwark against B. Perhaps B exists in spite of A. For example, "in the United States, illiteracy is higher in rural than in urban areas. Illiteracy is higher among Negroes than whites. Yet rural areas in the United States, and most American Negroes, are Protestant."[6] Does this mean that Protestantism is the same as illiteracy, that it causes illiteracy, and that it is not a bulwark against illiteracy? Of course not; many factors, unrelated to Protestantism, are involved. The same is true of Catholicism and communism (see Chapters 6 and 15 for more on this topic).

However, POAU uses that fallacious norm when concluding about Catholicism and communism. Some typical judgments by POAU after using its own rules of logic are: "a choice between clerical authoritarianism [Catholicism[7]] and Communistic totalitarianism

---

[2] *Ibid.* (March, 1955), p. 6.

[3] Glenn L. Archer, *Out of Bounds* (POAU, 1954), p. 9.

[4] C. Stanley Lowell, *Truth Series No. 4* (POAU), pp. 2–3.

[5] POAU, *Church and State* (January, 1957), p. 4.

[6] John J. Kane, *Catholic-Protestant Conflicts in America* (Chicago: Regnery, 1955), p. 177.

[7] Glenn L. Archer, *Separation and Spirituality* (POAU, 1956), p. 7.

is no choice at all . . .";[8] ". . . two roads . . . the one to Moscow, and the other to Rome . . . neither one of these roads is safe since the end of both is tyranny";[9] ". . . Catholicism and Communism . . . the only change is in the authority at the top. The rest is all the same."[10]

By applying the POAU principle of guilt by association to some POAU statements and actions, the organization can be made to condemn itself.

Reuben H. Markham, a Protestant, commented on a postwar visit to Russia by the current POAU president as follows:

> One illustration of an attempt by American Protestants to shine up to Bolsheviks is found in a 48-page booklet published by the American Russian Institute and distributed by the Communist Party throughout the U. S. It is called *An American Churchman in the Soviet Union* and was written by the Reverend Louie D. Newton, "with an Introduction by Bishop G. Bromley Oxnam. . . ." A superficial or a careful reading of this booklet leaves the impression that Dr. Newton is trying to persuade American Protestants that the Bolshevik Government grants religious freedom. . . .
>
> Dr. Newton . . . asked a group "of chosen leaders of the Baptists in the U. S. S. R." to give "a statement over their signatures for publication in the U.S."
>
> Naturally, they did. What would the secret police have done to them if they had refused to give a statement, praising the Soviet regime! Does it not occur to you that the Bolsheviks invited Dr. Newton to Russia precisely in order to get such a propaganda statement published in America?[11]

The American Russian Institute, publisher of the Newton booklet, was cited as a communist front in 1944[12] and is on the Attorney General's list (1949). The Institute's function is "specializing in pro-Soviet propaganda."[13] At a public hearing of the House Committee on Un-American Activities (21 July, 1953), Representative Clardy remarked about Newton's booklet: "I find it a considerable

---

[8] Archer, *Let's Think it Through* (POAU, 1956), p. 15.

[9] Archer, *Separation and Spirituality* (POAU, 1956), pp. 9–10.

[10] Lowell, *op. cit.*, p. 3.

[11] Reuben H. Markham, *Let Us Protestants Awake* (Madison, Wis.: American Council of Christian Laymen, 1949), p. 42.

[12] Edgar C. Bundy, *Collectivism in the Churches* (Wheaton, Ill.: Church League of America, 1958), p. 79, n. 6. Also: Attorney General's list of 1 November, 1955.

[13] *Guide to Subversive Organizations and Publications* (Washington: U. S. Government Printing Office, 1957), p. 16.

apology for the Soviet Russian system." Bishop Oxnam replied, "If you do, let me say I do not."[14]

Bishop Oxnam, POAU vice-president, appeared for several hours before the House Committee on Un-American Activities. He admitted belonging to several communist-front organizations. However, either he was associated with such groups before formal citation by the Attorney General, or he simply did not realize that the groups had been designated as communist. For those reasons the House Committee concluded, ". . . this Committee has no record of any Communist Party affiliation or membership by Bishop Oxnam."[15] But POAU's standards are not the same as the Committee's. If a Catholic bishop possessed Oxnam's record, one need not be a genius to predict POAU's conclusion about Catholicism and communism.

While testifying Bishop Oxnam admitted he was chairman of the Massachusetts Council of American Soviet Friendship (cited communist in 1944). The Russian spy, Dirk J. Struik, asked him to join.[16] He belonged to the Medical Bureau and North American Committee to Aid Spanish Democracy (communist)[17] and the American Committee for Spanish Freedom (communist).[18] Although former communist Manning Johnson in 1934 declared that Harry F. Ward was "the Red religious dean of the Communist Party in the religious field"[19] and although Bishop Oxnam knew Ward was a communist as to objective,[20] the Bishop praised Ward in 1939 and did not publicly reveal that Ward was a communist because of his personal friendship with him.[21]

Directly referring to Bishop Oxnam, Mr. Markham reflects:

> What kind of Christian leader is he who tells us a state bus for private schools [Constitutional] would lead us to enslavement and yet cooperate in an attempt to make us believe that there is "complete religious liberty" in the USSR where the state controls every form of thought expression, every school, every church building, every publishing concern, every youth organization . . . ?[22]

What conclusion can be drawn from this comment by Dr. John A. Mackay, current POAU vice-president, when POAU logic stand-

---

[14] Public Hearing of House Committee on Un-American Activities (21 July, 1953), Cited in full by *U. S. News and World Report* (7 August, 1953), p. 141.

[15] *Ibid.*, p. 142.
[16] *Ibid.*, p. 44.
[17] *Ibid.*, p. 107.
[18] *Ibid.*, p. 109.

[19] *Ibid.*, p. 127.
[20] *Ibid.*, p. 125.
[21] *Ibid.*
[22] Markham, *op. cit.*, p. 44.

ards are used? On 16 January, 1950, the *Presbyterian Outlook* and Religious News Service reported Mackay had

> . . . urged that the United States recognize the Communist government of China. . . .
> Dr. Mackay . . . said recognition was justified on the following grounds:
> (1) The excellent behavior of the Communist armies in their conquest of the China mainland;
> (2) The fact that missionary activity had not been disrupted;
> (3) The widespread view that China's communism will take a "different expression" than in Russia and Eastern Europe;
> (4) The overwhelming support of the people for the new regime, based largely on their disillusionment with the Nationalist government.[23]

In December, 1956, Dr. Mackay urged the National Council of Churches to send a delegation of American churchmen to Red China.[24] Herbert A. Philbrick, the famed F.B.I. counterspy, declared:

> . . . I was certainly shocked to read the Presbyterian Letter issued last October, 1953, over the signature of Dr. Mackay, and to note that it . . . contained all of the fundamental premises of Marxism, Leninism, and Stalinism concerning class struggle, imperialism, force and violence, and revolution."[25]

Paul Blanshard, POAU special counsel, was a socialist for a number of years during the 1920's. In July, 1932, Blanshard wrote an article entitled "Socialist and Capitalist Planning" which appeared in *The Annals of the American Academy of Political and Social Science:*

> If we gained control of the American government, we probably would begin with a complete revision of the national governmental system. We would do one of two things. We would write an amendment to the Constitution . . . or we would abolish the Constitution altogether. . . .[26]

Mr. Blanshard hoped "to accomplish that revolution peacefully"[27]

---

23 Edgar C. Bundy, *Collectivism in the Churches, op. cit.,* pp. 185–186.
24 *Ibid.,* p. 188.
25 *Ibid.,* p. 250, a letter to Mr. Bundy, 10 June, 1954.
26 *Who's Who in the POAU?* (Huntington, Ind.: Our Sunday Visitor Press, 1951), p. 102.
27 *Ibid.,* p. 103.

but writing in *Christian Century* in October, 1932, he concluded, "there would be some bloodshed."[28] In 1933, *World Tomorrow* described Blanshard as an "ex-Socialist." Mr. Blanshard's reaction was published in *World Tomorrow* (9 November, 1933):

> You wave your arm and dismiss us from the fellowship of American Socialism because we have recognized the obvious fact that the Socialist Party is dying and because, pending arrival of a new third party, we have decided to fight for progressive leaders and progressive programs within the older parties.[29]

Harvey M. Matusow, a former communist, told the Senate Security Sub-Committee that although Mr. Blanshard expressed a dislike for communism, the latter's book, *American Freedom and Catholic Power*, "adhered to the Communist line in relation to the Catholic Church."[30]

The *Protestant* has been cited as a magazine "which has faithfully propagated the Communist Party line under the guise of being a religious journal," and "with an eye to religious groups the Communists have formed religious fronts such as the . . . *Protestant*."[31] The publication was described in 1946 by former communist Louis Budenz in these words:

> . . . the Communists everywhere planned to wage war on the Catholic Church as the base for obliterating religion. . . . this policy was developed . . . namely, the program to arouse the Protestants against the Catholics in this country as a means of causing confusion in the United States . . . the magazine whose name is *Protestant* but which is engaged largely in being anti-Catholic. . . .[32]

In the *Protestant,* issue of June-July, 1942, these familiar names are listed as "editorial advisors": Louie D. Newton, G. Bromley Oxnam, John A. Mackay, Edwin McN. Poteat (former POAU president), and Rufus W. Weaver (POAU forebear of early 1940's; see Mr. Ebersole's account in Chapter 2).[33]

---

[28] *Ibid.* From the *Christian Century,* 19 October, 1932.

[29] *Ibid.,* p. 102.

[30] *The Pilot,* 6 September, 1952.

[31] *Guide to Subversive Organizations and Publications, op. cit.,* p. 107. Cited in 1944. The *Protestant* is identical with the *Protestant Digest.*

[32] Public Hearing of House Committee on Un-American Activities, *op. cit.,* p. 101. The *Protestant* was also cited in 1942, according to this Hearing.

[33] From Appendix IX (p. 1455) of a Report of the Special Committee on Un-American Activities, House of Representatives, 78th Congress, Second Session, on Communist Front Organizations with special reference to The National Citizens Political Action Committee.

Thus, the group that professes to defend our Constitution identifies itself with a movement working contrary to the principles of the same Constitution. Such is the contradiction when POAU *"logic"* is employed.

Once again, the author has no valid evidence to indicate that POAU is communistic. Many relationships with communist groups by POAU leaders may be explained by the fact that the leaders of POAU have in common with communist agencies the purpose of discrediting the Catholic Church at every opportunity. Such a purpose undoubtedly blinded certain POAU leaders to the true nature of the communist organizations to which they lent their names.

CHAPTER 5

AIMS AND INTERNAL CONFUSION

THE aims of POAU are concisely enumerated by the organization's *Manifesto* which was revised in January, 1957. A little study, however, demonstrates that these aims and other statements of purpose have been repeatedly contradicted by the organization in action.

POAU's "single and only purpose," the *Manifesto* says, "is to assure the maintenance of the American principle of separation of church and state upon which the Federal Constitution guarantees religious liberty to all the people and all churches of this Republic."[1] Again, "the First Amendment is the legal safeguard against unholy church and state alliances in America. To defend this law is POAU's purpose for existence."[2] The pertinent portion of the First Amendment that POAU professes to defend is: "Congress shall make no law respecting an establishment of religion, or prohibiting the free exercise thereof." The *Manifesto* explains how POAU intends to accomplish its self-appointed task. It states:

> Although the existing situation cannot be dealt with save by frankly taking account of the specific sources from which violations of the First Amendment originate . . . our [POAU] undertaking is *not* primarily directed toward these sources, *but toward those agencies of government — local, State, and Federal — which weakly yield to their demands.*[3] [Emphasis added.]

It is clear, then, that POAU's "single and only purpose" is to "assure the maintenance" of the First Amendment by directing action primarily toward "agencies of government."

[1] POAU, *A Manifesto* (January, 1957), p. 3. See also *Church and State* (October, 1948), p. 3.

[2] Glenn L. Archer, *Let's Think it Through* (POAU, 1956), pp. 14–15.

[3] POAU, *A Manifesto* (January, 1957), p. 4.

The preceding chapters make it clear that POAU has contradicted its "single and only purpose" a multitude of times. However, a few more examples of these contradictions are appropriate at this time.

POAU obviously has objected to foreign aid to Italy, "that Roman Catholic land," because funds given there are merely subsidizing "religious tyranny."[4] What has foreign aid to do with the First Amendment? Nothing whatsoever. POAU continually disapproves of Catholic marriage regulations.[5] Mr. Archer accuses one hundred and fifty Catholic groups — among them, the Catholic Press Association, Catholic Actors Guild of America, Knights of Columbus, and the National Catholic Educational Association — of "the reshaping and control of religious liberty."[6] Here Mr. Archer is certainly not directing POAU's action toward "agencies of government." Mr. Lowell, for his part, disapproves "of the kind of narrow, limited teaching done by brain-washed nuns and priests in parochial schools."[7] Again, and with no discernible relevance to POAU's "single and only purpose," he refers to the Catholic Church's "slavish adherence to educational and medical codes long since outmoded. . . ."[8] Just what have these things to do with the prohibition placed on Congress by the First Amendment?

This interesting declaration of Mr. Archer's may help to "clarify" POAU's real target: "the *only* real question before us is: *Do Roman Catholic* practices and philosophies help or harm the American tradition and law of church-state separation?"[9] Similarly, "in 38 states public funds are 'leaking' to various activities of this *one* denomination [Catholic]. To stop these leaks is POAU's job."[10] (Emphasis added.) What has happened to "those agencies of government" toward which POAU is supposed to be directing its attack? In view of such remarks, this *Manifesto* statement is farcical: "Our [POAU] controversy is not with any church, Roman Catholic or any other."[11]

If lawmakers or agencies of government act in a way displeasing to POAU, the organization does not direct its "controversy" pri-

---

4 Glenn L. Archer, *Separation and Spirituality* (POAU, 1956), p. 6.

5 Archer, *The Growing Struggle for Religious Liberty* (POAU), p. 2.

6 *Ibid.*

7 C. Stanley Lowell, *Truth Series No. 6* (POAU), p. 3.

8 Lowell, *Truth Series No. 4*, pp. 2–3.

9 Glenn L. Archer, *Let's Think it Through* (POAU, 1956), p. 5.

10 POAU, *Wake Up America!* (1957), p. 5.

11 POAU, *A Manifesto* (1957), pp. 9–10.

marily toward them. Instead, POAU excuses the government officials by such statements as "if they oppose, their political life will be endangered" by "Roman Catholic political pressure."[12] "There is a need of someone with courage . . . to equalize the [Catholic] pressures levelled against government officials. . . . Roman Catholic political action is on the march."[13] If legislatures irk POAU, they are described as receiving a "naked threat" by a hierarchy that urges Catholics "to destroy the political career of any man who dared to oppose."[14] We should logically expect POAU to flatly oppose this "Roman Catholic political action" that "is on the march." Therefore, we are amazed to read that Mr. Archer is responsible for another POAU contradiction: "the fault I find is not with the . . . right of Roman Catholics to organize for political action."[15]

It is obvious that POAU's actions are not limited to its "single and only purpose."

POAU affirms that it "does not concern itself with the religious teaching . . . of the many churches. . . ."[16] But Mr. Archer tells his POAU associates, "one must study its [Catholic Church's] laws and dogmas, its aims and actions all carefully designed to envelop whole nations and cultures."[17] But in another pamphlet, Mr. Archer declares, "the fault I find is not with the Roman Catholic faith (that is none of my business)."[18] Thus, Mr. Archer finds no fault with alleged Catholic dogmas (which are not supposed to be treated by POAU) that will "envelop whole nations and cultures." In an early 1958 letter, Mr. Archer expressed his desire to help sue any Catholic bishop or priest for "slanders" arising "out of that church's *teaching* . . ." concerning the marriage of Catholics outside the Church.[19] (Emphasis added.) An Americans United meeting in Boston on 20 January, 1958, heard an address on "Modern Problems of Mixed Marriages."[20] A POAU pamphlet by Mr. Blanshard criticallly "interprets" various articles of Canon Law: Canons 1094, 1099, 1399, 1374, 218, 127, and 128. In addition, Blanshard dis-

[12] Glenn L. Archer, *Let's Think it Through* (POAU, 1956), p. 9.
[13] *Ibid.*, pp. 9–10.
[14] POAU, *Church and State* (July, 1957), p. 1.
[15] Glenn L. Archer, *Let's Think it Through* (POAU, 1956), p. 13.
[16] POAU, *A Manifesto* (1957), p. 1.
[17] Glenn L. Archer, *Separation and Spirituality* (POAU, 1956), p. 8.
[18] Archer, *Let's Think it Through* (POAU, 1956), p. 13.
[19] Archer, a letter, Spring, 1958. See Chapter 12 for full quotation.
[20] J. Murray Marshall (Chapter president), form letter, January, 1958.

cusses various Catholic documents including an encyclical of Pope Leo XIII.[21] It might be objected that Canon Law does not pertain to religious teaching but rather to internal practices of the Catholic Church. However, POAU promises that "it is no part of our purpose to . . . oppose the teaching or internal practices of the Roman Catholic Church."[22]

POAU "does not concern itself with the . . . forms of worship . . . of the many churches."[23] But in Blanshard's book, which POAU describes as "indispensable,"[24] we read that ". . . many parish priests are operating on the lower level of popular superstition . . ."; that "the scapular racket has been promoted with renewed zeal . . ."; that "scapulars are not so important in the Catholic system of sorcery . . ."; that priests practice ". . . traditional magic . . ."; that the priest acts in ". . . the role of a 'good' magician. . . ."[25] This last quote is in apparent reference to the transubstantiation of the Mass. We are now far away from POAU's "single and only purpose," the defense of the First Amendment.

POAU "does not concern itself with the . . . ecclesiastical organization of the many churches."[26] But POAU-recommended reading declares that ". . . the American Catholic hierarchy . . . has never been assimilated. . . . it is an autocratic moral monarchy. . . ."[27] Mr. Lowell also treads upon "forbidden" ground when he critically remarks that "the rulers are the hierarchy; the ruled are the masses. . . . This is dictatorship with no chance for check or balance of any kind."[28] He also complains that the Pope is a "foreign potentate,"[29] and Mr. Blanshard is wary because the Pope is "a non-American."[30]

POAU alleges it does "not question the right of churches to operate their own school systems. . . ."[31] But it states "the principle [contained in the First Amendment] is being undermined by

---

21 Paul Blanshard, *Truth Series No. 5* (POAU), pp. 2–5.

22 POAU, *A Manifesto* (1957), pp. 3–4.

23 *Ibid.*, p. 3.

24 POAU advertisement attached to *Church and State* (April, 1958).

25 Paul Blanshard, *American Freedom and Catholic Power* (Boston: Beacon Press, 1958), pp. 263, 250, 245, 49.

26 POAU, *A Manifesto* (1957), p. 3.

27 Paul Blanshard, *American Freedom and Catholic Power* (1958), *op. cit.*, p. 14.

28 C. Stanley Lowell, *A Summons to Americans* (POAU), p. 3.

29 Lowell, *Truth Series No. 6* (POAU), p. 4.

30 Paul Blanshard, *Truth Series No. 5* (POAU), p. 3.

31 Glenn L. Archer, *Without Fear or Favor* (POAU, 1955), pp. 22–23.

15,000 parochial schools with their four million pupils taught by 120,000 garbed sisters. It is being destroyed in the minds of many additional children who are being brain-washed. . . ."[32] To say that Catholic schools brain-wash pupils in order to undermine a portion of the Constitution is about as close to shouting "Down with Catholic schools" as one can get without actually using those words.

POAU informs us that it is "no part of our purpose to propagandize the Protestant faith. . . ."[33] But it is really no surprise to find POAU involved in another contradiction: "Churches and ministers of your community will want to make the best use of Reformation Sunday. . . . POAU will be glad to send you copies of Reformation Sermons by G. Bromley Oxnam . . . and Glenn L. Archer; also a litany, 'The Faith of a Protestant.' "[34] The patriotic defense of the First Amendment seems to have been supplanted by Mr. Archer's sermons.

Other statements of POAU, aside from those describing its purpose, are contradictory. Mr. Lowell writes: "I want my child to learn the secret of American splendor — E Pluribus Unum [out of many, one]."[35] In the same pamphlet: "I will not send my child to a parochial school because I do not believe in dividing America."[36] First he recognizes that a unified nation is able to contain diverse groups and institutions; then he is afraid of "dividing America" by sending his child to one of these diverse institutions.

One POAU pamphlet handsomely declares that "the Roman Catholic people . . . are standing with us. . . . We believe that most of them are quite as appreciative of American freedom and quite as devoted to it as we are."[37] Again, "we should not be critical of the Catholic people as loyal Americans. . . ."[38] If the "Catholic people" are "loyal Americans" and "are standing with" POAU, why does the Americans United criticize Archbishop Richard J. Cushing for "straining the credulity of the American people" by asserting that "American Catholics rejoice in the separation of church and state"?[39] Why does it criticize Catholic lay groups of

---

[32] Archer, *Separation and Spirituality* (POAU, 1956), p. 4.

[33] POAU, *A Manifesto* (1957), p. 3.

[34] POAU, *Church and State* (September, 1950), p. 3.

[35] C. Stanley Lowell, *Truth Series No. 6* (POAU), p. 5.

[36] *Ibid.*, p. 4.

[37] Glenn L. Archer, *The Growing Struggle for Religious Liberty* (POAU, 1956), p. 6.

[38] POAU, *Church and State* (June, 1951), p. 6.   [39] *Ibid.*, p. 3.

"teachers . . . lawyers . . . doctors . . . nurses . . . actors . . .
policemen of that faith" as trying to "tie up the larger groups of
which they are a part and render them ineffectual in the struggle
for freedom"?[40] If Catholics are "loyal Americans," why this insulting POAU reference to the Catholic laity: "the Catholic shock
troops are ordered by their headquarters in Rome to adopt the
attitude of the Pharisee. . . the dictator of the Vatican seeks world
unity through conquest"?[41]

At a Boston lecture, Mr. Lowell was asked if he objected to
laws declared constitutional by the Supreme Court. He replied
in the negative.[42] POAU as a whole does not object to Supreme
Court decisions, for in regard to religious education POAU "pro-
nouncedly approves any arrangement consistent with the Constitution as interpreted by the Supreme Court. . . ."[43] Also, POAU
affirms, "we stand with the Supreme Court."[44] As usual, there are
inconsistencies appearing elsewhere in POAU literature. For instance, POAU referred to a Supreme Court decision concerning
bus transportation for parochial school students as follows: "the
wisdom of such a concession can still be debated . . . the 4 judges
who dissented . . . applied the First Amendment more rigorously
and reasonably than the majority."[45] In addition, POAU objects
to granting Federal funds for sectarian hospitals[46] and free textbooks for pupils of private schools;[47] both of which have been
declared Constitutional by the Supreme Court. But when the Catholic hierarchy (1948) questioned the logic of a Supreme Court opinion, POAU exclaimed that "the Hierarchy dared to denounce the
U. S. Supreme Court and sought to inflame and confuse the public
mind. . . ."[48] POAU apparently thrives on double standards.

Within one paragraph Mr. Blanshard is able to refer to the
"lofty moral purpose" of the Catholic Church and also describe
the Church as following "intolerant policies."[49] POAU finds it pos-

---

[40] Glenn L. Archer, *The Growing Struggle for Religious Liberty* (POAU, 1956), p. 4.

[41] POAU, *Church and State* (March, 1950), p. 4.

[42] C. Stanley Lowell, a lecture, Arlington Street Church, Boston, Mass., 8 p.m., 23
September, 1957.

[43] POAU, *Church and State* (October, 1948), p. 3.

[44] Glenn L. Archer, *Without Fear or Favor* (POAU, 1955), p. 2.

[45] *Ibid.*, p. 19.

[46] *Ibid.*, p. 26.

[47] POAU, *A Manifesto* (POAU, 1957), p. 12.

[48] POAU, *Church and State* (January, 1949), p. 2.

[49] Paul Blanshard, *American Freedom and Catholic Power* (1958), p. 4.

sible to speak of the Church's "cultural domination"[50] in Spain,
and also to report that "Spanish youths ignore church movie censors."[51] The First Amendment is really lost in the shuffle at this
point. One begins to wonder if it were ever in the deck.

Mr. Blanshard advances norms whereby anti-Catholic groups
can be recognized: "anti-Catholic fanatics in the forties and fifties
of the last century caricatured priests . . . and spread wild rumors
that Catholics were plotting to capture the country by armed re-
bellion."[52] POAU's monthly organ portrays a stupid-looking individual dressed in a cassock and wearing what appears to be a
beret but is supposed to be a biretta. He is gazing at a document
labeled "Constitution of the U. S.," and the drawing is captioned
"Unfamiliar Catechism."[53] In 1957, POAU published a drawing
of a priest in a cassock and alb and wearing a biretta. In his left
hand he holds a breviary and in his right a paintbrush, with which
he is painting "censored" on sixteen books. Regarding "armed re-
bellion," POAU apprehensively asks its readers, "is Roman Catholic
action in the armed forces now going underground?"[54] When POAU
read that some Catholics wanted to organize a war veteran group,
it reported approvingly that "Dr. Clyde R. Miller of New York at
once addressed a letter to President Truman protesting that this
indicates that a group in America, under the influence of a foreign
power (the Vatican) with possible undisclosed aims, could utilize
this force for private ends, even to subversive purposes."[55]

After glancing at this wide range of POAU activities, the reader
will realize that any resemblance of the following POAU statements
to fact is purely fictitious: "the only people who do not like POAU
are those who do not like the First Amendment,"[56] and "we [POAU]
are the Roman Catholic's best friend."[57]

What is the significance of these contradictory statements issued
by POAU? Why has POAU declared that its "single and only purpose" is the maintenance of the First Amendment; that it will
"not concern itself with the religious teaching, the forms of worship,

---

[50] Glenn L. Archer, *Let's Think it Through* (POAU, 1956), p. 10.

[51] POAU, *Church and State* (June, 1951), p. 5.

[52] Paul Blanshard, *American Freedom and Catholic Power* (1958), p. 12.

[53] POAU, *Church and State* (November, 1949), p. 3.

[54] *Ibid.* (October, 1956), p. 7.

[55] *Ibid.* (August, 1948), p. 4. Miller was on POAU National Advisory Council.

[56] Glenn L. Archer, *Let's Think it Through* (POAU, 1956), p. 15.

[57] Archer, *Separation and Spirituality* (POAU, 1956), p. 12.

or the ecclesiastical organization," etc., of the Catholic Church or any other? Obviously, the organization has consistently violated those pious aims. Why were those righteous statements of purpose issued in the first place? The answer is in one vital word: support. By setting up the patriotic aim of defending the First Amendment, POAU has produced the flag around which the boys can rally. To charges of "bigotry" and "anti-Catholic" POAU replies by pointing to the noble words of its *Manifesto*. Occasionally the strategy works and authorities find themselves giving support to POAU. Such was the case with Rev. Dr. Ralph Lord Roy, author of *Apostles of Discord*. Roy's work is a study of recent Protestant hate groups in which he treats POAU, but "emphatically" excludes it from the ministry of hate. He does concede that there are individuals within POAU that might lead it into the arena of anti-Catholicism. In exonerating the organization from "hate" charges, Dr. Roy refers to the *Manifesto*, stating it made "meticulous disavowals of any anti-Catholic animus" and that POAU's objection to Catholicism was not born out of hate but under the banner of "Separation of Church and State."[58]

Roy terms a "hate group" as

. . . any group . . . seeking to exploit the Christian religion to justify racial or religious hate, discord and dissension. . . .[59]

Dr. Roy differentiates between "anti" and "hate" groups and Mr. Archer states "persons who use the word 'anti-Catholic' to characterize POAU are speaking carelessly. . . . The record shows that POAU has adhered to the principles and objectives . . . in its *Manifesto*. . . ."[60] After a comparison of the actions of other groups cited by Roy (e.g., the American Protestant Defense League) and the actions of POAU it is left to the reader to decide whether Roy's partial definition of hate groups is more representative of POAU than is the *Manifesto*.

Since POAU's actions do not coincide with its purposes and objectives, assent should not be given to any POAU declaration until the situation has been investigated. When this is done, assent will be practically impossible.

---

[58] Ralph Lord Roy, *Apostles of Discord* (Boston: Beacon Press, 1953), p. 147.

[59] *Ibid.*, p. 5.

[60] POAU, *Church and State* (May, 1953), p. 2.

PART II

RANDOM CASE HISTORIES

CHAPTER 6

POAU vs. CARDINAL MINDSZENTY

IN MARCH, 1949, POAU decided to depart from its "single and only purpose" by commenting upon the trial of Cardinal Mindszenty, the Hungarian primate. The organization adopts the role of motion-picture critic with this prophecy:

> The ink is not yet dry on all the stories pouring into the American press concerning the trial of Cardinal Mindszenty, but the enterprising movie magnate, Jack L. Warner, intrepidly announces that his studio will interpret the affair on celluloid.
>
> This will be a "topical drama" indeed! . . . It is as likely to be lurid as it is unlikely to be intelligent.[1]

But even though "the ink is not yet dry on all the stories," POAU feels well qualified to "interpret the affair" in print:

> There is real tragedy in the Hungarian situation. . . . The tragedy lies in this: *two powerful and inordinately ambitious forces are struggling for complete control, and in this struggle the people figure no more importantly (in the eyes of the combatants) than a bone over which two dogs are fighting.* On the one hand there is totalitarian Communism; on the other, that church which claims to represent the "one true faith.". . . Other churches, less politically ambitious, have become involved because the two principals in the contest, in their blind fury, see either ally or enemy in everyone.[2] [Emphasis added.]

That portion which is italicized was sent to the POAU national office, but the source was not divulged. The word "forces" in the italicized section was followed by the words "Catholicism and

---

[1] POAU, *Church and State* (March, 1949), p. 2.
[2] *Ibid.*

45

Communism" enclosed in parentheses. POAU was asked if it believed that there was any truth to the statement, or whether the
quotation should be dismissed as anti-Caholic. Mr. Lowell replied
that he would not say that it

> should be disregarded as purely anti-Catholic. . . .
> I think there is truth in the part which says that "two powerful
> and inordinately ambitious forces (Catholicism and Communism) are
> struggling for complete control." Regarding the part which says that
> "in this struggle the people figure no more importantly (in the eyes
> of the combatants) than a bone over which [two] dogs are fighting," I
> would say that there is truth in it but that it is stated in rather an
> exaggerated way.[3]

Mr. Lowell, then, believes the statement to be basically true,
although a section "is stated in rather an exaggerated way." Not
everyone agrees with this analysis. Dr. Bela Fabian wrote a book
in 1949 about Cardinal Mindszenty and the Hungarian situation.[4]
Dr. Fabian is a Hungarian-born Jew who was a prisoner of the
Russians in 1915 and of the Nazis in 1944.[5] Dr. Fabian declares:

> My undying admiration for Joseph Mindszenty is not a product of
> Catholic partisanship. . . . It is based solidly upon the love of human
> freedom and honesty which we have both held throughout our lives.
> . . . Regardless of the fact that Mindszenty is a Prince Primate of
> the Catholic Church and I am a Jew . . . we have always worshipped
> the same God.[6]

In 1928, Dr. Fabian was president of the Hungarian Independent
Democratic Party, and he is currently in this country as chairman
of the Federation of Former Hungarian Political Prisoners. In
describing Cardinal Mindszenty Dr. Fabian remarks:

> He was most assiduous in his concern for the poor, and would go
> to great lengths to see that they were not hungry. . . "He had com-
> plete respect for the honest faith of a religious Jew.". . . [He said:]
> "Let [Catholics] work with cordial love for everyone regardless of
> his beliefs" . . . Everywhere one read and heard [the communist line]
> that Mindszenty was . . . in every way an enemy of the people.[7]

POAU describes the Catholic Church in Hungary as one of the

---

[3] C. Stanley Lowell, a letter, 17 April, 1958.
[4] Bela Fabian, *Cardinal Mindszenty* (New York: Charles Scribner's Sons, 1949).
[5] *Ibid.*, pp. 2, 5.   [6] *Ibid.*, pp. 1–2.   [7] *Ibid.*, pp. 56, 76, 121.

"inordinately ambitious forces" that are "struggling for complete control" and is "politically ambitious." But Dr. Fabian tells us that in Catholic Hungary freedom was granted all Christian denominations in 1848, and Jewish groups were given freedom equal to that of Christian bodies in 1894.[8] Is that an example of a Church seeking "complete control" — a "politically ambitious" Church? Dr. Fabian continues to explode the POAU myth by quoting the anti-nazi and anti-communist Dr. Aurel Kern of the Hungarian Ministry of Home Affairs (1947):

> "Mindszenty's political philosophy was firmly based on the principles of western democracy. He utterly refused to admit the possibility of any totalitarian doctrine. Particularly obnoxious to him were the racial theories of Nazism."[9]

Thus, a Prince Primate of a Church which POAU affirms to be seeking "complete control" possesses a political philosophy "firmly based on the principles of western democracy." Dr. Fabian proceeds:

> The Churches — and especially the Roman Catholic and Presbyterian Churches — were the repository of Hungarian traditions of freedom and unity. . . . Repeatedly [Cardinal Mindszenty] sent letters to the Government [communist] demanding that it cease abridging human rights. . . . By early 1946 it had become clear that Mindszenty was the Russians' "Enemy Number One" in Hungary. But so thoroughly did he have support of the democratic forces of the country that political barriers to an open attack against him had to be removed as a first step.[10]

In the light of these remarks about a leader of the Catholic Church who possesses a political philosophy based on "principles of western democracy," who is opposed to those "abridging human rights," and who, therefore, "was the Russians' 'Enemy Number One,' " the following false comment by POAU's Mr. Archer is not only insulting but borders on the absurd:

> [Catholicism] . . . needs revision in line with democratic principles: that the carryovers in canon law from medieval times need restudy in light of more humane principles; that a clericalism so much like Communism in its dialectics is not the answer to man's yearning for spiritual freedom.[11]

---

[8] *Ibid.*, p. 113.   [10] *Ibid.*, pp. 114, 119, 121.
[9] *Ibid.*, p. 75.   [11] Glenn L. Archer, *Let's Think it Through* (POAU), p. 15.

Returning to POAU's 1949 account, we are told that

> Had Cardinal Mindszenty come into court with cleaner hands, he
> would be better qualified to play the role of Christian martyr. . . . he
> refused to recognize the Hungarian republic and advocated a return
> to monarchy . . . he urged Catholics to boycott the government. . . .[12]

Dr. Fabian relates that *after being drugged* the Cardinal "confessed" that Father Joseph Kozi-Horvath had sent reports to
Mindszenty of a meeting with Archduke Otto about returning the
monarchy. The meeting allegedly took place on 12–14 December,
1946. But

> Kozi-Horvath in an interview with representatives of the French
> press in Paris, said, "That part of Cardinal Mindszenty's confession
> which refers to me is demonstrably completely untrue. At the times
> mentioned I was still behind the Iron Curtain in Soviet-occupied
> territory which I was quite unable to leave and the Archduke equally
> unable to enter. It was not until September 1, 1947, that I was able
> to cross the border and escape Russian jurisdiction."[13]

The "confession" also declared that the Cardinal talked with
Otto at Chicago in 1947. But at the time this talk was supposed
to have taken place, Cardinal Mindszenty was in Canada.[14]

POAU declares the Cardinal "refused to recognize the Hungarian
republic." Now Hungary was indeed declared a republic in 1946,
with the anti-communist Zoltan Tildy, a Protestant minister, its
president. Nonetheless, Mindszenty and others realized that the
communists called the shots because of their infiltration into key
government positions.[15] By 1949, it was obvious that Hungary was
not a true republic, but actually was controlled by a communist
regime. Therefore, to describe Cardinal Mindszenty as refusing
"to recognize the Hungarian republic" is to deceive the uninformed.
Hungary was as much a republic as Russia is a democracy. If
Mindszenty "urged Catholics to boycott the government," he was
merely urging Catholics not to support a government that was
republic in name but communist in fact.

POAU continues its "foreign affairs" analysis by declaring that
the Cardinal "threatened with excommunication any parliament

---

[12] POAU, *Church and State* (March, 1949), p. 2.
[13] Fabian, *op. cit.*, p. 176.
[14] *Ibid.*, p. 184.
[15] *Ibid.*, p. 117.

members who voted to abolish compulsory religious education."[16] Whether the Hungarian Primate "threatened" or did not threaten is not known to this writer. But what is grossly misleading is the reference to "compulsory religious education." The obvious connotation is that the Cardinal desired a monopoly on the "compulsory" religious education.

Dr. Fabian informs us that when the nationalization of schools began as a first step toward abolishing religious education and injecting Marxist texts into the schools, *both Catholics and Protestants* were so opposed that the communists were forced temporarily to withdraw the plan.[17] A Hungarian writer's interview with Mindszenty is reported as follows:

> He [Cardinal Mindszenty] says that the Church is merely defending the rights of the parents to choose what kind of education they wish to give their children and what sort of school they want them to attend. *The Church does not wish a school monopoly,* he says, but the State does. Whereas over sixty-percent of the schools had formerly been in sectarian hands [all faiths] these had now all been taken over by the State in order to indoctrinate the children with Communism.
>
> "We want to keep our schools," he says. *"We freely acknowledge the right of the State* to build its schools but where there is a Catholic school it belongs to us."[18] [Emphasis added.]

As previously indicated, POAU's reference to "compulsory religious education" is misleading. However, our Washington friends continue by writing that Mindszenty "was the largest landowner in Hungary, and the chief opponent of land reform. . . ."[19]

It is probably true that Cardinal Mindszenty "was the largest landowner in Hungary," but by virtue of being the leader of the Hungarian Church, not because of personal wealth. The Jewish, Presbyterian, and Catholic Churches were all wealthy and large landholders, together possessing 65 per cent of the nations schools.[20]

In 1945, "the landed estates of Hungary were confiscated for redistribution to the people . . ." and all business and industrial activity were placed in the hands of a State monopoly.[21] Dr. Fabian reports that

---

[16] POAU, *Church and State* (March, 1949), p. 2.
[17] Fabian, *op. cit.,* p. 123.
[18] *Ibid.,* pp. 128–129.
[19] POAU, *Church and State* (March, 1949), p. 2.
[20] Fabian, *op. cit.,* p. 114.
[21] *Ibid.,* p. 104.

Mindszenty himself had long known that land reform was essential to the happiness and well-being of his country, but he steadfastly opposed its institution under Russian pressure. He felt that it should wait until a Parliament legally elected by the Hungarian people could instigate it carefully and carry it out in such a way that it would really benefit the country. He disapproved of the cutting up of the great estates according to the Russian plan into such tiny strips that no one would make a living on one of them. . . . It was no more than a trick, he decided, to bring about the working of an undisclosed plan.[22]

The Cardinal was correct. The undisclosed plan was that since the peasants were unable to make a living on such small strips, the rural areas were unable to export foodstuff to the cities which then would struggle with famine. Thus, Hungary would settle for the collective farms the Russians always wanted to establish. What about the former landowners? Eugen Varga, Stalin economic adviser on Hungary, said, "As to the former owners of the land we are not concerned with them. They are a class rightly condemned to perish."[23]

Dr. Fabian concludes by stating that

Later one of the [communist] charges against him was that he had joined the landed proprietors in their opposition to the distribution of land to peasants; actually it was precisely because Mindszenty knew that the plan as it was being carried out would rob the peasants of their land that he opposed the Communist procedure. It is perhaps significant that when five hundred acres of land of the episcopate of Veszprem were exempted from distribution and given to Mindszenty as a reward for his opposition to the Nazis, he promptly placed it at the disposal of the episcopate.[24]

There are other POAU remarks about Cardinal Mindszenty and Hungary that do not stand the test of history or reason. But this POAU conclusion is truly remarkable: "Whatever the true facts may be it is clear the church-state confusions of Hungary . . . have no attraction to free Americans who have enjoyed church-state separation."[25] Of all the conclusions that could possibly be written, that one is the most fallacious. Because we are "free Americans" we *should* concern ourselves with the "confusions" of Hungary. Many responsible groups have concerned themselves with Hungary. The following organizations condemned the Mindszenty trial (prior

---

[22] *Ibid.*, p. 105.   [24] *Ibid.*, pp. 106–107.
[23] *Ibid.*, p. 106.   [25] POAU, *Church and State* (March, 1949), p. 2.

to March, 1949): American Jewish Committee, Jewish Labor Committee, Jewish War Veterans, and B'nai B'rith. Bishop W. T. Manning of the Protestant Episcopal Church, and Dr. Daniel A. Poling denounced the trial.[26] President Truman called the trial "infamous" and conducted by a "kangaroo court."[27] An exiled Hungarian Unitarian declared "no confession ever made in a Communist court can be taken for the truth. This [is] an axiom."[28] But POAU wishes the Cardinal had come into court "with cleaner hands." This is still the official POAU position, for late in 1956 POAU referred its readers to the POAU account of 1949.[29] The Hungarian Freedom-Fighters did not agree with POAU that the Cardinal is a leader of a Church which considers the people no more "than a bone over which two dogs are fighting." One of the first acts of the Hungarian rebels against communism was to free their imprisoned Cardinal.

At a 1957 National POAU Conference in Los Angeles, a POAU speaker asked, "How can we prevent the immigration of Hungarian Catholics to the United States? . . . America needs quality, not quantity! POAU is the only bastion of freedom in America!"[30] No comment.

---

[26] *The Pilot*, 12 February, 1949.

[27] Fabian, *op. cit.*, p. 197.

[28] *The Pilot, op. cit.*

[29] POAU, *Church and State* (December, 1956), p. 3.

[30] N.C.W.C. *Bulletin* (March, 1957), p. 6. The comment was made by Mr. Walter Montano, formerly a Catholic seminarian, now editor of *Our Christian Heritage* (new name for *The Converted Catholic*) which is published by Christ's Mission, a group antagonistic toward Catholicism. Mr. Montano spoke at POAU's Conference even though "POAU finds some material of value in the publications of Christ's Mission, but does not endorse them" (POAU letter, 11 December, 1957).

CHAPTER 7

CATHOLIC HOSPITALS AND MEDICAL ETHICS

MISSOURI and Louisiana are areas in which Catholic nursing Sisters have formulated elaborate schemes to gain control of public hospitals. Such is the substance of POAU reports. The Americans United inform us of a ". . . plan of a Catholic religious order to take over a $900,000 public hospital . . .";[1] and about a "Marine hospital given to Roman Catholic order."[2] Those sensational disclosures will be treated in the first portion of this chapter.

Next, we shall investigate POAU's charges that Catholicism maintains a "slavish adherence to . . . medical codes long since outmoded";[3] that Catholic hospitals "subscribe to a medieval medical code which contravenes in many instances the enlightened medical and legal code of this country";[4] that "Catholic hospitals operate, not according to the laws of our states or according to the laws of the United States. . . ."[5]

POAU, now completely oblivious to its "single and only purpose," takes on the role of commentator — well qualified, no doubt — on medical codes. The relevance of the First Amendment in this area is scarcely clear, and POAU does not bother to explain it.

---

[1] POAU, *Church and State* (May, 1957), p. 1.

[2] *Ibid.* (November, 1953), p. 8.

[3] C. Stanley Lowell, *Truth Series No. 4* (POAU), pp. 2–3.

[4] Glenn L. Archer, *The Ramparts We Watch* (POAU, 1957), p. 9.

[5] POAU, *Church and State* (February, 1954), p. 5. That absurd statement was issued by Emmett McLoughlin, a speaker at a POAU Conference.

— 1 —

CATHOLICS ELBOW EVERYONE ASIDE

In November, 1953, a story appeared in *Church and State* under the intriguing caption "MARINE HOSPITAL GIVEN TO ROMAN CATHOLIC ORDER." The article says:

> The city of St. Louis, St. Louis County and the city of Kirkwood, Mo., were all elbowed aside recently by the Sisters of St. Joseph of Carondelet, a Roman Catholic order, which was given a government hospital by the United States Department of Health, Education and Welfare without payment of any kind and in preference to the public agencies which bid for it. Formerly operated by the U. S. Public Health Service, the Marine Hospital at 525 Couch Avenue, Kirkwood, was given to the Church order as "surplus."[6]

The Acting Chief of the Division of Surplus Property Utilization of the U. S. Department of Health, Education and Welfare was contacted in order to verify the facts in this case. It is not surprising that the story told by POAU and that told by the U. S. Government differ. In the words of the Department of Health, Education and Welfare:

> Prior to the time that the Public Health Service discontinued using this facility for a hospital, applications were received from the Board of Education, Kirkwood School District R-7, Mid-West Bible and Missionary Institute, St. Louis Chiropractic Health Center of St. Louis, State of Missouri, St. John's Hospital, Sisters of St. Joseph, and the Bethesda Hospital Association.[7]

Even to the extent of listing just exactly whom the Sisters of St. Joseph "elbowed" out, POAU is inaccurate.

The remainder of HEW letter presents the entire case so well that it is now quoted almost in entirety. After listing all the applicants for the hospital facility the letter continues:

> We received reports and recommendations from members of Congress, the City of Kirkwood, the State Department of Health, and the Public Health Service to the effect that the Marine Hospital at Kirkwood should be retained as a general hospital. On the basis of this recognized general hospital need, we administratively determined that no further

---

[6] *Ibid.* (November, 1953), p. 8.
[7] A. K. Haines, a letter, 9 May, 1958.

consideration would be given to applications for educational purposes, for chiropractic hospitals, or for use for chronic disease, convalescent or geriatric hospitals.

As a result of this determination, there remained three eligible applicants. These were the City of Kirkwood, the Sisters of St. Joseph of Carondelet, and the Sisters of Mercy of St. John's Hospital. On October 2, 1953, the Sisters of Mercy of St. John's Hospital, St. Louis, Missouri, withdrew its application for the property. The application of the City of Kirkwood proposed that the hospital would be operated by the Lutheran Charities Association on behalf of the City. However, when the deadline date was reached for the award of the hospital to the successful applicant, no specific or binding commitments had been entered into by the City of Kirkwood and the Lutheran Charities Association respecting the operation of the property by the Lutherans on behalf of the City.

A review of the applications led to the conclusion that of the two applicants, the Sisters of St. Joseph had the better program and was better equipped to operate both from a financial and technical viewpoint. The director of the Missouri State Department of Health favored the application of the Sisters of St. Joseph. On October 31, 1953, the Marine Hospital was conveyed to the Sisters of St. Joseph of Carondelet.

Experience to date, as is apparently indicated by the successful conversion, modernization, equipment, and activation of the St. Joseph Hospital, would appear to support the soundness of judgment exercised by this Department in award of this facility. Our reports indicate that approximately $1,000,000 has been spent for the remodeling, equipping, and furnishing of the hospital. Dedication ceremonies were held September 26, 1954, and the Kirkwood Messenger News article on this dedication indicates that 3,000 persons attended. Mayor William L. Berthold spoke on behalf of the City of Kirkwood, extending greetings and welcome, and Dr. H. Edmund Mack, Chairman of the Committee on Health, Education, and Welfare of the Chamber of Commerce, promised the backing of the business men. L. Gordon Davis of the County Council extended greetings and welcome on behalf of the St. Louis County Government.[8]

The facts brought out by the HEW letter completely discredit the inexcusable inferences made by POAU. Instead of the Sisters of St. Joseph elbowing out anyone, it is apparent that of all the applicants they alone could fully meet the requirements of the U. S. Department of Health, Education, and Welfare. The leading

---

[8] *Ibid.*

dignitaries that turned out to welcome the Sisters into the community had no feeling of being "elbowed aside." POAU's implication that the Sisters were given a hospital over the "bids" (implying monetary bids which was *not* the case) of others is misleading.

Returning to the POAU article, we read about the amount of money spent by the Sisters in order to remodel, furnish, and equip the hospital. The POAU figure was $498,000.[9] The HEW letter says that approximately $1,000,000 was spent for the purpose. This error, a minor point perhaps, on the part of POAU, is mentioned as a preview of the mathematical problems that plague the group. Some of these problems are brought out in Chapter 14.

— 2 —

LOUISIANA, LAW AND ETHICS

The May, 1957, issue of *Church and State* carried as a lead story the exposure of a hospital "give-away" plan to a group of Catholic nursing Sisters. POAU claimed to have saved the citizens of Ponchatoula and Hammond, Louisiana, from losing their new hospital to the Catholic Church. Since hospitals are not given away very readily, even to Catholics, a closer look at the facts and their greater implication in regard to POAU treatment of Catholic medical ethics might be worthwhile.

According to POAU:

> Citizens of Ponchatoula and Hammond, Louisiana, with the help of POAU leaders, scored a quick victory in April against the plan of a Catholic religious order to take over a $900,000 public hospital that was to have been paid for by public taxation. By threatening court action, a determined local committee on separation of church and state forced the abandonment of the "give-away."[10]

Now that we are acquainted with the accusations, a closer scrutiny of the situation will show, at best, conflicting reports.

There never has been an attempt by Catholic Sisters to assume control of the hospital. Several years ago, the local hospital committee requested the clergymen of the District to assist the committee by checking with all religious denominations for an operating agency which would be able to administer the proposed hospital

---

[9] POAU, *Church and State* (November, 1953), p. 8.
[10] *Ibid.* (May, 1957), p. 1.

under control of the Hospital Board and in accordance with Louisiana law.

The Dominican Sisters were contacted as to the possibility of their administering the hospital. In 1957, after trained personnel had been made available to them, the Sisters contacted the Board in order to discuss the possibility of administering the hospital.

POAU has given a completely different slant to the procedure by which the nuns were to function. The Sisters had simply answered a request for help that had gone out through the Protestant ministers in the area. True to their traditions, the Catholic Sisters responded to a community need as they had in the War of 1812[11] and the Civil War.[12] Unmindful of such acts of civic responsibility POAU reports that nuns are sometimes referred to as "faceless women."[13]

Returning to POAU's fiction, let us examine what action POAU took to prevent the alleged "give-away." The Americans United state:

> Meeting in Baton Rouge with legal advisers who included POAU Special Counsel, Paul Blanshard, the group organized itself into a Committee for the Separation of Church and State. . . .[14]

The committee contacted each member of the Board by letter explaining to each that he would be responsible for the "illegal" expenditures of tax funds. POAU attributes the subsequent resignation of four of the five members of the Board to this letter.[15]

Four of the five Board members did attempt to resign, but not for the reason circulated in the pages of *Church and State*. It simply is not accurate to conclude that the "letter of legal warning" had in itself caused the resignation of the four members. Furthermore, it was not known to the general public nor to the commissioners that the committee of local citizens who had drafted the letter were under the guidance of POAU. Like many other American communities of comparable size and circumstances, Hammond, Louisiana, had been accustomed to handling its own internal affairs in a peaceful, tolerant manner. A more valid reason for the

---

[11] C. E. McGuire (ed.) *Catholic Builders of a Nation* (Boston: Continental Press, Inc., 1923), p. 280.

[12] *Ibid.*, pp. 181–182.

[13] C. Stanley Lowell, *Captive Schools*, (POAU, 1959), p. 2.

[14] POAU, *Church and State* (May, 1957), p. 1.

[15] *Ibid.*

attempted resignations is that the commissioners feared, and wished to forestall, any possible interference in local affairs by such an organization as POAU.[16]

POAU reports that its letter reminded the Hospital Board that

> The Louisiana constitution also forbids any preference or discrimination . . . and . . . that under the proposed rule "non-Catholic physicians, nurses, and patients" would be deprived of standard medical remedies.[17]

As this was to be a public hospital open to all people, a religious order could not function as administrator if it discriminated against patients of other faiths. The Hospital Board took action to assure that the $900,000 hospital would operate according to recognized standards. The Board of Hospital Commissioners met with the Parish Medical Society and discussed the medical practices that would be adhered to if the Sisters administered the hospital. After a thorough study the Parish Medical Society reported that it found nothing objectionable in the medical practices followed by the Dominican Sisters. To the contrary, the medical doctors concluded that the observance of the medical code followed by the Sisters would lead to early accreditation of the hospital.[18]

The Parish Medical Society and the Board of Hospital Commissioners were satisfied that Catholic hospitals are in no way second-rate or "medieval," but not POAU. In March, 1958, *Church and State* quotes from a complaint filed with the Louisiana Courts that there

> are a number of areas of medical practice wherein the best and most informed medical opinion as to the course of action required for the welfare of patients conflicts with the tenets of the Roman Catholic Church.[19]

Just who the "best and most informed" medical people are POAU does not divulge. It was not the Parish Medical Society, as it had already approved the awarding of the hospital to the Sisters. We can assume that the American Medical Association is fairly well informed on medical practices and has ready access "to the best and most informed medical opinions." Certainly the AMA is not

---

[16] Two Commissioners later withdrew their resignations.

[17] POAU, *Church and State* (May, 1957), p. 1.

[18] In May, 1959, *Church and State*, POAU reported on three other public hospitals which it accused of following "Catholic limitation on . . . medical procedures."

[19] POAU, *Church and State* (March, 1958), p. 2.

under the control of the Catholic Church; consequently, its opinion can be recognized as being impartial in medical matters. The AMA was questioned on accusations made by Americans United not only in regard to this situation, but also in regard to the entire ethical code followed by Catholic hospitals. The AMA was asked to comment on a 1955 Archer statement entitled *Without Fear or Favor,* addressed to all "the Senators and Representatives of the United States, and to the American people."[20] He charged that the Catholic

> . . . church definitely forbids many medical measures which are permitted in non-Catholic hospitals. Frequently it discharges from its staff doctors who do not conform to this denominational code. . . . The books of instruction for denominational nurses instruct them to discriminate in a specific way against patients who request the services of non-Catholic clergymen.[21]

In May, 1957, before "a cheering audience of 12,000" Southern Baptists Archer reiterated the charge by stating that doctors practicing in a Catholic-affiliated hospital

> . . . must subscribe to a medieval medical code which contravenes in many instances the enlightened medical and legal code of this country.[22]

The American Medical Association speaking through its Law Department and Judicial Council answered the following questions regarding these charges: First: Do Catholic hospitals prohibit medical measures which are permitted in all non-Catholic hospitals? The AMA Law Department says:

> . . . the statement attributed to POAU is so general that it is meaningless. I would suspect that in general what is meant is that in Catholic hospitals sterilization procedures for economic, social and non-therapeutic reasons are not permitted. *This is also true in many other hospitals.* . . . The position of Catholic hospitals on this subject is well defined and strict.[23] [Emphasis added.]

Second: What is to be said of doctors being dismissed for not conforming to Catholic medical ethics? The AMA says:

---

[20] Glenn L. Archer, *Without Fear or Favor* (POAU, 1955), front cover.

[21] *Ibid.,* p. 18.

[22] Glenn L. Archer, *The Ramparts We Watch* (POAU, 1957), p. 9.

[23] Edwin J. Holman (executive secretary of AMA Judicial Council), a letter, 10 January, 1958.

The rule of law is that private hospitals may adopt such rules as in their judgment are deemed satisfactory. Whether any private hospital, Catholic or non-Catholic, adopts rules relating to the practice of medicine within its confines would seem to be the prerogative of the hospital. . . .

Insofar as medical practice is concerned doctors who are accorded staff privileges in Catholic hospitals have agreed to be bound by the regulations of the hospital. *They are not forced to accept such regulations.*[24] [Emphasis added.]

Some of the errors in *Without Fear or Favor* could have been averted had Archer consulted the AMA and in particular the 23 July, 1955, issue of the *Journal of the American Medical Association*. On page 1132 the *Journal* comments:

Under [the] power to prescribe reasonable rules and regulations, it has been held [by the courts] that the governing board of a public hospital may refuse to allow a duly licensed physician and surgeon to practice his profession in the hospital. Such an exclusion must not, however, be based on grounds *that are unreasonable, arbitrary, capricious, or discriminatory.* [Emphasis added.]

It might be that Mr. Archer and the POAU medical experts are aware of this rule of law concerning public hospitals and are referring to private hospitals. Again the AMA *Journal* reports:

It has long been held that the board of trustees of a private hospital has the right to adopt rules and regulations relating to the qualifications and responsibilities of its staff members. . . .[25]

The *Journal* goes on to quote from the case of the United States *vs.* American Medical Association, 28 F. Supp. 752., which said in part:

Permission to practice in such a hospital [private] is not a right on the part of an applicant doctor but is only a privilege which can be extended or withheld from him at the will of, or at the discretion of, the particular hospital.[26]

It should be clear that a hospital may close its doors to a doctor, if that doctor violates the rules and regulations of the hospital; the one exception being if the rules are ". . . unreasonable, arbitrary,

---

[24] *Ibid.*
[25] "Medicine and the Law," *Journal of the American Medical Association* (9 April, 1955), p. 1342.
[26] *Ibid.*

capricious, or discriminatory." A question that might be asked is: Do the ethical and religious directives for Catholic hospitals fall in this category (unreasonable, etc.)?

Mr. Archer has declared that Catholicism "imposes its own code of ethics on doctors practicing in the hospitals it controls, even though this code at certain points outrages the code of the medical profession."[27] In a POAU-recommended book, Mr. Paul Blanshard states his opinion of the question:

> . . . Protestant and Jewish religious organizations . . . do not have the exclusive and archaic rules of medical practice that separate Catholic hospitals from American public hospitals. . . . Catholic hospitals . . . subject even non-Catholic doctors, nurses, and patients to the rigid limitations of the Catholic medical code.[28]

Mr. Lowell in an article published in the *Christian Herald* in September, 1958, and later released by POAU as a pamphlet made the statement that:

> The Roman Catholic Church has its own medical code which differs markedly from the code of the American Medical Association.

Where Mr. Lowell and his colleagues got their information is not known, but it was not from the AMA. In answer to a letter of inquiry concerning Catholic medical practices the executive secretary of the AMA Judicial Council reports:

> *I am familiar with the ethical and religious directives for Catholic hospitals as well as the Principles of Medical Ethics of the AMA. There is nothing in the former which contravenes the latter.*[29] [Emphasis added.]

If POAU is to persist in its charge that Catholic hospitals "subscribe to a medieval medical code," then by self-admission the American Medical Association is also "medieval." And every doctor who upholds the medical ethics of the AMA must conclude that he is practicing a code which "contravenes in many instances the enlightened medical and legal code of this country."[30] Such a conclusion is as ridiculous as POAU's original accusation.

---

[27] Glenn L. Archer, *The Growing Struggle for Religious Liberty* (POAU, 1956), p. 4.

[28] Paul Blanshard, *American Freedom and Catholic Power* (1958) (Boston: Beacon Press, 1958), p. 159.

[29] Holman, *op. cit.,* 17 October, 1957.

[30] Glenn L. Archer, *The Ramparts We Watch* (POAU, 1957), p. 9.

Third: Do the books of Catholic moral theology instruct nurses to discriminate against patients who request the services of non-Catholic clergymen? POAU claims discrimination exists.

Again, the AMA found the answer quite simple. It said:

> . . . Section 58 of the ethical and religious directives for Catholic hospitals provides especially for the spiritual care of non-Catholics.[31]

Specifically, Section 58 reads:

> While avoiding odious proselytism, we must not be indifferent to the spiritual needs and desires of non-Catholics; and everything consonant with our principles must be done for them. In particular, when a non-Catholic patient asks to have his minister or rabbi called this request should be honored.[32]

It is difficult to say just when POAU added that fantasy to their list but it was uttered by an excommunicated Catholic priest whom POAU hired in 1954 as its principal speaker at the Sixth Annual Convention. POAU states that the defrocked priest proved his statement by making reference to page 88 of *Moral Theology* by Heribert Jone.[33] This book is easily accessible and inexpensive; consequently, POAU has no recourse when it is criticized for making another error of omission. The POAU quote is as follows:[34]

> Sisters in a hospital may not summon a non-Catholic minister for a dying person to assist him in death.

What Jone actually says is this:

> Sisters in a hospital may not summon a non-Catholic minister for a dying person to assist him in death. For a very weighty reason (e.g., public welfare) they may inform the minister that a patient desires to see him. It seems lawful even for them to prepare a little table for his use in religious ministrations.[35]

In his first sentence, Jone simply asserts that nursing Sisters may not summon a non-Catholic minister, i.e., if the patient does not make such a request. However, if the patient desires a minister,

---

[31] Holman, *op. cit.*, 17 October, 1957.

[32] *Ethical and Religious Directives for Catholic Hospitals* (St. Louis: The Catholic Hospital Association, 1957), p. 11.

[33] POAU, *Church and State* (February, 1954), p. 5.

[34] *Ibid.*

[35] Heribert Jone, *Moral Theology* (Westminster, Md.: The Newman Press, 1957), p. 88.

the Sisters may inform the minister, and even "prepare a little table for his use in religious ministrations." The expression, "non-Catholic minister," means "not only a Protestant minister, but also a Jewish rabbi and a schismatic priest. In a word . . . all official ministers of non-Catholics. . . ."[36] The POAU speaker, Mr. Emmett McLoughlin, has obviously quoted out of context.

Paul Blanshard writes that "Until recently Catholic medical manuals instructed Catholic nurses to discriminate against non-Catholic clergymen . . . when non-Catholic patients were dying."[37] Blanshard then quotes a portion of a 1946 Catholic book in a way which gives the reader the impression that a Catholic nurse, at that time, could not summon a non-Catholic minister to comfort a dying non-Catholic patient.[38] He indicates that it was not until 1956 that a Catholic nurse could summon a minister under those circumstances. A *1946* Catholic booklet on ethical procedures contradicts Mr. Blanshard:

> May Catholic nurses send for non-Catholic ministers to attend non-Catholic patients for religious purposes?
>
> If a non-Catholic patient asks to see a non-Catholic minister of religion, the Catholic nurse ought to inform some non-Catholic relative or friend to send for the minister.
>
> If that is not possible, the Catholic nurse herself may notify the the non-Catholic minister of the patient's desire.[39]

This does not restrict such a summons by a Catholic nurse to the circumstances of a dying patient.

Mr. Blanshard gives the false impression that it was only in 1956 that a Catholic nurse could effect the presence of a non-Catholic minister. According to a Catholic source Catholic nurses could make such arrangements back in 1848.[40]

— 3 —

BIRTH CONTROL

The subject of birth control is an issue in the field of both

---

[36] Gerald Kelly, S.J., *Medico-Moral Problems* (St. Louis: The Catholic Hospital Association, 1958), p. 320.

[37] Blanshard, *op. cit.*, p. 151.

[38] *Ibid.*

[39] L. Rumble and C. M. Carty, *Quizzes on Hospital Ethics* (St. Paul: Radio Replies Press, 1946), p. 48.

[40] Kelly, *op. cit.*, p. 321.

medical and personal morality. Catholic hospitals and doctors do not endorse, publicize, nor advocate what is popularly termed "birth control."

As used in this book, "birth control" means engaging in the marriage act while directly and intentionally doing something either before, during, or after the act which would render its performance incapable of resulting in conception regardless of natural physiological circumstances. Thus defined, birth control is always and always has been declared grievously sinful in all circumstances by the Catholic Church.

POAU regards legal proscriptions on birth control information as "archaic."[41] Legal prohibitions of such information exist in Massachusetts and Connecticut. In 1953, POAU reported that "for the thirteenth time in 74 years, the Connecticut legislature has defeated a bill authorizing doctors to prescribe contraceptives. . . . This means that the state continues to force Roman Catholic 'morality' on all the citizens of the state."[42] Massachusetts law "gives state sanction to the Roman Catholic doctrine on the subject."[43] The implication is that the birth-control legislation in those two predominantly Catholic states are "Catholic laws." POAU accurately places the original birth-control legislation in Connecticut back into the nineteenth century. The Massachusetts law was passed in 1879.

> Certainly in 1879 the Catholics of Massachusetts [and Connecticut] were in no position to dictate or pressure the legislature into passing a law that was not widely approved by Protestants. . . . The so-called birth control laws of Massachusetts and Connecticut are (if they are to have any religious label) Protestant laws which so far Protestant and Catholic citizens in the exercise of their constitutional freedom and responsibility have united (wisely or unwisely in anyone's free opinion) to keep on the books. But to Mr. Blanshard [and POAU] the exercise of American freedom by Catholics is a threat to American freedom.[44]

It is only in the past decade that Catholics in Massachusetts and Connecticut have approximated 50 per cent of the population,

---

[41] POAU, *Church and State* (May, 1957), p. 7.

[42] *Ibid.* (July, 1953), p. 3.

[43] *Ibid.* (February, 1952), p. 6.

[44] James M. O'Neill, *Catholicism and American Freedom* (New York: Harper and Brothers, 1952), p. 155.

and that figure includes children who are not of voting age. With this background, at least one flaw is obvious in Mr. Blanshard's questions for "any Catholic candidate for the presidency." The question is asked in his POAU-recommended discourse *American Freedom and Catholic Power* (1958):

> 3. Your Church denies the right of both non-Catholics and Catholics to receive birth-control information, and in such states as Massachusetts and Connecticut its power has been sufficient to make prohibition of birth control legally binding. Do you personally approve or disapprove of your church's policy on this subject?[45]

Naturally, any faithful Catholic approves his "church's policy on this subject." But Mr. Blanshard has not even approximated, the "church's policy" on birth control. The reader immediately recognizes the falsity of the charge that the Church had or has "power" to make prohibition of birth control "legally binding." The statutes in question enacted the Protestant morality of the Protestant majority, and are being sustained by groups of all faiths, inasmuch as no one faith has a majority of voting-age members. Second, Mr. Blanshard misrepresents the "church's policy" when he declares that Catholicism "denies the right of both non-Catholics and Catholics to receive birth-control information." *The Pilot*, Boston archdiocesan weekly, declares: "moreover, the Church plainly cannot legislate for any but her own members. The unfortunate aspect of the whole matter is that Paul Blanshard knows very well the proper answers to his own questions."[46]

Must a Catholic offer positive resistance to birth control? Obviously, a conscientious Catholic will not vote for birth-control statutes. To do so would be contrary to his conscience, and, therefore, wrong in the eyes of both Catholic and Protestant morality. But must a Catholic campaign for laws, local or national, that prohibit birth control, and thereby deny "the right of . . . non-Catholics . . . to receive birth control information"? The answer is no.

> In answer to the question proposed, therefore, a Catholic would be bound to say that he approves of the policy of his church in relation to birth control. This would not mean, however, that he would be bound to offer positive resistance to non-Catholics, who, presumably

---

[45] Blanshard, *op. cit.*, p. 350.
[46] *The Pilot*, 11 January, 1958,

in good conscience, teach that birth control is allowable and advocate its practice.[47]

The Catholic Church's policy toward birth control is that it is wrong under any circumstances. Only in the sense that the Church is enforcing the natural law is it correct to refer to the "church's policy" on birth control. Ultimately, the "policy" is that of the Creator. The natural law is that law which is recognizable by unaided reason and usually by the conscience; reason is able to discern that "the will of the Creator established this law for all mankind in order that the necessary purpose of man's being or a part of his nature be fulfilled."[48] The Catholic Church opposes birth control because it militates against the natural law established by God, i.e., hinders "man's being or a part of his nature" from being fulfilled. Just what that portion is of man's nature which will be prevented from proper fulfillment we shall discuss presently, but first it is interesting to note the motive that POAU ascribes to the Church for her opposition to birth control:

> Go into a Roman Catholic home and you will find anywhere from five to fifteen. It takes no great mathematical skill to see where that brings us in a few generations. It has just about brought us there. The hierarchy's hostility to birth control has paid off. Their adherents are now numerous enough to challenge American traditions with good chance of success.[49]

According to the October, 1958, *Church and State*, the Church opposes birth control in order that her members will quickly multiply, become a majority, and gain "cultural domination" of the country.

> This is nonsense. The Catholic Church does not command Catholic husbands and wives to have even one child. *She considers it more than normally meritorious for them to have no children,* if they mutually and perpetually give up the use of the marriage right for the love of God. She only maintains that the free use of the marriage

---

[47] *Ibid.,* 7 June, 1958. Opposition to birth control need not be based on theology. To that extent, the motive for opposition is not a desire to legislate the doctrine of *any* Faith.

[48] D. F. Miller, *What Laws Can the Church Change?* (Liguori, Mo.: Liguorian Pamphlet Office, 1955), p. 6.

[49] C. Stanley Lowell, *A Summons to Americans* (POAU), p. 6.

right involves the acceptance of whatever children God may send them.[50] [Emphasis added.]

There is nothing in Catholic moral teaching that says Catholics must have families "from five to fifteen."

In Mr. Blanshard's revised *American Freedom and Catholic Power,* we find another reason alleged for Catholicism's attitude on birth control:

> Perhaps Catholicism's unrealistic attitude on this subject goes back in part to the negative attitude of celibate priests toward the enjoyment of married life. If sex is essentially sinful, then its enjoyment should be counterbalanced by certain obligations and penalties. In the Augustinian conception the sexual act was sinful in itself, and the essence of the original sin in the Garden of Eden was the concupiscence which accompanied the act of generation. For the priest the method of escape from this sin is perpetual virginity. Ordinary people compensate for their sin by fulfilling their obligation to create children. . . . The dutiful Catholic must not use medical or mechanical devices to avoid his duty. So runs the Catholic philosophy that lies behind the opposition to birth control.[51]

So runs the Blanshard-POAU fabrication of teaching that is not "Catholic philosophy." There is no "duty" imposed upon Catholics to have children and "ordinary people" do not "create children." Catholics believe that parents co-operate with God, who creates the soul. Creation means to produce something from nothing. "Ordinary people" do not create, only God. Furthermore, there is no "negative attitude of celibate priests." Mr. Blanshard indicates that this "negative attitude" is one which regards "sex" and the "sexual act" as "essentially sinful." Catholics regard marriage as a sacrament instituted by Christ Himself.

> The marriage contract is a contract by which two competent persons of opposite sex give to each other the exclusive and irrevocable right over their bodies . . . for the procreation and education of children.[52]

Mr. Blanshard and POAU would have us believe that Catholicism teaches that Christ instituted the sacrament of marriage and

---

[50] D. F. Miller, *Why Is Birth Control Wrong?* (Liguori, Mo.: Liguorian Pamphlet Office, 1955), pp. 7–8. See note 59.

[51] Blanshard, *op. cit.,* pp. 164–165.

[52] Heribert Jone, *Moral Theology* (Westminster, Md.: The Newman Press, 1957), p. 466.

also that the marriage act is "essentially sinful" and "sinful in itself." That is absurd. The Church teaches "the union of husband and wife represents the union between Christ and His Church."[53]

Mr. Blanshard's next false statement refers to the priest's "method of escape from this sin" as "perpetual virginity." If the Church regarded the marriage union as "sinful," she would hardly allow married men of certain rites to become priests. However, the Catholic Church generally requires celibacy for her priests in order to better imitate Christ, Himself unmarried; when asked "whether He expected men not to marry, our Lord replied, 'Not all men will refrain, but those to whom it is given. He that can do so, let him do so.' "[54]

Next Blanshard misrepresents the "Augustinian conception" that "the sexual act was sinful in itself." Blanshard is apparently referring to the teaching of St. Augustine of Hippo. Contrary to Mr. Blanshard's misrepresentation, St. Augustine wrote that "relations with one's wife when conception is deliberately prevented" are "unlawful and impure."[55] Augustine did not believe that "the sexual act was sinful in itself," but only in certain circumstances.

The sixth major error of Blanshard in seven sentences is ascribing to "Catholic philosophy" the position that "the essence of the original sin in the Garden of Eden was the concupiscence which accompanied the act of generation." In Catholic teaching "the essence of the original sin" has nothing whatsoever to do with such "concupiscence." According to the Catholic catechism, the essence of original sin is that Adam and Eve "disobeyed God" symbolized by the eating "of the fruit of a certain tree in Paradise."[56] The doctrine of original sin is not, as Mr. Blanshard and POAU term it, "Catholic philosophy," but rather, Catholic (and Protestant) *theology.*

Now that we have learned what the Catholic motive for opposition to birth control is *not,* let us briefly elaborate on what that motive *is.* Birth control contravenes the natural law by intrinsically frustrating a "necessary purpose of man's being or a part of his nature." The primary purpose of marriage — according to Catholic

---

[53] F. B. Cassilly, *Religion: Doctrine and Practice* (Chicago: Loyola University Press, 1958), p. 304.

[54] Rumble and Carty, *Radio Replies,* Vol. III (St. Paul: Radio Replies Press, 1942), p. 283.

[55] *Ibid.,* Vol. I, p. 263.

[56] J. I. Malloy, *A Catechism for Inquirers* (New York: Paulist Press, 1927), p. 14.

teaching — is "the procreation and education of children." Birth control frustrates that primary purpose. According to our definition of "birth control," stated earlier, its practice would not permit conception even if natural physiological conditions were such that conception would be possible. Therefore, birth control is condemned by the Catholic Church.

An inescapable corollary to this discussion is "rhythm." Rhythm means "the practice of periodic abstinence from marital relations, during periods of more probable fertility, in order to avoid the conception of children."[57] That is quite different from the procedure of birth control where *even if natural physiological circumstances were propitious,* conception would be prevented by the very essence of the practice. With rhythm there is no positive attack by the married on the primary purpose of marriage because of the way the marriage act is performed. Rhythm takes advantage of the natural cycle of fertility; the only hindrance to conception is due to a natural physiological phenomenon (cycle of fertility) originating from the action of nature. Absence of conception *per se* is *not* the criterion for judging subordination of marriage's primary purpose; the criterion is whether the spouses interfere with the natural process of reproduction, thereby rendering conception impossible regardless of physiological condition.

Use of this natural cycle of diminishing and increasing fertility is, sometimes, licit and enables the married to fulfill in a lawful manner a secondary purpose of marriage, "the showing of mutual love between husband and wife and the avoidance of the wrong use of sex."[58] However it can be practiced only if serious reasons demand its use. Thus, rhythm enables the married not to thwart the primary purpose of marriage while fulfilling its secondary purpose, and at the same time reducing the probability of children because of certain grave reasons. These "grave reasons" to justify the use of rhythm temporarily or permanently "must be either: 1. medical (e.g., ill-health of wife); 2. eugenic (e.g., great probability of bringing forth defective children); 3. economic (e.g., poverty); 4. social (e.g., inescapable dependence on others, or being dependent on others)."[59]

---

[57] J. D. Conway, *What They Ask of the Rhythm* (Notre Dame: Ave Maria Press, 1956), p. 3.

[58] Miller, *Why Is Birth Control Wrong? op. cit.,* p. 28.

[59] *Ibid.,* p. 30. Rhythm may be used permanently if necessary.

It is inexcusable for POAU to intimate that the Catholic Church sponsors a policy which results in families of "five to fifteen," and which opposes family limitation under all conditions. The *goal* of family limitation is not *per se* condemned by Catholicism; however, the *means of limitation* may be.

Although the thesis of this chapter in no way depends upon the following testimony, it is worthwhile to recall that the American Medical Association has stated that there is nothing in Catholic medical ethics that contravenes in any way the AMA ethical principles. In regard to POAU charges that Catholic ethics outrage the medical profession and are long since outmoded, the AMA forcefully declares:

> . . . if you care to pursue it further, you will find that the *statements made by POAU do not bear close scrutiny, nor can they be supported in fact.*[60] [Emphasis added.]

---

[60] E. J. Holman, *op. cit.*, 17 October, 1957.

CHAPTER 8

PUBLIC AND PRIVATE EDUCATION

SINCE its inception in November, 1947, POAU has waged relentless war against the Catholic parochial schools, and against what it presents as Catholic attitudes in the whole area of public education. To be sure, from time to time POAU declares righteously that it is not opposed to the right of Catholics to have their own school.[1] What it says, and would like Catholics and Protestants to believe, is that POAU is only opposed to

> The bigoted opposition of the Roman Catholic Church to the American public school system.[2]

POAU is not opposed to the existence of Catholic parochial schools. It is only opposed to allowing American children to attend these schools. This is brought out in a POAU "Truth Series" pamphlet titled *NO — I WON'T SEND MY CHILD TO A ROMAN CATHOLIC PAROCHIAL SCHOOL HERE'S WHY . . .*

> I disapprove of the kind of narrow limited teaching done by brainwashed nuns and priests in parochial schools. Such persons . . . are kept throughout their life under the most rigid mental strait-jacket imaginable. Training of this kind may qualify for citizenship in a totalitarian state, but it is not adequate for a citizen of a free country.[3]

This pamphlet concludes with the "reassuring" statement that

> This is no attempt to interfere with the freedom of the Roman Catholic Church to operate its sectarian schools. . . .[4]

---

[1] C. Stanley Lowell, *Truth Series No. 6* (POAU), p. 5.
[2] Glenn L. Archer, *Out of Bounds* (POAU, 1954), p. 7.
[3] C. Stanley Lowell, *op. cit.*, p. 3.
[4] *Ibid.*, p. 5.

POAU says it has set "forces in motion" that will save the American public schools from being crushed by the "dictatorial power of Roman clericalism." It has announced that the first step in its "remedial program" of correcting Church-State separation violations is to gather the facts of the violations "accurately" (*Truth Series No. 1*).

Analysis of a few POAU fact-gathering episodes provides a novel interpretation of the word "accurately."

— 1 —

NEW MEXICO AND MISSOURI

POAU has asserted that Dixon, New Mexico, is a place where the Catholic Church was "asserting power over the public school." This situation was effected by "controlled state executives" and by "servile," "religiously biased county administrators."[5] POAU sent a lawyer to Dixon with a hope of "breaking the grip of Catholic sectarianism on the public school system" and to help effect a "transition from the existing Church-monopoly of the schools."[6]

The factual account of the Dixon affair reads quite differently:

> For a number of years Catholic Sisters had been employed in thirty small schools in the State of New Mexico where the Catholic population was predominant, where it was almost impossible to procure lay school teachers because of the isolated character of the towns or villages, and because the schools, in most instances, had been parish schools, and continued to be the property of the Sisters.
>
> Some non-Catholic parents might not have been completely satisfied with this arrangement, but they preferred it to the taxation which would be levied on the community for a new public school. . . . The first opposition arose in September, 1947, and it was due to agitation from the outside. During 1946, private subscriptions were gathered by some of the Protestant people in the community for the purpose of building a new public school entirely free from religious influence. . . .
>
> But because of these complaints, the Archbishop of Santa Fe, who inherited the situation and never gave any thought in either direction concerning the legality of the practice, sent a letter to all the Sisters in public schools forbidding them to teach religion during school hours,

---

[5] POAU, *Church and State* (10 July, 1948), p. 3. The issue states that opinions therein are "for your information only" and are not "policy determinations."

[6] *Ibid.* (April, 1949), pp. 1, 7.

forbidding them to bring the children by bus before the school day opened, and asking them to remove from the walls any religious emblem.

That the people of New Mexico wanted the Sisters to teach in these schools is clear from the fact that Governor Mabry [non-Catholic], the State School Superintendent . . . the State School Budget Auditor, applied to District Judge E. T. Hensley, of Santa Fe, to dismiss the suit which would bar Catholic Nuns from teaching in the state schools. . . .

The State Superintendent of Schools had said repeatedly that Nuns teaching in the public schools were there at the behest of the local population; that lay teachers would be very hard to procure for such schools situated in out-of-the-way places.

. . . [POAU] probably never read the following editorial which appeared in an El Paso daily back in 1924:

"In refutation of the charge that Catholics are the enemies of the public school the El Paso papers could point to the fact that every public school building erected in New Mexico was made possible by Catholic votes. We have had to rely on the Catholics of the state to carry all of our public school bond elections. The Catholics are in the majority in New Mexico, and could have defeated our schools had they been opposed to the public school system. . . ."

Even though the Archbishop of Santa Fe has withdrawn the Sisters POAU wants the agitation to continue.[7]

POAU calls the Dixon affair part of a "campaign" by the hierarchy "to destroy the public school."[8] The El Paso editorial refutes such a myth. If POAU-approved statements that members of Catholic organizations ". . . are carefully guided by the hierarchy into ways of separation and monopoly" and ". . . have priestly 'advisors' [who] serve as a supreme authority in many cases"[9] are true, then why has not the Catholic majority in New Mexico defeated public school bond issues instead of enthusiastically approving them?

Catholic religious were employed by New Mexico residents because no other teachers would apply for posts in remote sections. Therefore, thirty schools — not a "Church-monopoly of the schools" — were staffed by the Sisters at the request of the populace.

[7] *Who's Who in the POAU* (Huntington: Our Sunday Visitor Press, 1951), pp. 52–55.

[8] POAU, *Church and State* (February, 1950), p. 1.

[9] Paul Blanshard, *American Freedom and Catholic Power* (1958) (Boston: Beacon Press, 1958), pp. 42–43.

Catholic authorities were not aware of any violation of law on their part. When such a possibility was drawn to the attention of the Archbishop he instructed the Sisters to avoid presenting topics or objects of a religious nature to the students. Catholic authorities do not deliberately transgress laws. If a law is inadvertently violated, it is only just that such a violation be corrected. In the Dixon case, apparently there was religious teaching in the public school, and this practice violated a state statute. When the violation was called to the attention of the Archbishop, he took action to remedy the situation. It is inexcusable for POAU to report that affair as a plot "to destroy the public school."

Another POAU attempt to imply that the hierarchy is encroaching upon the public schools occurs in 1951 when the Washington organization declares that in Franklin County, Missouri, a POAU affiliate is instigating legal action "to halt sectarian encroachments on the state's public school system."[10] The case was decided by the Supreme Court of Missouri in 1953.[11]

The long Court opinion states that the Catholic-operated schools allegedly responsible for "sectarian encroachments" were placed in the category of public schools by *"induction into* the free public school system."[12] (Emphasis added.) The opinion concludes that the public school districts did the inducting, not the Catholic Church. The Court decided that the schools were not eligible for public financial support because they were located on Catholic property, were conducted by Sisters, and that the Catholic students were taught religion outside the premises of the school in a nearby building.

POAU asserts that the Missouri Supreme Court "upheld unanimously" the decision "that the teaching sisters . . . were not free to accept the American policy of church-state separation in good faith."[13] The Court said nothing whatever about the Sisters not being "free to accept" *any* "American policy." During a previous case involving the *exact same* issue the Missouri Supreme Court affirmed:

In reaching this conclusion we recognize that the members of these

---

[10] POAU, *Church and State* (May, 1951), p. 2.

[11] Berghorn, *et al. vs.* School District No. 8, Franklin County, Missouri, *et al.*, April, 1953.

[12] *Ibid.*, p. 5.

[13] Glenn L. Archer, *Without Fear or Favor* (POAU, 1955), pp. 13–14.

noble orders are inspired only by the most unselfish and highest
motives; that parochial education is an embodiment of one of the
highest ideals that man may enjoy. The Supreme Court of the
United States found that parochial education has been "long regarded
as useful and meritorious."[14]

Since the Court praised the Sisters as being guided by the "highest motives," and termed parochial education as embodying "the
highest ideals," it is absurd that POAU should try to intimate that
the Sisters are "not free to accept" the American policy that is
embodied in the First Amendment. Certainly POAU does not mean
to imply that the Missouri Court considers not accepting the First
Amendment as one of the "highest motives" and as one of the
"highest ideals."

— 2 —

BRADFORDSVILLE, KENTUCKY

Marion County, Kentucky, had three high schools: namely, St.
Francis, St. Charles, and Bradfordsville. The two former were
staffed by nuns, the last by lay teachers. Bradfordsville High was
closed in 1954 because the enrollment fell below 100 students — the
minimum for state accreditation. Subsequently, legal proceedings
were begun against the Marion County School Board, composed of
three Catholics and two Protestants. The complaint charged the
Board with discriminating against Bradfordsville High and its predominantly Protestant student body by discontinuing certain courses
at Bradfordsville and by not running school buses on Catholic holydays of obligation. The complaint stated St. Francis and St. Charles
Highs were closed on Catholic holydays of obligation and that their
libraries contained much Catholic literature.

In June, 1956, the Kentucky Court of Appeals ruled in favor
of the appellants and cited the Board for discriminating against
Bradfordsville as charged.[15] The case was appealed but the decision
of June, 1956, was affirmed.[16]

On the surface this looks like a victory for POAU, but actually
it is not. Not satisfied with redressing the wrong in accordance with

---

[14] Harfst, *et al. vs.* Hoegen, *et al.,* 7 July, 1942.
[15] Wooley *vs.* Spalding, Court of Appeals of Kentucky, decided 22 June, 1956.
[16] Spalding *vs.* Wooley, Court of Appeals of Kentucky, decided November, 1957.

the spirit of its *Manifesto,* POAU went on to present the opinion of the court in the group's own way.

An Archer pamphlet states:

In Marion County, Kentucky, a Roman Catholic board of education built its public education program to suit Roman Catholic tastes, heedless of the wishes and desires of other creeds and citizens. *This board closed the public high school at Bradfordsville, depriving 373 children of one year of school* — children whose parents did not wish their children to be taught by nuns at St. Francis and St. Charles — schools public in legal structure, but Roman Catholic in function. *This board has so far refused to obey the court's order to open the Bradfordsville school,* remove the Roman Catholic literature from the public schools, quit discriminating against its fellows, *cease from using the buses as property of the Roman Catholic Church.* Every contention I made in the Kentucky case was upheld by the Appellate Court. My charges may have been "monstrous" but they were valid and true.[17] [Emphasis added.]

The only completely true statement here is that the Board did close Bradfordsville High. The court opinion of 22 June, 1956, will be used to indicate how Mr. Archer has confused the situation. Archer says 373 children were deprived of schooling when Bradfordsville closed; the court states the school closed because it fell below 100 students. The Court noted that the School Board's actions had affected Bradfordsville's enrollment, but at no time had the enrollment approximated 373 students. Mr. Archer cannot be referring to children whose parents refused to let them attend St. Francis or St. Charles schools because the Court opinion states:

Generally, the county school transportation system in the western part of the county is designed and utilized to transport Catholic students to St. Francis or St. Charles, and to convey the children who adhere to the Protestant religion, and who reside near St. Charles, to the Lebanon School even though the Lebanon School is in another independent school district, where their tuition is paid by the county board of education.[18]

At no time does the Court mention anyone being deprived of schooling. Certainly it would have if such were the case.

Archer's pamphlet, originally a speech, delivered in August, 1956,

---

[17] Glenn L. Archer, *Let's Think it Through* (POAU, 1956), pp. 11–12.
[18] Wooley *vs.* Spalding, *op. cit.*

to a Presbyterian group, asserts that the School Board disobeyed the Court and refused to reopen the Bradfordsville school. The case was decided in June, 1956, and since July and August are school vacation months it was obviously not feasible to open the school at once.

It is possible that the Court ordered Bradfordsville High reopened at a later date and the Board indicated it would not comply with the order. Although plausible this is not the case. The ruling of 22 June, 1956, ordered the School Board to re-establish a school in the eastern section of the county (where Bradfordsville High was located) or establish a central county high school.

The Court did not order Bradfordsville High reopened. This is made perfectly clear in the appeal opinion of 15 November, 1957. The Court said:

> We are convinced . . . that better educational opportunities are being furnished at the Lebanon city school than could be at Bradfordsville. Also, *reopening the Bradfordsville school would merely fan the dying flames of controversy*.[19] [Emphasis added.]

In July, 1954, *Church and State* carried a story indicating POAU's warped sense of fair play. It commented that Bradfordsville residents were considering a protest march to the state capitol emphasizing they would not tolerate the closing of the Bradfordsville school, etc. The group, organized by a POAU Kentucky affiliate, stated it would "withhold all their taxes" unless the county high schools were equalized. Although apparently endorsing the move, POAU was very careful not to commit the National office.

Ironically, in March, 1957, the parents of parochial school children in Augusta, Maine, threatened to send their children to public schools unless they were provided bus transportation to the parochial school. *Church and State* was horrified, stating, in April, 1957, that the Augusta parents were "using the parochial school children as a club to coerce the school board." It continued:

> They [Catholic parents] threatened to confuse and even wreck the public schools by "jamming" them with 900 parochial pupils.

Neither threatened action took place, but that is not the point. POAU condoned the potentially illegal Bradfordsville action and

---

[19] Spalding *vs.* Wooley, *op. cit.*

condemned the Augusta move. The action contemplated by Augusta parents was unusual, but the parents were requesting a service declared constitutional by the U. S. Supreme Court. The Maine Supreme Court ruled that Augusta had no legislative authority to finance such service, although a "properly worded enabling act" by the State legislature *would be* constitutional (*Springfield, Mass. Daily News,* 25 May, 1959).

The Bradfordsville episode is not dead. An attempt has been made to have four of the five Board members removed from office for misconduct.[20] The State Superintendent of Public Instruction and the State Board of Education refused to take action on the charge. The Kentucky Court of Appeals has sustained the action of the state education officials but the case was appealed on 31 October, 1958.

— 3 —

DO NOT DIVIDE AMERICA

POAU does not "believe in segregating our schools by religious faith. The advantage of our American public school system is that it serves all creeds without distinction." The Americans United affirm:

> The Roman Catholic enclave in our country is a divisive influence. Three and a half million [now close to five million] children, separated from other American children . . . will not be a force for unity in the America we know and love. . . .
> [Catholic] schools . . . build walls of division between groups.[21]

In effect POAU is denouncing parochial schools — Catholic or otherwise. By that attitude, POAU is opposing a Supreme Court decision which denied an Oregon law that took "from parents their freedom to 'direct the upbringing and education' of their children by sending them either to parochial or to private non-sectarian schools of approved educational standards"[22] (Pierce *vs.* Society of Sisters, 1925).

Actually, of course, and contrary to the POAU implication that

---

[20] Hogan *vs.* Kentucky State Board of Education, *et al.,* Court of Appeals of Kentucky, October, 1958.

[21] C. Stanley Lowell, *op. cit.,* pp. 3, 4.

[22] R. E. Cushman, *Leading Constitutional Decisions* (New York: Appleton-Century-Crofts, Inc., 1958), p. 144.

parochial schools do not serve all creeds without distinction, it is a known fact that non-Catholics may and do attend Catholic schools.

The issue of divisiveness revolves about the theory that if we associate closely with other people, we will, as a result, develop a bond of brotherhood. But Dr. John Kane, well-known sociologist, says:

> The notion that to know people intimately is to love them is just a bit naive, as divorce statistics in the United States appear to indicate. The most intense prejudice toward Japanese was most common on the West Coast although people there had an opportunity of coming into contact with them. It is much less in the East where few Japanese live. . . . The mere fact of having children of different faiths and different races in the same classroom is not in itself enough to destroy prejudice and discrimination. It depends on the circumstances under which people meet and the intensity of prejudice they hold toward minorities which they encounter. This information is available in any fundamental text on social psychology.[23]

Dr. Kane further questions whether individual public schools always do have minorities represented, since people of the same social and racial group tend to live in the same areas, and school districts have been formed with that fact in mind. However,

> Secondary Catholic schools and other private schools either have no such districts or as in the case of the former they are apt to be so broad that persons of all social classes, races and ethnic groups are represented. . . .[24]

Professor James M. O'Neill shows if parochial schools were divisive (which he denies), opposition to them would not solve the "problem" even if we grant the opponents' faulty assumptions:

> . . . The assumption that students in public schools do not know who is Protestant, who Catholic, who Jewish, seems possible to intelligent people only if they have had little or no contact with public schools. If the knowing of these differences means hostility and suspicion among the pupils, then homes and schools [public] seem obviously to be failing in ways that would not be cured by eliminating parochial schools. . . .[25]

---

[23] John J. Kane, *Catholic-Protestant Conflicts in America* (Chicago: Regnery, 1955), p. 113.

[24] *Ibid.*

[25] James M. O'Neill, *Catholicism and American Freedom* (New York: Harper and Brothers, 1952), p. 93.

If separate religious groups result in "dividing America," as is the result from the "Roman Catholic enclave in our country," we will have to stop going to our separate churches; we will have to abolish the armed forces' chaplain "enclave"; etc. If, indeed, religious differences are a "divisive influence," the only logical solution is to unite America by either abolishing religion or forcing everyone to conform to religion "X."

Secretary Folsom of the Department of Health, Education and Welfare has referred to the "rich diversity of both public and private educational institutions," and said we therefore have

> avoided the pitfalls of nationally controlled education.
>
> We believe that a system based on freedom of the mind and unshackled right of inquiry will accomplish more than a system based on conscription and regimentation.[26]

The 1958 president-elect of the American Association of School Administrators, executive voice of the nation's public schools, declared that private-public school relations were "better than ever." He continued,

> It is my belief that good public school administrators should support private schools . . . [because] under the American system of universal education, people must have freedom to choose between the two systems because *it is essential to our national welfare.*[27] [Emphasis added.]

In contrast POAU terms the country's largest private school system as "dividing America" and as building "walls of division."

— 4 —

FOREIGN CONTROL

POAU warns that Catholic schools are under foreign control inasmuch as such institutions are "directed by officials who are under the control of a foreign potentate [how POAU loves that word "potentate"!] . . . who is the dictator of the Vatican State in Italy."[28] The absurdity of the statement is best shown by quoting from a recent study on private schools done by the Federal Government.

---

[26] *The Pilot,* 22 March, 1958.
[27] *Ibid.*
[28] C. Stanley Lowell, *op. cit.,* p. 3.

In one way or another every enterprise, public or nonpublic, that is conducted within a State is subject to the authority of the State. State legislatures [not the Vatican] determine the extent of such regulation through statutes. . . .

. . . In the normal operation of their activities, non-public schools must accept responsibilities prescribed by law for the conduct and care of the children and youth they enroll . . . they may be expressly required to provide educational programs that compare favorably with the programs required in public schools of like nature.

In a number of States if a nonpublic school fails to comply with the standards established for compulsory education, the State may require conformance or deny the school the right to serve children of compulsory school age.[29]

The teaching of religion is the main difference between the curriculum in a Catholic school and a public school and since Catholic schools are accredited in every state, there must be nothing in that religion which transgresses standards established for public schools. If religion constituted a threat to such standards, the State could ". . . require conformance or deny the school the right to serve children of compulsory school age." Religion, the only subject controlled by the "dictator of the Vatican State in Italy," is not considered by the states as something that detracts from the general education of a child or as something that is "alien," and "not adequate for a citizen of a free country."[30]

Many states have laws requiring nonpublic schools to place certain subjects in the curriculum. Arkansas, for example, requires a course "instilling into the hearts of the various pupils . . . an understanding of the United States and . . . a love of country and . . . a devotion to the principles of American government."[31] Rhode Island requires a course in which "the principles of popular and representative government" are taught.[32] Catholic schools in those states give such courses; consequently the POAU implication that children in parochial schools do not learn "American loyalties" is absurd.[33]

Related to the question of "foreign control," is the question of

---

[29] U. S. Department of Health, Education and Welfare, *The State and Nonpublic Schools* (Washington: U. S. Government Printing Office, 1958), pp. 9, 11.

[30] C. Stanley Lowell, *op. cit.*, pp. 2, 3.

[31] U. S. Department of Health, Education and Welfare, *op. cit.*, p. 37.

[32] *Ibid.*, p. 129.

[33] C. Stanley Lowell, *op. cit.*, p. 3.

Catholics on public school boards. POAU fears that if "tax-supported school systems . . . come under the domination" of Catholics, such boards "are in danger of losing their 'public' character."[34] As Mr. Dale Francis remarked:

> That sounds to me suspiciously as if someone is urging taxation without representation because, while the POAU may forget, Catholics don't forget their tax money is buying public school[s]. . . . And when it comes to spending that tax money they want to know the what-fors, they don't want to wonder where the green stuff went.
>
> I think many non-Catholics fail to realize how much public school education is helped by Catholics. Say there is a town with 100 school age children, and $50 per pupil is set aside for their training. Then 50 of these children don't go to public schools but to Catholic schools. That means there will be $100 per pupil [of the public school], and that extra $50 is coming from the money set aside for the Catholic child in a Catholic school. . . .
>
> So whether he uses the schools or not, a Catholic has a citizen's right to speak out on how the schools are run.[35]

— 5 —

FEDERAL AID AND SCHOOL BUSES

Concerning federal aid to education POAU maintains that *the* "Catholic position" is to advocate aid if parochial schools are included, and to oppose the aid if Catholic schools are excluded.[36] Actually, there is no "Catholic position" on this question to which Catholics must adhere. As Professor O'Neill remarks, Catholics hold a number of views on the matter, such as;

1. Opposed to any federal aid to education as a threat of federal control.
2. Approve it if limited only to "areas of need."
3. Approve it if given without discrimination, as partial support only, to all schools that educate American children in accordance with the educational standards of the individual states.
4. Approve it only for schools under *public* control — i.e., oppose it in any form (even health and safety measures) for children attending Catholic schools, as endangering specifically Catholic education.[37]

---

[34] POAU, *Church and State* (July, 1953), p. 2.
[35] *Our Sunday Visitor*, 23 June, 1957.
[36] POAU, *Church and State* (October, 1951), p. 2.
[37] O'Neill, *op. cit.*, pp. 100–101. He mentions two additional viewpoints.

When, therefore, an individual Catholic priest or bishop expresses an opinion on Federal aid to education, that man is speaking as a citizen and is only rendering *his* view, which others may accept or reject.

The school bus issue of Connecticut attracted wide publicity. When the Connecticut legislature approved the bus measure, POAU termed it "Archbishop O'Brien's bill"[38] and a "parochial school bus subsidy bill." Factually, the legislation pertained to *all* private schools. The Associated Press reported, "the measure provides that any town or city in Connecticut if the voters dictate in a referendum can provide bus service for private non-profit schools."[39] The bill passed the legislature by the tie-breaking vote of a Congregationalist and was signed by Connecticut's Jewish governor. Nonetheless, POAU says it was "Archbishop O'Brien's bill."

In 1947, the Supreme Court of the United States declared bus transportation a public welfare benefit which did not violate the First Amendment; POAU consistently opposes that opinion.

POAU worked to defeat the Connecticut bill and charged that Archbishop O'Brien urged Catholics "to destroy the political career of any man who dared to oppose."[40] The Archbishop urged no such thing. The bishops of Connecticut issued a pastoral letter which stated that the affair was "of the most acute concern" to the faithful, especially "since more than sixty-two percent of the children born in Connecticut in 1956 are Catholic."[41] The letter urged Catholics to observe carefully the action taken by their representatives. No threats were hurled at the legislature. If some Catholics approved their representatives' action, they would probably vote for them in the next election; others could conceivably vote against them for performing the same action. The Archbishop was not telling Catholics how to vote, nor does he have any authority to do so in such a matter. He was merely informing the faithful about an issue that concerned them.

The POAU argument against bus transportation for all school children is as follows:

> To treat bus transportation for children in parochial schools as a detached welfare service is to be completely unrealistic [the U. S.

---

38 POAU, *Church and State* (July, 1957), p. 1.
39 *Springfield (Mass.) Republican,* 1 June, 1957.
40 POAU, *Church and State* (July, 1957), p. 1.
41 *The Pilot,* 8 June, 1957.

Supreme Court thinks otherwise]. We would not spend tax money to transport people to church just because it contributed to their personal welfare.[42]

People are not compelled by the State to attend church, whereas children are compelled to attend school. The Americans United notwithstanding, bus transportation is classed as welfare legislation (Supreme Court, Everson Case — 1947). The Fourteenth Amendment declares in part, "Nor shall any State . . . deny to any person within its jurisdiction the equal protection of the laws." In the Hayes Case the United States Supreme Court declared "equal protection" meant "That all persons shall be treated alike, under like circumstances and conditions, both in the privileges conferred and in the liabilities imposed."

In what way does "equal protection" apply to bus transportation? The state provides bus transportation to aid children in complying with compulsory school attendance laws and to protect them from the hazards of the highway. The equal protection guarantee requires that all share this state-provided benefit who attend an approved school. Parochial schools are approved schools. The Supreme Court of Mississippi asserted that "the state is under duty to ignore a child's creed, but not its need. . . . The state which allows the pupil to subscribe to any religious creed should not, because of his exercise of this right, proscribe him from benefits common to all" (Chance Case).

In many states parochial and private school children are excluded from forms of welfare legislation. However they are permitted to walk on tax-supported sidewalks which are classified as welfare legislation that should benefit all children.

Even if it were true that a parochial school also benefits from bus transportation, such a fact cannot deprive the child of its equal rights under the Constitution (U. S. Supreme Court, Everson Case).[43]

It is interesting to read this remark by Mr. Blanshard, POAU special counsel:

Those bills which exempt tuition payments to colleges have won much support on purely humane grounds. . . .

---

[42] Glenn L. Archer, *Without Fear or Favor* (POAU, 1955), p. 20.
[43] Robert White, "Are They Step Children?" *The Catholic Home Journal* (March, 1957), p. 13 ff. All since note 42 is based on this article.

It seems natural to extend such exemptions to any taxpayer, whether he chooses a public, a Catholic or Methodist college.

The real danger comes when such exemptions are extended to tuition payments for elementary and secondary schools.[44]

Mr. Blanshard leaves the area of bus transportation and advocates or at least does not oppose tuition exemptions on the college level — even for payments to Catholic colleges. If that is not a violation of "church-state separation," why does he balk at such exemptions on the elementary and secondary level? They are called a "real danger." Only *private* schools on the elementary and secondary levels have tuition payments. Catholic parochial schools are the largest element in the private system, and therein lies the "real danger" to Mr. Blanshard and POAU.[45]

— 6 —

THE BIG GUN: CANON 1374

The first of POAU's three "special questions . . . to every Catholic candidate for president or vice-president of the United States" is:

> The Canon Law of your church (Canon 1374) directs all American Catholic parents to boycott our public schools unless they receive special permission from their bishops. Do you personally approve or disapprove of this boycott rule?[46]

POAU presents a completely fictitious teaching of canon law, and then asks Catholic candidates if they "personally approve" the rule. Just why the POAU straw man is fictitious is indicated by *The Pilot* of Boston. The Catholic weekly in specific reply to POAU states in part:

> The text of canon 1374, in English translation (by Abbo-Hannan, in "The Sacred Canons") is as follows:
> "Catholic children shall not attend non-Catholic schools, neutral schools or mixed schools, that is, schools that are also open to non-

---

[44] *The Humanist* (published by American Humanist Association, Yellow Springs, Ohio), Vol. XVII, No. 3 (May–June), p. 183.

[45] Although Blanshard does not oppose tax exemption for tuition payments to sectarian colleges, he does oppose bus transportation for all school children regardless of creed. See his and POAU's fallacious *The Bus Wedge.*

[46] POAU, *A Ten Year Balance Sheet* (mimeographed, 1958), p. 3.

Catholics. Only the Ordinary is competent to determine, in accordance with the norm of instruction of the Apostolic See, in what circumstances, and with what safeguards to overcome the danger of perversion, the conducting of such schools can be tolerated." [Some translate this as "attendance at such schools," etc.]

THE WORD "BOYCOTT" does not appear in the text of the canon. It is *not correct,* therefore, to say that the Church "directs all American Catholic parents to boycott our public schools. . . ." What the canon actually states is that Catholic children shall not attend the schools mentioned. A better translation of the Latin "Pueri catholici ne frequentent" would perhaps be "Catholic children should not attend these schools." This meaning would seem to be more consistent with the provision of the second part of the canon which authorizes the bishop to grant exceptions to the general rule.

In relation to this second part of the canon, it is *not correct* to say that Catholics are forbidden to attend public schools "unless they receive special permission from their bishops.". . . The law as it stands would permit a bishop to insist upon this condition, but does not require him to do so. Each bishop will decide for his own diocese the extent to which attendance by Catholics at the schools mentioned will be allowed. Where there is no explicit ruling from the local authorities, it may be assumed that the bishop sees no reason for alarm in the existing situation and is satisfied to deal with it by applying the general principle set down in canon 1374.

It will be noted that the term "public school" does not appear in the text of the canon. Instead, the canon enumerates three kinds of schools which Catholics are urged to avoid because of the dangers to their faith which these schools may be presumed to afford. By non-Catholic school is meant one in which a non-Catholic religion is taught and recommended. The reason for the Church's objection to such schools is obvious, but it should be noted that they are not usually public schools.

A MIXED SCHOOL is one which is indifferent to religion, and which admits pupils of any and all religions in such a way as to encourage the leaders of each group under the auspices of the school to provide religious instruction for its own members. Here again it is not our public schools which are singled out, since it is the policy of American public schools to exclude religious instruction entirely. . . .

A NEUTRAL SCHOOL is one from which the teaching of religion is completely excluded. The exclusion of religion from the public schools had been considered mandatory by some proponents of the public school system. In recent times, however, this policy has been severely criticized by many non-Catholics as it applies to the public schools. Regardless of the reasons for the criticism, it obviously indicates that Catholics are not alone in considering the exclusion of religion from the public schools to be undesirable. From the Catholic point of view the neutral school is objectionable because it excludes the possibility of the direct influence of religion upon education which Catholics, along with many non-Catholics, hold to be desirable.[47]

According to *Webster's Dictionary* "boycott" has the element of combining against. Catholics are not against public schools in the sense that they will not support those schools. And certainly there is no plot to destroy or undermine public education by Catholics (see next section).

Catholics simply believe that public education with its exclusion of religion is not the ideal education for *Catholic* children. Therefore, whenever and wherever possible, Catholic children will be sent to Catholic schools. That attitude *does not in any way* mean or imply that Catholics have to destroy, weaken, or "capture" public education. This still would be true even if *all* Catholic children could be accommodated in Catholic schools.[48]

— 7 —

CATHOLIC SUPPORT OF PUBLIC SCHOOLS

First, it is appropriate to outline briefly the general Catholic position regarding education. One Catholic source paraphrases an encyclical of Pius XI as follows:

> Now education is, in essence, a thing meant to prepare man for the ultimate purpose of his existence. This ultimate purpose — or last end — is God. . . . For a Christian education aims at securing the Supreme Good, that is to say, God, for the souls of those being educated, and the maximum well-being for human society.
>
> Education is the responsibility of *three distinct,* and necessary, societies, says the pope; they are the Family and the *State,* which are natural societies, and the Church which is a supernatural society. . . .
>
> The Church's rights derive, in the first place, from the command laid upon it by the divine founder, Jesus Christ, when He said:

---

[47] *The Pilot,* 7 June, 1958.

[48] POAU often remarks that the Catholic Church uses "coercion" by means of "clerical dictators" (priests) to make Catholics send their children to parochial schools. If a Catholic does not voluntarily send his child to a parochial school, the Church cannot coerce him to do otherwise, in contrast to the power of the state to exercise coercion in this matter (POAU references: see *Truth Series No. 6*).

"Teach ye all nations whatsoever things I have commanded you . . . even to the consummation of the world."

"To watch over the entire education of *her* children . . . is the Church's inalienable right." She can never cease to care whether her children are exposed to doctrinal or moral evil. . . .

The Family rights, then, come before the rights of the State; its rights are something the State must not violate. . . . existence comes from the parent and not from the State. . . .

Yet the parents' rights to educate their children are neither absolute nor despotic. They are subordinated to the ultimate purpose of the children's existence, and to the natural and divine law.[49] [Emphasis added.]

Referring specifically to the State, Pius XI affirms:

Accordingly, unjust and unlawful is any monopoly, educational or scholastic, which, physically or morally, forces families to make use of government schools, contrary to the dictates of their Christian conscience, or contrary even to their legitimate preferences.[50]

The injustice of such a monopoly applies to both the Catholic and non-Catholic State.[51]

Although "education belongs pre-eminently to the Church, by reason of a double title in the supernatural order, conferred exclusively upon her by God Himself [and] absolutely superior therefore to any other title in the natural order,"

it pertains to the State, in view of the common good, to promote in various ways the education and instruction of youth. . . . It should, moreover, supplement their work [family and church] whenever this falls short of what is necessary, *even by means of its [the State's] own schools and institutions*.[52] [Emphasis added.]

Therefore, "education is the responsibility of three distinct and necessary societies . . . the Family and the State . . . and the Church." Since the family preceded the State, and since the State is a collection of many families working for the common welfare, the rights of the family in education take precedence over those of

---

49 P. Hughes, *The Popes' New Order* (New York: Macmillan Company, 1944), pp. 194–197. Paraphrase from *Divini Illius Magistri,* December, 1931.

50 Anne Freemantle (ed.), *The Papal Encyclicals* (New York: Mentor, 1956), p. 226. From *Rappresentanti in Terra,* December, 1929.

51 J. A. Ryan and F. T. Boland, *Catholic Principles of Politics* (New York: Macmillan Company, 1940), p. 333.

52 Freemantle, *op. cit.,* p. 227.

the State. The Catholic Church also has rights in the sphere of education since Christ commissioned her to teach. No one of the three societies can claim a monopoly of education because education is the responsibility of all three. The State may establish its own schools when the effort of the other two societies "falls short of what is necessary."[53]

In this light, it is inexcusable for POAU to say:

> American members of the Roman Catholic hierarchy frequently deny that they are opposed to the public school system, but Church law and the actions of the Pope prove contrary.[54]

This assertion of POAU can only be the result of gross ignorance about a subject it is supposed to be informed on because the American hierarchy in 1919 declared that

> the State has a right to insist that its citizens shall be educated. . . . the State has the right to establish schools and take every other legitimate means to safeguard its vital interests against the dangers that result from ignorance.[55]

POAU calls Cardinal McIntyre "a noted enemy of the public schools" because "more than 80 new parochial schools have been built during his service as Archbishop of Los Angeles."[56] Catholics prefer to build parochial schools. That is their constitutional privilege. Because of his exercise of a democratic preference, POAU terms Cardinal McIntyre an "enemy" of public schools. By such reasoning, everyone sending children to any private school is an "enemy" of public schools. The real "enemy" seems to be POAU, in that it opposes and labels as "enemy" anyone who democratically and constitutionally prefers a nonpublic education. Cardinal McIntyre himself has declared:

> *Both* systems [public and private schools] make a profound and indispensable contribution to the American scene, and it is the way of wisdom to acknowledge in *both* systems a noble partnership in education. . . .[57] [Emphasis added.]

[53] The State always may establish schools to prepare citizens for civic duties and for military service, provided the rights of both family and Church are respected (cf. Freemantle, *op. cit.*, p. 226).

[54] POAU, *Church and State* (January, 1953), p. 1.

[55] R. M. Huber (ed.), "Pastoral Letter of 1919," *Our Bishops Speak* (Milwaukee: Bruce Publishing Company, 1952), p. 62.

[56] POAU, *Church and State* (January, 1953), p. 1.

[57] N.C.W.C. release, 29 August, 1955.

That quotation demonstrates that one is able to build "80 new parochial schools" and still not oppose the public education system.

In 1955, the American hierarchy affirmed: ". . . the plain physical fact of the [public] school system is a matter for unanimous congratulation."[58]

Despite this 1955 statement, POAU early in 1956 uttered a statement that the hierarchy has a "master plan," and that the ultimate goal "is to obtain control of all education." What the hierarchy really wants is "clerical domination" and "monopoly."[59] In view of the bishops' praise of public education, and the Pope's remarks about educational responsibility belonging to *three* distinct societies, the POAU diatribe is gross error.

A favorite device of POAU is to present some statement made by a priest or bishop as official doctrine that all Catholics must believe. POAU never makes the distinction between opinion and doctrine. For example, a Catholic priest is reported to have written a pamphlet entitled *May an American Oppose the Public School?* POAU makes a big point of the fact that the pamphlet "was published in 1937 under the Imprimatur of the late Patrick Cardinal Hayes, and has never been repudiated by the hierarchy."[60] In the pamphlet, the priest-author is said to have written: "Our first duty to the public school is not to pay taxes for its maintenance."[61]

First of all, POAU is up to its old trick of implying that everything published with an *imprimatur* is Catholic doctrine which all must believe until "repudiated by the hierarchy" (see Chapter 1 of this book). The statement of the priest regarding public schools is his own opinion. Catholics are able to distinguish such opinion from the essentials of the Faith. POAU is not able to do so because it does not know the first thing about Catholic doctrine, and if it did then its ramblings would not be in conformity with what it knows to be the truth.

All such statements can be accepted or rejected by individual Catholics. In fact, one priest ("clerical dictator" to POAU) wrote:

---

[58] "The Place of the Private and Church-Related Schools in American Education," *The 1956 National Catholic Almanac* (Paterson: St. Anthony's Guild, 1956), p. 519.

[59] Glenn L. Archer, *Separation and Spirituality* (POAU, 1956), p. 4.

[60] POAU, *Church and State* (May, 1952), p. 4.

[61] For the sake of argument it will be assumed that the priest actually said this. However, one should never assume anything as true simply because POAU prints it. The pamphlet in question has not been located by the author.

"I am also suggesting that the best place for pamphlets describing the public schools as *Our National Enemy No. 1* is the ash-can."[62] POAU should now feel quite secure, for that statement has the *imprimatur* of Cardinal Spellman.

Monsignor James E. Hoflich, superintendent of grade schools for the St. Louis archdiocese, asserted that Catholics have a grave obligation to continue to support public education. He commented that "The educational atmosphere as a whole is weakened if one set of schools is weak. We feel that all schools should be as good as possible." Another Catholic educator, Richard Chidress, professor of constitutional law at St. Louis University, said Catholics have a "moral obligation" to support public schools:

> The fact that we have schools of our own does not remove our obligation to the public welfare. We have a moral obligation to see that all children in our communities receive at least a minimal level of education.[63]

According to POAU such apparently innocent statements are really a part of a sinister "master plan" by the hierarchy. One wonders why POAU does not publish a photostat of this "master plan."

— 8 —

CONCLUSION

A letter from a county superintendent of public schools refutes many of the POAU charges discussed in this chapter:

> I wish to say that Catholic nuns have been teaching in Dubois County for over sixty years, and there has never been unfavorable reaction of the general public to their presence. Many of the nuns teaching in the elementary schools have M. A. degrees [where is the "mental strait-jacket"?]. They are licensed by the state and hired by the trustees. They meet all the requirements as public school teachers [even though "brainwashed"?] and comply with all county and state regulations. . . . They are under the supervision of the county or city superintendent [where is the "alien" control by the "foreign potentate"?] and teach the state adopted texts [but POAU says nuns do not understand "American loyalties"]. . . .

---

[62] G. H. Dunne, *Religion and American Democracy* (New York: America Press, 1949), p. 27.
[63] *The Pilot*, 22 March, 1958.

They are some of the best teachers, and there is perfect harmony [what about "dividing America"?] between Catholics and Protestants in this county as far as schools are concerned, and we are opposed to any outside forces that would destroy this harmony . . . I have heard of the so-called POAU before. . . . We live under a free representative government not dominated by POAU, and that is democracy.[64]

---

[64] John H. Teder (Dubois County, Indiana), a letter, 10 January, 1958.

CHAPTER 9

CENSORSHIP?

BECAUSE of the wealth of literature that has been written about Catholic principles of "censorship," that aspect of the problem will be discussed only briefly. For a readable and thorough account of Catholicism's philosophy on "censorship," Father Harold C. Gardiner's *Catholic Viewpoint on Censorship* (Hanover House, 1958) is recommended.

Strictly speaking, censorship is the result of the action performed by a government official empowered to examine written or printed matter, motion pictures, and the like, in order to forbid publication if objectionable. Should the official decide that a certain book shall not be published, then the citizens will not be able to read that book regardless of their wishes. The publisher of the book is legally restrained from printing the volume. If he disobeys, the government can apply legal sanction.

The Catholic Church, obviously, does not and cannot exercise censorship in this manner. As Professor O'Neill remarks:

> The effectiveness of the Church in the area that is inaccurately called "censorship" depends wholly upon the *voluntary* acceptance of the Church's guidance by those who read or listen.[1]

If a Catholic refuses to heed the voice of the Church on this matter, the Church cannot force him to obey. Spiritual penalties, of course, may be inflicted, but there is nothing in the nature of those penalties — in contrast to government penalties — that forces or compels a person to obey. Therefore, Catholic agencies such as

---

[1] J. M. O'Neill, *Catholicism and American Freedom* (New York: Harper and Brothers, 1952), pp. 115–116.

92

the National Office for Decent Literature may criticize, guide, and influence but they cannot "censor." NODL cannot "force" anyone nor "impose" anything on anyone if people do not co-operate voluntarily. If criticism and voluntary acceptance of that criticism is to be termed "censorship," then those who use the word in that sense should explain precisely what they mean because for the ordinary individual "censorship" implies some type of official compulsion that can be enforced.

POAU, however, never explains what it means by "censorship." The group uses the word indiscriminately, and lets the reader's imagination do the rest. NODL is referred to as "a non-public Roman Catholic censorship group,"[2] and an "active private censorship group" that engages "in double-talk when denying that it used coercive tactics."[3] For the purposes of this chapter, "censorship" will be used as defined in the previous paragraph, i.e., non-governmental criticism and voluntary acceptance of that criticism.

— 1 —

FOUR RULES, NODL, AND THE LEGION

There are four rules that present an excellent norm by which minority groups should regulate their actions in the area of censorship within a pluralistic society. These rules are heartily endorsed by Catholics, lay or clerical:

1. Each minority group has the right to censor for its *own* members in order to protect and adhere to the special standards held within the group.

2. No minority group has the right to demand that government legally enforce that group's standards upon all the people.

3. Any minority group has the right to work toward elevation of standards of public morality through measures of persuasion and pacific argument.

4. No minority group has the right to impose its own religious or moral views on other groups, through the use of the methods of force, coercion, or violence.[4]

The only place for confusion is the differentiation between "per-

---

[2] POAU, *Church and State* (November, 1956), p. 8.
[3] *Ibid.* (June, 1957), p. 5.
[4] H. C. Gardiner, *Catholic Viewpoint on Censorship* (New York: Hanover House, 1958), p. 125.

suasion and pacific argument" and "methods of force, coercion, or violence" in Rules 3 and 4 respectively. Specifically, the distinction we are looking for revolves around the practice of what is called "boycott." Some say boycott is simply a means of "persuasion and pacific argument"; others maintain that it is a method of "force" or "coercion" and hence illicit under the terms of Rule 4.

POAU considers boycott as something bad and a threat to freedom and democracy. The group tells us that "the secular press is throttled by fear of boycotts" by Catholics, and that is regarded as one of the "onslaughts" against religious liberty.[5] Again, "Two of America's best-known magazines are being made the targets of boycotts launched by leaders of the Roman Catholic hierarchy"; Catholics were "asked to boycott *Newsweek* and *Reader's Digest*."[6] It is evident that even if the boycott is confined to action by a minority group, as in the above case, POAU still regards such action as objectionable.

The American Civil Liberties Union disagrees with POAU. In a 1951 official statement, the ACLU declared that

> It recognizes as far as legal right is concerned, the use of . . . the organization of a specific and primary boycott even when [it implies] some degree of coercion.[7]

What is a primary boycott?

> A primary boycott occurs when a threat not to patronize is directed only against the offending party (employer, bookseller, film exhibitor, etc.); a secondary boycott arises when the threat not to patronize is extended to induce a third party or parties to join in the refusal of patronage.[8]

Therefore, if Catholics boycott a certain magazine, such action is quite within their rights. But if Catholics try to make other groups of citizens boycott the magazine, such a practice is not within their rights, i.e., a secondary boycott.

In this connection, the daily papers recently reported that an agency of the National Education Association urged a "boycott in classrooms" of *Life* magazine. The agency declared, ". . . your most effective weapon will be to question the continuation of sub-

---

[5] POAU, *Church and State* (June, 1949), p. 1.

[6] *Ibid.* (September, 1951), p. 3.

[7] Gardiner, *op. cit.*, p. 173, n. 1.

[8] *Ibid.*, p. 132.

scriptions to the *Life* and *Time* publications in your school. . . ."
Thus, a primary boycott was urged. The general manager of *Life*
quite correctly replied that it is *"the privilege of any American to
boycott anything he wants to."*[9] (Emphasis added.) But when a
New York City school board wanted to boycott *The Nation* because the magazine published articles by Paul Blanshard which
ridiculed Catholic views, POAU called such action by the board
"unconstitutional, undemocratic and unwholesome."[10] POAU did
not comment on the *Life* boycott. Presumably, if the National
Education Association agency had boycotted *Life* because the magazine misrepresented Catholicism, POAU would have termed such a
boycott "unconstitutional, undemocratic and unwholesome."

POAU to the contrary notwithstanding, American law recognizes
the constitutional and democratic nature of primary boycotts.

It seems, then, that the practice of a primary boycott is a
measure of "persuasion and pacific argument" and not one of the
methods of "force, coercion, or violence." Thus, according to Rule
3, the boycott may be licitly used by a minority group "to work
toward elevation of standards of public morality."

The NODL Code declares:

> The National Office for Decent Literature has been established to
> safeguard the moral and spiritual ideals of youth. . . .
> The NODL fulfills its function, in part, by offering to responsible
> individuals and organizations an evaluation of current comic books,
> magazines and pocket-size books. . . .
> . . . After giving the dealer a NODL list which he may keep, the
> team should ask permission to examine the racks. . . . When a team
> finds objectionable titles, a member should courteously ask that they
> be removed from sale. . . .
> . . . *the list is not to be used for purposes of boycott or coercion.*[11]
> [Emphasis added.]

It is quite clear that NODL does not violate any of the four
rules stated. It does not even wish its list used for boycott. If the
list is used for boycott or coercion, such use is in spite of, not
because of, NODL regulations. Therefore, it is typical of POAU
to refer to the "works on the boycott list of the NODL."[12]

[9] *Springfield Daily News,* 9 April, 1958.
[10] POAU, *Church and State* (August, 1948), p. 3.
[11] Gardiner, *op. cit.,* pp. 110, 112, 115.
[12] POAU, *Church and State* (November, 1956), p. 8.

Since NODL merely circulates a list of objectionable paperback books — a list that can be accepted or rejected — it is ridiculous to report that censorship (in any sense) is "imposed" by NODL.[13] If dealers will not remove objectionable titles from the racks, no boycott or coercion is to be practiced.

POAU has echoed the criticism that the end result of NODL action deprives others of the opportunity to buy books that otherwise would have been present on the newsstand racks.[14] That is ridiculous. NODL efforts are directed only at paperbacks. If a person really wants to obtain a book, he may easily procure a hard-back copy from the library or bookstore. In addition, it is perverse thinking to label the result of constitutional actions by NODL as deserving "special rebuke."[15]

The Legion of Decency is a Catholic agency which distributes a list that rates films. Catholics are urged not to see those films that are indecent and immoral. Catholics are also urged to stay away from theaters showing such films as a matter of policy. Therefore, the most drastic result that may be effected by Legion policy is a primary boycott. Such a boycott does not violate our four rules and is "the privilege of any American."[16]

— 2 —

BRITANNICA AND MARTIN LUTHER

POAU reported this sinister event in 1949; namely, next to the

> . . . publishing offices of the "Encyclopaedia Britannica" in Chicago . . . [an] office has been established, with the following legend on the door: "Catholic Committee on the Encyclopaedia Britannica." The editors of the Encyclopaedia submit their copy to the neighboring office for censorship.[17]

---

[13] *Ibid.* (June, 1957), p. 5. POAU is echoing ACLU criticism.
[14] *Ibid.*
[15] *Ibid.*
[16] Contrary to some opinion, a Catholic does not *necessarily* commit a sin by viewing even a condemned picture. See Gardiner, *op. cit.,* p. 97. For those desiring a very complete understanding of the Legion and NODL, Father Gardiner's book is an excellent source.

Some Catholic groups will undoubtedly be found that attempt to violate the four rules listed at the beginning of the chapter. Such organizations possess more zeal than good sense, although the lack of good sense is permissible under the Constitution.

[17] POAU, *Church and State* (September, 1949), p. 3.

The only "legend" in that report is truth. POAU was forced to retract the story when contacted by *Encyclopaedia Britannica's* general counsel, who said,

At no time has a "Catholic Committee on the *Encyclopaedia Britannica*" existed. At no time has there been an office adjacent to *Britannica's* offices with such a legend on the door. At no time have the editors of the *Encyclopaedia Britannica* "submitted" copy for the Encyclopaedia to any Catholic committee for censorship.[18]

At no time is POAU to be considered reliable without personal intensive investigation of its legends.

The film *Martin Luther* received national publicity when its scheduled appearance on WGN-TV was canceled by the Chicago station in December, 1956. It is difficult to imagine a more intense reaction had Luther himself been denied access to WGN studios. POAU exploited the incident for all it was worth; not until October, 1957, did *Martin Luther* disappear from the pages of POAU's *Church and State*.

In January, 1957, POAU sent "telegrams to the House Committee on Un-American Activities and the Federal Communications Commission . . . demanding investigation of the banning of the film. . . ." Mr. Archer called the cancellation as worthy of investigation as "subversion by Communist organizations." POAU "ridiculed the claim" that "the suppression of the TV program had not been directly ordered by the Roman Catholic Church."[19] A POAU reprint of a *Christian Century* article proclaimed that the incident "is the beginning of tyranny."[20]

In February, POAU changed its mind and said the ban was "placed by Chicago Station WGN-TV."[21] In March, "sectarian censorship" caused the ban.[22] But during April it was again "WGN-TV's ban."[23] However, the following month saw POAU declare that the film was banned "by Roman Catholics."[24] The only factor that

---

[18] *Ibid.* (November, 1949), p. 2. It should be mentioned that John Courtney Murray, S.J., has served *Britannica* for some time as an adviser on Catholic subjects. In 1959 two other Jesuit scholars were added to assist Father Murray (*Information*, June, 1959).

[19] *Ibid.* (January, 1957), pp. 1, 8.

[20] POAU, *Censorship in Chicago* (1957), p. 1.

[21] POAU, *Church and State* (February, 1957), p. 1.

[22] *Ibid.* (March, 1957), p. 1.

[23] *Ibid.* (April, 1957), p. 3.

[24] Glenn L. Archer, *The Ramparts We Watch* (POAU, May, 1957), p. 9.

remained constant was that *Martin Luther* did not get televised by WGN.

Fact Number 1: WGN-TV received several phone calls protesting the scheduled showing of *Martin Luther*. Although it is quite conceivable that groups desiring to promote Catholic-Protestant friction made the calls, it is more likely that individual Catholics originated the protests. We, at least, will assume that Catholics in the Chicago area were responsible for the phone calls to WGN. Fact Number 2: WGN-TV canceled the *21 December, 1956,* showing of *Martin Luther* as a result of the protest calls. Thus, WGN is the agency that "banned" the film scheduled for December, and the phone calls provided the motivation for that cancellation.

Certain individuals made use of their American freedom to protest a scheduled film. The TV station was free to show or to cancel the film. WGN was not subjected to "tyranny." The station was faced with a question of deciding freely either to show or not to show the film. After deliberation, the free choice of canceling the December televising of the film resulted. POAU terms that situation "subversive to American freedom," and an "un-American activity."[25] The *Martin Luther* cancellation could be variously described as "poor judgment," "good judgment," the result of "bad taste" on the part of some Catholics, the result of "proper action," "stupid action," etc.; but one description that *cannot* be *validly* ascribed to the *Luther* cancellation is that it is "subversive to American freedom." The cancellation was the result of exercising American freedom. Catholics were free to protest or not to protest; WGN was free to televise or not to televise. Exercising one's democratic right of free choice in that matter cannot be rationally termed an "un-American activity."

Many were the published errors about the cancellation. POAU printed all of them. It is not surprising that several false statements appeared in the press. Mr. Ward L. Quaal, general manager of WGN, Inc., and the person responsible for the December cancellation, wrote that "Unfortunately, most of the persons who have written about the incident have not bothered to inquire as to the true facts."[26]

POAU implies that the "suppression" of *Martin Luther* was

---

[25] POAU, *Church and State* (January, 1957), p. 8.
[26] Ward L. Quaal, a letter, 6 March, 1958.

"directly ordered by the Roman Catholic Church."[27] The arch-diocese of Chicago denied any part in protesting the *Luther* tele-vising. POAU says that the archdiocese "lamely denies."[28] Mon-signor E. M. Burke, chancellor of the Chicago archdiocese firmly declared:

> We have sought through radio and television to present the Cath-olic faith in a positive manner. *We certainly do not wish, and have never wished, to deny the same opportunity to those of other religious beliefs.* The honest expression of a religious viewpoint is not merely a democratic right; it is indispensable to a democracy. If a television station deems that the *Martin Luther* film is a positive presentation of religious beliefs, and then decides to show it, we will not protest the decision in any way whatsoever.[29] [Emphasis added.]

But many months after the cancellation, POAU reports:

> The successful bigot campaign to censor Martin Luther from station WGN-TV in Chicago last spring was apparently sponsored by the Chicago archdiocesan office. Msgr. Edward Burke . . . denied this. The fact remains, however, that he was seen by reputable witnesses to emerge from the WGN office just an hour or so before the show-ing was canceled.[30]

POAU does not think it advisable to reveal the names of the "reputable witnesses." Mr. Quaal, general manager of WGN, spe-cifically denied the POAU charge:

> The archdiocesan officials did not contact me or any other official of the station regarding the Luther film and did not make any request that the film not be shown.
> I have no knowledge of any visit of a Catholic priest to the WGN offices just before the film was cancelled. Our station, in common with other radio and television stations, has many visitors each day. If a Catholic priest visited the station at the time you mention, his visit had nothing to do with my cancellation of the scheduled showing of the film.
> . . . I do not believe that the telephone calls protesting against the film were inspired by the archdiocese.[31]

---

[27] POAU, *Church and State* (January, 1957), p. 8.
[28] *Ibid.* (March, 1957), p. 7.
[29] *The Christian Century* (27 March, 1957), pp. 379–380.
[30] POAU, *Church and State* (October, 1957), p. 2.
[31] Quaal, *op. cit.*

If Catholic publications protested against the film, such a fact was unknown to Mr. Quaal:

> In all probability Catholic publications did voice protests against the film after I cancelled the showing on December 21. However, I made no attempt to inform myself on this and have no information regarding it. So far as I know, no Catholic publication in the Chicago area protested the showing of the film before my cancellation.[32]

POAU again attempts to imply that the cancellation was the result of some plot by the Catholic Church:

> Actually, according to Robert E. A. Lee, executive secretary of Lutheran Church Productions (producer of the film), the station had "privately told us that it was at the receiving end of pressure from high Roman Catholic sources." After the storm broke, however, spokesmen for Samuel Cardinal Stritch and the Chicago chancery asserted that there had been no official protest from the Church or the Cardinal and any complaints from Catholics were "an individual matter if they saw fit to protest against a film they consider historically inaccurate, if not downright insulting."[33]

When POAU asserts that there was no "official" protest by the Church, the group implies there was some unofficial protest. Such an implication is false. There was no protest of any type from Church officials. Concerning the alleged statement of Mr. Lee:

> Of course, you must realize that Mr. Lee was, at the time of the incident, completely obsessed with the idea there was a gigantic Catholic conspiracy to prevent the showing of the film his organization was engaged in promoting. In this frame of mind, it would have been easy for him to misconstrue the most innocent statements.
>
> Mr. Lee does not identify in the words ascribed to him the person to whom he refers in saying "the station privately told [us]." I [Mr. Quaal] can categorically state that I have never made any such statement in any of the group meetings which Mr. Lee attended or on any other occasion. Furthermore, I do not believe that any member of my staff would have made such a *false statement*.[34] [Emphasis added.]

Now that it is clear that the archdiocese had nothing to do with the calls or any other "suppression" tactics, we may state, for the sake of argument, that the phoned protests originated from Catholic

---

[32] *Ibid.*
[33] POAU, *Church and State* (February, 1957), p. 6.
[34] Ward L. Quaal, a letter, 19 May, 1958.

laymen, and that such protests motivated WGN to cancel the *21 December, 1956,* showing of *Martin Luther.* But the Catholic protests were *not* the reason why *Martin Luther* was *never* shown by WGN. As Mr. Quaal relates:

> The film had been scheduled by our Program Department for tele-casting on Friday evening, December 21, 1956, the beginning of the Christmas holiday vacation of that year. The scheduled program was included in advance program listings published by Chicago newspapers for that week. When the scheduling of this film was brought to my attention by telephone calls from members of the public who had seen the program listings, I decided that any film which could be con-sidered, rightly or wrongly, an attack upon the religious faith of any of our listeners was not appropriate program material *during the Christmas holiday season.* I, therefore, cancelled the scheduled broad-cast, *intending at that time to reschedule it after the Christmas holi-days.* However, *the campaign of abuse and vilification which was immediately instigated against the station and me* because of such cancellation *and the threats of proceedings before the Federal Com-munications Commission* [such as the POAU threat] *caused me to reconsider. Any rescheduling* of the film while this campaign was in progress and such threats were being made *would have been an abject surrender to pressure groups.*[35] [Emphasis added.]

Catholic protests motivated, therefore, a *temporary* cancellation of the film. Mr. Quaal intended to schedule *Martin Luther* at a later date. But owing to the action of other groups which protested the temporary cancellation and which tried to pressure the station into an immediate showing, Mr. Quaal decided to *permanently* defer televising *Martin Luther.* To televise the film "would have been an abject surrender to pressure groups." The most prominent of these "pressure groups" was the Chicago Action Committee whose chairman was Dr. John W. Harms, a member of POAU's National Advisory Council.[36] Had it not been for the protests spearheaded by the Action Committee, WGN would have rescheduled the film as intended.

POAU sharply attacked WGN when POAU thought the station had permanently canceled *Martin Luther* (actually it was only a temporary deferment). POAU complained that the station had surrendered to "Roman Catholic pressure," but when the station

---

[35] *Ibid.,* 6 March, 1958.
[36] POAU, *Church and State* (March, 1957), p. 7.

refused to surrender to non-Catholic "pressure groups," POAU still condemned WGN. Apparently, POAU only considers Catholic protests as "pressure," whereas non-Catholic "pressure groups" are merely a manifestation of a "national drive against the suppression of the film."[37] Actually, this "national drive against the suppression of the film" was the direct cause for the film's *permanent* cancellation. Ironic, but true.

The next bit of POAU deception is its report that the American Civil Liberties Union "would join others in protesting the ban formally to the FCC."[38] It is true that the Chicago ACLU branch supported the Action Committee for Freedom of Religious Expression in subsequent FCC hearings. But:

> It is important to note . . . that the Radio-Television Panel of the ACLU National Office, at a meeting held February 5, 1957, expressly determined, after consideration of the entire matter, that the national ACLU should not intervene in the present proceeding in support of the Petition [of the Action Committee] and that it should not make any accusation of censorship against WGN-TV.[39]

Washington attorneys Frank S. Ketcham and Seymour Krieger prepared the Action Committee's petition. They objected to the cancellation by WGN because the station had "entered into a valid contract."[40] Such grounds are entirely invalid because the agreement with the film owner "did not . . . obligate our station to actually televise the film."[41] In addition, the contract between that station and the film's sponsor gave the latter "no right to insist that any particular film be used at any time. We did not, therefore, breach any contract with any film owner, advertiser or any other party, in cancelling the scheduled broadcasting of this film."[42]

The Federal Communications Commission never took action on the petition of the Chicago Action Committee; in fact, in April, 1957, the Committee requested the FCC to permit *withdrawal* of the petition. Without further action, the FCC allowed the petition to be withdrawn.[43] POAU declared that the petition was with-

---

[37] *Ibid.*, p. 1.

[38] *Ibid.* (February, 1957), p. 6. An ACLU official gave POAU that information.

[39] Hearing before the FCC (File No. BLCT-519, 1 March, 1957), *Opposition of WGN, Inc.*, p. 1.

[40] POAU, *Church and State* (March, 1957), p. 7.

[41] Quaal, a letter, 19 May, 1958.

[42] *Ibid.*

[43] *Ibid.*, 6 March, 1958.

drawn because the Committee's "purpose is not punitive."[44] The National Council of Churches said the film cancellation "travesties the First Amendment to the constitution of the United States."[45] Does this mean that the Chicago Committee for Freedom of Religious Expression does not desire to punish WGN for an action that "travesties the First Amendment"? Why did not the Freedom Committee take WGN to court if the station violated the Constitution? The answer is obvious; there was no First Amendment violation, FCC violation, "freedom" violation, or any other type of violation, and the Committee knew it. The Committee simply wanted to see *Martin Luther* televised and attempted to pressure the station by raising as great a clamor as possible. After another station had agreed to televise the film, the Committee admitted in FCC testimony:

> The immediate goal of the Action Committee, which was to make this important film available to the people of Chicago, will have been achieved.[46]

As WGN surmised,

> Thus the Action Committee stands convicted by its own words. It is just another pressure group which sought to force WGN, Inc. to program a particular film.[47]
>
> If the Commission were to yield to this unbelievable demand of Petitioner, every radio station and television station in the country would, in effect, be programmed by pressure groups working through the Commission, and not by the station licensee.[48]

So ends a senseless conflict in which the only thing violated was the desires of some people to see a certain program televised at a particular time on a given channel. Your authors' desires in that connection have been often violated; perhaps they should write the FCC and the Un-American Activities Committee, and correct this sinister threat so "subversive of American freedom."[49]

[44] POAU, *Church and State* (April, 1957), p. 3.

[45] *Ibid.*, p. 8.

[46] Hearing before the FCC (File No. BLCT-519, 28 March, 1957) *Comments of WGN, Inc. Concerning the Action Committee Request for Withdrawal of Petition,* p. 2.

[47] *Ibid.*

[48] Hearing before FCC (1 March, 1958), *op. cit.,* p. 5.

[49] If POAU must get excited over something, perhaps it should write the Un-American Activities Committee about the Churchmen's Commission for Decent Publications, a Protestant group representing 80 per cent of the entire U. S. Protes-

tant membership according to one of the group's officials, former Congressman O. K. Armstrong. He said that he hopes "the commission will eventually receive support comparable to that given by Catholics to the National Office for Decent Literature" (*The Register,* 29 September, 1957).

Space does not permit enumeration of the many valid reasons for Church censorship. Father Gardiner's book is an excellent source for such information. Let it be mentioned here, however, that the Church is not afraid of her doctrines being "exposed" as false, etc., and, therefore, censorship is urged. On the contrary, it is because her doctrines are true that she does not wish her faithful to be deceived by error. Every Catholic is not so informed on doctrinal matters that he is unable to be deceived by false statements. As mentioned in Chapter 1, there is nothing in the nature of a false statement that causes a person immediately to recognize the errors. For example, how many readers immediately recognized the seven errors in the seven sentences of Blanshard quoted in Chapter 7?

CHAPTER 10

CITIZENSHIP AND CATHOLICS
IN PUBLIC OFFICE

—1—

TO COMBAT the American Catholic hierarchy is an obsession with POAU. In 1953 and again in 1958 it sought to have the State Department invoke the Immigration and Nationality Act of 1952 (McCarran Act) against members of the hierarchy. In 1953 POAU "demanded that Archbishop O'Hara should lose his American nationality because, contrary to the McCarran Act, he is serving a foreign state as a diplomat under an oath of allegiance to its head."[1] The Archbishop was papal nuncio to Ireland.

The State Department declared POAU's assertions to be invalid and Senator McCarran himself had earlier declared that the Archbishop had not risked his citizenship by serving as nuncio.[2] POAU countered that the State Department had "completely side-stepped the major questions of law," and had evaded most of the issues.[3] The crux of the POAU position rests on the false assumption that bishops and papal nuncios take "an oath of allegiance" to a "government of a foreign state."[4] Catholic apologists have testified to the point of literary exhaustion that

---

[1] POAU, *Church and State* (April, 1953), p. 1. NOTE: The Archbishop is Gerald P. O'Hara and not John Cardinal O'Hara.

[2] N.C.W.C. release, 23 February, 1953.

[3] POAU, *Church and State* (April, 1953), p. 1, and (July, 1953), p. 1.

[4] *Ibid.* (July, 1954), p. 6.

105

Neither a papal nuncio nor any Catholic official in the service of the Church takes "an oath of allegiance to a foreign power." [The oath] is purely a doctrinal matter and involves no civil allegiance.[5]

No civil allegiance is afforded the Vatican by any American Catholic — lay or cleric. The State Department reiterated in July, 1957, that

> It had found no evidence of any law or regulation requiring papal nuncios to take an oath, affirmation or declaration of allegiance to the state of Vatican City, nor did it have any evidence that they took any such oath, affirmation or declaration.
>
> Mr. Blanshard himself had furnished no such evidence. . . .[6]

This did not deter POAU; three months later it declared that Catholic bishops have a "primary allegiance to the head of a foreign state."[7]

In July, 1954, Paul Blanshard announced in a letter to *The Christian Century* that POAU was dropping the issue. Mr. Blanshard stated, "Possible legal action . . . must wait for the right circumstances."[8] He concluded that further action seemed "untimely" because (1) Archbishop O'Hara was no longer papal nuncio to Ireland; (2) a stronger violation of the McCarran Act might arise in the future; (3) the risk of defeat in court based on the technicality of lack of sufficient economic interest.[9] Thus POAU exits after a year of harassment in order to "await a more timely opportunity to make the legal challenge."[10]

At first appearances the "time" arrived accompanied with a "stronger violation" when U. S. cardinals prepared to journey to the Vatican to participate in the election of Pope John XXIII. POAU seized the opportunity to allege that if the cardinals took part in the papal election they would risk loss of their nationality by violation of the 1952 McCarran Act. The POAU statement continued that if Secretary Dulles did not warn the cardinals of the

---

[5] N.C.W.C., *op. cit.*

[6] Letter from Loftus E. Becker of the State Department (29 July, 1957) to POAU. Quoted in full by *The Pilot,* 10 August, 1957.

[7] POAU, *Church and State* (October, 1957), p. 5.

[8] *Ibid.* (July, 1954), p. 6.

[9] *Ibid.*

[10] *Ibid.*

consequence of their action then POAU's ". . . legal remedies will not be exhausted."[11]

Secretary Dulles did not issue any warning and the cardinals took part in the conclave. The State Department did issue a statement asserting that the cardinals had not jeopardized their citizenship because "the real significance of such an election is religious."[12]

It is logical to assume that POAU would now resort to the "legal remedies" it referred to in the October press release. But again, the Americans United "side-step" the issue. In December, 1958, *Church and State* confessed that it did not really expect the State Department would take any action. And in January, 1959, POAU cushioned its own exit by asserting that while it would like to take the case to court technicalities prevented it from doing so. It claimed that it would be difficult "to get status in court on an issue of this kind" because POAU did not have the "special interest" necessary for admittance into court.[13]

Certainly participation in a "foreign election" is the type of "strong violation" Mr. Blanshard was seeking in July, 1954. And what happened to the "legal remedies" POAU was ready to use in October, 1958? Did someone at POAU headquarters blunder, or, as is more likely, did POAU realize that it did not have the semblance of a case against the cardinals and again backed out to await a mythical "stronger violation"?

— 2 —

CATHOLICS IN PUBLIC OFFICE[14]

Just what is the POAU position with regard to Catholics holding public office? Does it feel that Catholics have the same right as others to seek any and all offices of public trust in this country? As might be expected, its statements have shown no easily definable position. On several occasions it has with righteous indignation denounced the religious labeling of candidates for public office.

Earlier in this volume, it was shown that although POAU pro-

---

11 *Boston Globe*, 15 October, 1958. This displays POAU's odd sense of religious liberty.

12 *The Advocate* (Catholic weekly), 7 November, 1958.

13 POAU, *Church and State* (January, 1959), p. 2.

14 The specific questions that POAU addressed "special" to Catholic candidates are treated elsewhere in this volume. See Chapters 7, 8, 11, and 14.

fesses not to be opposed to the existence of parochial schools, it is opposed to anyone attending them. The same might be said of its position on Catholics in political life. POAU declares that certainly a Catholic has the right to hold public office, but it adds that no one should vote for a Catholic until he has been examined by the POAU religious testing service.

The establishment of this "service" by POAU resulted in serious internal discord. Because of it, POAU lost the services of its able research director, Mr. Stanley Lichtenstein. More will be said of Mr. Lichtenstein later.

In 1951 POAU used the uproar over President Truman's nomination of General Mark Clark as United States Ambassador to Vatican City (POAU opposed) to denounce the practice of attaching religious labels to political candidates. *Church and State* regretted

> . . . that some citizens have not yet learned the folly of casting their votes in political elections according to the religious labels of the candidates.[15]

The article briefly recognized areas where POAU thought a candidate ought to be asked religious orientated questions, and then continued:

> . . . nothing could be more futile and self-defeating than the circulation of lists of candidates with "Protestant," "Catholic," and "Jew" after each name. Such labels give no clue whatsoever to the actual position of the candidate involved on any public issue. . . . It is the voter's job to make the candidates take a stand — and then to vote accordingly without regard to religious labels.[16]

A year later, in November, 1952, *Church and State* appeared to continue on the same high plane when in restrospect it complimented itself for the "no religious label" position it had taken in Justice Clark's August, 1949, appointment to the Supreme Court. President Truman appointed Tom Clark, a Protestant, to succeed Justice Frank Murphy, a Catholic, who died in 1949. POAU advised the President that he need not feel precedent required him to name another Catholic to succeed Murphy, stating that:

> The sole question, properly considered, was the individual merit or lack of merit of the appointee and not any religious or political label which might be attached to him.[17]

[15] POAU, *Church and State* (December, 1951), p. 2.
[16] *Ibid.*   [17] *Ibid.* (November, 1952), p. 3.

POAU advised the President to appoint a man "of the same high caliber" as Murphy, "but not necessarily a Catholic."

As if to establish complete objectivity in the situation the same *Church and State* editorial concluded by reprimanding political leaders who felt that party tickets must contain a mixture of Catholic, Protestant, and Jewish candidates. It also criticized the Brooklyn, New York, Protestant Council of Churches for publicly lamenting over the small number of Protestant judges in local courts. It asserted:

> Every judgeship should go to a man qualified to be a judge — and not to a "Catholic judge," a "Protestant judge," or a "Jewish judge."[18]

If such statements as these were representative of POAU policy, then there would be no quarrel, but unfortunately they are not and POAU has never adhered to them. The statements complimenting the President for his bias-free selection of Justice Clark were made in 1952 — but Justice Clark was appointed in 1949. After three years POAU states that its major concern was the professional qualifications of the man and not his religion. In 1952 there was no immediate "danger" of a Catholic being appointed to the Court; therefore, POAU could be "objective" and "adhere to the principles of the *Manifesto*."

Whether or not POAU actually "advised" President Truman concerning Murphy's successor is not known. If it did, no mention was made of it in the succeeding issues of *Church and State*. Since POAU terms itself an "action group" it seems that it would publicize any contact it had with the President of the United States. However, assuming that the organization did intervene, the intervention was not to ask the President to be free of religious bias in naming Murphy's successor. It was to "pressure" him politely into the realization that no precedent had been established and that he did not have to name another Catholic to the Court. The danger of having Truman appoint a Catholic was more important to POAU than the appointment of a man "of the same high caliber as Justice Murphy."

The real danger of having another Catholic on the Court did not materialize until September, 1956, when Judge William J. Brennan (Catholic) was named as associate justice. POAU did not comment on the appointment until March, 1957, and then it was to

---

[18] *Ibid.*

say suspiciously that it had investigated Brennan's record and found him to be 100 per cent American and a Catholic besides. Apparently the investigation took six months. More recently it admitted that after studying Justice Brennan's record it found nothing that indicated "personal subserviance to Catholic as against Constitutional principles." It did insinuate that Justice Brennan's assertion that nothing in his religion hindered him in any way from performing the functions and trusts of his office would not be accepted by all elements of the Catholic press. *Church and State* told its readers that it would report any opposition from the Catholic press to Brennan's "repudiation of papal supremacy over any aspect of his judicial conduct." If we can assume that *Church and State* kept its word and did examine Catholic publications, then not one word of criticism was uttered against Brennan because *Church and State* mentions him only once in the next eighteen issues and that was to list him as having attended the annual Red Mass in Washington, D. C., along with Chief Justice Warren and four other members of the Court.

POAU statements calling for objectivity and bias-free selection of public officials does not represent actual POAU opinion. POAU has always been critical of Catholics in public life. In May, 1948, *Church and State* asserted:

> The Catholic Church exercises political control beyond its numerical importance. . . . With not more than one-sixth of the voting population of the United States Roman Catholic, here are interesting figures on the present Congress . . . [the article goes on to list all denominations represented, the point being that Catholics numbered 77 in the House and 10 in the Senate].[19]

The article concluded with the remark that there was "little evidence of Protestant conviction" in Senate voting.

If the voter is to disregard religious labels as POAU suggests, then why should he be expected to become concerned over the lack of Protestant conviction in Senate voting? If United States senators voted primarily as Protestants, then in effect we would have an established Church in violation of the same First Amendment that POAU alleges it is dedicated to uphold.

Again in 1948 POAU concerned itself with "religious labels" of Federal officeholders. It criticized President Truman for opposing

---

[19] *Ibid.* (May, 1948), p. 2.

certain displaced-person legislation passed by the Eightieth Congress. Truman believed the legislation discriminated against Catholics and Jews. *Church and State* ignored the Jewish connection and asked:

> Was the President making a bid for the Catholic vote? When the President also pleads that religious bias in making government appointments be disregarded, is he seeking to justify the alleged disproportionate number of Catholics in Washington offices?[20]

In August, 1948, POAU is criticizing the President for acting the way it supposedly recommended that he act in August, 1949. If a situation has two sides — and most of them do — POAU is most frequently on the one less favorable to Catholics. Since Truman also believed the legislation discriminated against Jews, why didn't POAU accuse the President of reaching for the "Jewish vote"? What kind of plot existed in Truman's support of the new state of Israel?

In January, 1950, just months after its plea for the appointment of a Supreme Court justice of the same "high caliber" as Justice Murphy, POAU accused Catholic judges in general of participating in a plot to control United States Courts. *Church and State* commented that POAU had exposed the Church's attempt

> . . . to substitute Roman Catholic ecclesiastical law for American law in American courts presided over by Roman Catholic judges. It is with such dangerous threats to America's free institutions . . . that POAU contends.[21]

What judges is POAU referring to?

Catholics have served on the United States Supreme Court for over 111 years of this country's existence. Twice Catholics have served as Chief Justice of the Court. Assuming that our executive officials in government follow POAU's recommendation that "Every judgeship should go to a man qualified to be a judge," then POAU can bury forever its ludicrous accusation that ecclesiastical law is replacing American law in the courtrooms of Catholic judges.

In recent years POAU has become upset over the prospect of a Catholic in the White House. It seems to have assumed almost singlehandedly the task of preventing any such "drastic" occurrence. In July, 1956, when there was no Catholic candidate seri-

---

[20] *Ibid.* (August, 1948), p. 3.   [21] *Ibid.* (January, 1950), p. 1.

ously looming as standard-bearer for either major party, POAU thought it safe enough to waste a few lines in *Church and State* to propagandize its continued opposition to religious labels on candidates. At this time, several Catholics, among them Mayor Wagner of New York City and Senator J. F. Kennedy of Massachusetts were being mentioned as possible vice-presidential nominees. POAU realized that neither of these men was a serious contender for the nomination, hence it seemed safe enough in 1956, to refrain from raising the ghost of 1928.

But the whole country, POAU included, was startled when Senator Kennedy almost secured the vice-presidential nomination. The Americans United wasted no time in dropping its parlor manners. The September issue of *Church and State* informed its readers that it was "shocked by certain events" of the Democratic convention.

After bridging the gap, in a 150-word paragraph from apathy to hostility toward a Catholic candidate, POAU embarked on a course more in keeping with its past actions. What "shocked" POAU was the fact that "not a newspaper in America asked" the American people "to analyze or to candidly discuss the significance of a Catholic president in the development of our national life."[22] The answer might be that the American newspaper editors realized that the entire question had been aired in the religious and secular press only a scant 30 years before. At that time New York's Catholic Governor Alfred E. Smith was seeking the Democratic nomination. He was challenged to express his views on Church-State separation and to answer whether or not his Catholicity would interfere with his duties as president. The controversy was originally aired in the *Atlantic Monthly*. Governor Smith was asked:

> Is not the time ripe and the occasion opportune for a declaration, if it can be made, that shall clear away all doubt as to the reconcilability of [the Catholic Church's] status and her claims with American Constitutional principles?[23]

It was hoped Smith's inquisition would bury forever the false charges of an overlapping and irreconcilable loyalty to Church and government. Governor Smith answered every charge, and the bulk of the press was and still is satisfied with his answer.

[22] *Ibid.* (September, 1956), p. 2.
[23] Charles C. Marshall, "An Open Letter to the Honorable Alfred E. Smith," *Atlantic Monthly* (January–June, 1927), pp. 540–549.

A look at a few press reports of 1928 might help to relieve POAU and show it that there is no danger, just prejudice.

The *New Orleans Item* reflected:

> Gov. Smith's statement . . . is merely a well-worded declaration of what every intelligent citizen already understands. It probably won't appeal to the massive type of intellect that keeps itself awake nights by its sage apprehension of the sudden appearance of the papal fleet in the Potomac River. . . .[24]

The *Houston Post-Dispatch* in Texas commented:

> The insinuation that members of one religious group are less loyal to American Institutions than members of another deserves to be branded as the rankest bigotry and slander, utterly without foundation in fact.[25]

Most certainly POAU is questioning an American's loyalty when it publishes a list of "special questions . . . to every Catholic candidate for president or vice-president of the United States."[26]

The Literary Digest commented that the lay press was almost unanimous in applauding the stand made by Governor Smith and that much of the Protestant press backed him. One such periodical, the Universalist *Christian Leader* denounced Smith's inquisitors by stating:

> We let Catholics pay taxes, enlist in our army, lay down their lives for the flag, and then propose to say to them, "the highest office you can not hold because in the very nature of the case, you must be disloyal." It has been monstrous, how monstrous has not been realized. . . .[27]

So runs the press comment of 1928.

POAU has charged that today's press remained silent concerning Kennedy's bid for the nomination because it feared "Catholic political reprisals."[28] A more logical and valid reason is that the press saw no cause for alarm and is satisfied to let the editorials of 1928 answer POAU's fears. Today's press has followed the advice of the *Christian Leader*, in that to even raise the issue would be "monstrous" bigotry.

In September, 1956, *Church and State* declared that it alone

---

24 *The Literary Digest* (30 April, 1927).
25 *Ibid.*
26 POAU, *A Ten-Year Balance Sheet* (1958), p. 3.
27 *The Literary Digest* (14 May, 1927).
28 POAU, *Church and State* (September, 1956), p. 2.

was "ready and willing" to ask religion-orientated questions of *all* candidates for public office. It said it would ask them as "insistently of Roman Catholic officials as of any other." It reasoned that "Every candidate must be required to demonstrate whether he is loyal in practice to the concept of church-state separation."[29]

It even reiterated its 1951 statement, saying that it

> . . . opposed the indiscriminate and wholesale labelling of candidates by denomination, believing that this practice may lead to bigotry and abuse. *Church and State* has suggested as an alternative that voters should address searching questions on church-state policy to *all* candidates and then make a choice on the basis of the answers.[30]

Here POAU speaks of two main things: (1) opposition to "wholesale labelling" of candidates, and (2) addressing questions to "all" candidates. POAU is not guilty of point number 1. It has never attempted to label any candidates other than Catholics. But neither has it satisfactorily directed questions to *all* current candidates. On 25 February, 1958, Mr. Archer released a statement concerning the resignation of POAU research director Stanley Lichtenstein. Mr. Archer mentioned the POAU questionnaire for Catholic candidates and said the organization was considering releasing in "the near future" a questionnaire for non-Catholic candidates.[31] To date nothing has been released and whatever POAU now does concerning a Protestant questionnaire will come too late and will be recognized as an attempt to regain prestige that was lost through the Paul Blanshard-authored *Questions for a Catholic Candidate,* published in January, 1958.

POAU has addressed questions to presidential candidates in the past. In October, 1956, it asked President Eisenhower, Mr. Stevenson, Vice-President Nixon, and Senator Kefauver to comment on three questions:[32]

1. Federal aid for sectarian educational institutions;

2. Federal aid for sectarian hospitals as provided by the Hill-Burton Act;

3. Appropriations for a personal representative or official ambassador to the Vatican State.

These questions asked the four candidates might be classified

---

[29] *Ibid.*

[30] *Ibid.* (January, 1957), p. 5.

[31] Glenn L. Archer, *Statement Concerning Stanley Lichstenstein,* 25 February, 1958.

[32] POAU, *Church and State* (November, 1956), p. 4.

as "truly political."[33] But the Blanshard-authored questions of January, 1958, addressed especially to Catholic candidates were not entirely political. They concerned at least two false assumptions: (1) that Catholics boycott public schools, (2) that Catholics are opposed to separation of Church and State as known in this country. The third question concerned an ambassador to the Vatican. Potential candidates for the presidency might well be asked to reveal their sentiments on this issue, but it should not be asked as a "special" question and in a special setting to Catholic candidates.

To dispose of the third question, Catholics as a body have never asked for an ambassador to the Vatican. In recent times four names have been associated with this issue — those of Presidents Roosevelt and Truman, and their appointees to the Vatican, Myron Taylor and General Mark Clark. Since all four men were 32nd- or 33rd-degree Scottish Rite Masons, the charge of effective Catholic pressure for an ambassador at the Vatican is absurd. The Masons are not in the employ of the Vatican and would most certainly resent being accused of being duped by the Catholic Church.

The questions directed to all Catholic candidates are prototypes of exactly the things POAU says it cannot tolerate. POAU says that it will not be a party to a "blanket boycott" of Catholic candidates; nevertheless, its questionnaire is directed at all Catholic candidates. Nowhere is there found the name of any candidate for public office who also happens to be a non-Catholic. Since the questions are not directed to any one individual, they must be as a general "boycott" of all Catholic candidates. Such a position is in complete violation of POAU's slogan of "forget his religion and vote for the man according to his record" and its opposition to boycotts.

---

[33] On 2 June, 1958, on the television show "The Big Issue," Senator Eugene J. McCarthy, a Catholic from Minnesota, commented that no candidate could object to any questions asked that were "truly political." Belatedly, and with comparatively little fanfare, POAU addressed 5 questions to just plain "Presidential candidates" (*Truth Series 11*, July, 1958). But those queries were unsuccessful in giving POAU the reputation of being "objective," for their tone made it obvious that they were directed toward Catholics: one question even had a special section for Catholic candidates so the readers would not miss the point; one sentence in the *Series* ominously referred to "talk about a Roman Catholic President." Every query was linked to religion to the extent that none could be called "truly political." POAU's original three "special questions" were not revoked, nor was there any mention of special questions for non-Catholics.

It is within the scope of this work to remark on the right of POAU to ask such questions in the first place. In asking "special" questions, POAU exonerates itself from violation of Article VI of the United States Constitution which provides that "no religious-test shall ever be required as a Qualification to any Office or public Trust under the United States." In April, 1958, *Church and State* carried as a lead story an article to the effect that Senator Kennedy had announced he regarded the "Questions for Catholic Candidates" as a violation of that Article. POAU airily replied that Article VI

> does not apply in any way to the three questions . . . suggested by POAU. The Constitutional article applies to the right of an American citizen to serve as an officeholder. POAU has always opposed any such religious test for public office and is in complete agreement with Senator Kennedy in opposition to such a test.
>
> The three questions suggested for Roman Catholic candidates by the leaders of POAU were simply designed to disclose to the voters the attitudes of Catholic candidates concerning certain anti-democratic policies of the Catholic hierarchy.[34]

POAU is fence-sitting when it says it opposes and always has opposed a formal government-sponsored religious test, but does not object to questions asked by individual groups. Unfortunately for POAU the organization has voiced an opinion (other than that stated) which indicates that *any* religion-orientated question constitutes a religious test, and is a violation of Article VI. POAU took this position when it was young and striving to be recognized as a responsible organization. This goes back to March, 1953, and ambassador-designate to Italy, Clare Booth Luce. There was some speculation as to whether or not she were going to function in the dual capacity of ambassador to Italy and unofficial United States representative to the Vatican. POAU opposed any diplomatic ties with the Vatican, and the Vatican indicated that it was not receptive to any unofficial representative. *Church and State* reported that Mr. Archer submitted a formal statement to the Senate Committee on Foreign Relations. The statement was in opposition to a "religious test" for Mrs. Luce, and said in part:

> If the founders of this republic could return today and observe the trend of public comment on the nomination of Mrs. Clare Booth Luce . . . they would be profoundly disturbed — for the discussion

---

[34] POAU, *Church and State* (April, 1958), p. 1.

has emphasized the religious affiliation *of the nominee in disregard of Article VI of the Constitution of the United States.* . . . I respectfully submit this statement to the Senate Committee on Foreign Relations in the hope that it may help to dispel the unhealthy atmosphere which has arisen.[35] [Emphasis added.]

Mr. Archer is clearly opposed to public speculation on Mrs. Luce's qualifications for her job, when that speculation is centered about her religion. He recognizes it as a violation of Article VI of the Constitution and admits that our own founding fathers would be "profoundly disturbed" at such an occurrence. But POAU must tell us just what it is that makes questions asked by the general public a violation of Article VI; whereas, questions asked by POAU are to be regarded as being in complete harmony with our traditional concept of Church-State separation. When others ask such questions they are "disregarding" our Constitutional safeguards; when POAU asks them they are necessary in order to knock down the "shield" of religion behind which a Catholic candidate allegedly hides. POAU cannot continue to administer religious tests with one hand and with the other pass out statements proclaiming it is and always has been opposed to such tests.

In 1876 our country was confronted with a "Catholic" candidate for the presidency in the person of Republican James G. Blaine. Born of a Catholic mother and a Presbyterian father, Blaine was reared a Presbyterian. During his unsuccessful bid for the presidency he was subjected to a wave of anti-Catholic feeling. A prominent Methodist bishop referred to him as a "crypto-Catholic."[36] In 1883 a pamphlet entitled *Our Republic in Danger* denounced Blaine's "Romish" actions in sending one of his daughters to Paris to be educated in a "Romish" convent and allowing another daughter to be married by a "Romish" priest to an ex-officer of the Papal Swiss Guard.[37]

For the most part Blaine ignored these attacks but at their onset in 1876 he expressed his views in a letter to a friend, Professor James King. After the attacks of 1883, Blaine's friends published the letter as an answer from Blaine himself. It reads in part:

[35] *Ibid.* (March, 1953), p. 2.

[36] D. S. Muzzey, *James G. Blaine: A Political Idol of Other Days* (New York: Dodd, Mead and Company, 1934), pp. 5–6.

[37] G. Myers, *History of Bigotry in the United States* (New York: Random House, 1943), p. 220.

. . . I will never consent to make any public declaration on the subject religion in politics, and for two reasons: First, because I abhor the introduction of anything that looks like a religious test or qualification for office in a republic where perfect freedom of conscience is the birthright of every citizen; and, second, because my mother was a devoted Catholic. I would not for a thousand presidencies speak a disrespectful word of my mother's religion.[38]

Mr. Blaine was not the only presidential candidate to resent such questions as a "religious test." Governor Alfred Smith also considered the questions asked him as a religious test. The questions asked Smith do not differ basically from those currently asked by POAU. Both question the loyalty of Catholics to the United States Constitution. Both claim that Catholics would be influenced in civic responsibilities by a supposed allegiance to the Vatican. Dean Francis Sayre of the Washington Episcopal Cathedral clarified this latter point when he spoke along with Mr. Archer on the television show "The Big Issue." Dean Sayre commented on the assumption that Catholics cannot be conscientious officials because they have a higher allegiance. He said:

I think this accusation does an injustice to my Roman brethren. I would say that the allegiance given by Roman Catholics is not to a foreign power, but to the Lord and in this they are virtually no different from Protestants. We too owe an allegiance to the Lord which is over and above and beyond the allegiance we owe to the state. . . . No Christian can grant to the state an absolute right over his conscience.[39]

Again POAU is able to "cover" itself by saying, with documentation, that it agrees in principle with Dean Sayre. POAU would simply refer to J. M. Dawson's book, *Separate Church and State Now*. Dr. Dawson is one of the founders of POAU and the early portions of his book develop the same basic idea as expressed by Dean Sayre. Nevertheless, POAU's actions show that it has no intention of allowing Catholics to be masters of their own conscience. All matters must be submitted to POAU for scrutinization and its stamp of approval.

The *New York Times*, which is generally known for its forthright and excellent reporting, saw no danger in a Catholic securing the vice-presidential nomination in 1956. If it had, POAU would

---

[38] Muzzey, *op. cit.*, p. 16.   [39] *The Pilot*, 7 June, 1958.

have exploited the *Times'* remarks in order to show that POAU was on the side of right. In 1927, the paper did run an editorial on the test Governor Smith had been asked to take. The *Times* reported in words that should have prevented POAU or anyone else from ever again raising the question of a candidate's religion. It said Governor Smith

> set his foot upon a hideous prejudice, a slimy and un-American superstition which has been threatening to dominate our public life, but which after this will scarcely dare to raise its head in the open.[40]

Today it is generally realized that the business of questioning a Catholic candidate's loyalty to the Constitution is quite absurd. Mr. Archer was forced to tell the truth when he was backed into a logical corner by Mr. Spivak, moderator of the nationally televised "The Big Issue." POAU's executive director admitted under close questioning by Mr. Spivak that, in substance, "a Catholic can be a good president and a good Catholic at the same time."[41] Despite that momentary concession, POAU continues to imply that a Catholic candidate must always be on guard to resist the pressures of a hierarchy which is ever ready to grab special privileges. POAU's Dr. Mackay uses that line of thought as his theme song;[42] there is always the mysterious and sinister "hierarchy" seeking to pressure the all but helpless Catholic officeholder into violating the Constitution, in word or spirit, in order to grant special privileges.

Ever since the earliest days of our country, Catholic spokesmen have unequivocally asserted that there is nothing in the Catholic Faith that obligates a Catholic to effect a change in the Constitution regardless of circumstances. POAU refuses to recognize the fact. Obviously, the goal of POAU is not compatible with such a fact. If the organization admitted that Catholics are able to be just as loyal to the Constitution as anyone else and not violate Catholic principles by so doing, there would be no "Catholic threat" to the First Amendment, POAU's "single and only purpose." If there is no threat, POAU can no longer claim a patriotic purpose for its existence.

At times, POAU attempts to brush aside Catholic declarations

---

[40] Cited by *Current History*, "The Pope and the Presidency," C. H. Fountain (March, 1928), p. 767.
[41] Archer on "The Big Issue," 1 June, 1958.
[42] As on *ibid*.

of unconditional allegiance to our Constitution by implying that the Vatican issues *two* sets of instructions — one to deceive the public; the second, the real policy, given only to the hierarchy. For example, POAU quotes a source in apparent approval:

> . . . there are two teachings, one public for propaganda purposes, one private for guidance of the hierarchy.[43]

Cardinal Cushing of Boston has emphatically denied that the hierarchy is "under secret orders or commission from Rome."[44] A typical POAU reaction would be to say that the Archbishop was secretly ordered by Rome to deny secret orders. Perhaps if POAU could substantiate its charge with *valid* evidence, people might believe the Americans United. To date, no evidence — valid or otherwise — has been presented.

Among the most recent of the myriad statements issued by authoritative Catholic sources, proclaiming loyalty to the Constitution, is the one by Archbishop Alter of Cincinnati:

> I can categorically state that there is no doctrine of the Catholic Church which places upon its members the obligation to work for a change in respect to that religious freedom which is guaranteed to all of us by the Constitution of the United States.[45]

The Catholic Encyclopedia contains this passage which should allay the fears of POAU:

> The Catholic Church recognizes unreservedly the inviolability of constitutions confirmed by oath, of traditional laws, and regular religious compacts, because a breach of the constitution, of allegiance, of a treaty, or of an oath is a grievous sin, and because the Christian moral law prescribes loyalty to the State as an obligation strictly binding in conscience.[46]

In the light of such statements, it must be agreed that any questions directed "special" to a Catholic candidate, and which imply that such a candidate cannot fully uphold the Constitution because of his religion, are the result of, as the *New York Times* asserted, "a hideous prejudice, a slimy and un-American superstition."[47]

---

[43] POAU, *Church and State* (February, 1953), p. 3.

[44] *The Pilot,* 17 May, 1958.

[45] *Ibid.,* 9 February, 1957.

[46] J. Pohle, "Toleration," *The Catholic Encyclopedia,* Vol. XIV (New York: Robert Appleton Co., 1913), p. 772. Reprinted with permission of the Gilmary Society, New York City.   [47] *Current History, op. cit.*

CHAPTER 11

SINISTER SIGNS

—1—

THE CHRISTOPHERS AND CHAPLAIN SECRECY

MANY have been the innuendoes of POAU that create an aura of mysteriousness and subversiveness regarding the activities of the Catholic Church and her members. For example, Reverend James Keller was the object of one POAU article that declared:

> The *Detroit News* and other papers print a column called "Three Minutes a Day." The author is listed as "James Keller." A number of POAU readers have written in with the complaint that "James Keller" is none other than the Rev. James Keller . . . and head of The Christophers. . . .
> . . . Why does he hide his identity? . . .
> Other clergymen writing for the press frankly state their connection. Why does Father Keller conceal his? . . .[1]

How POAU could seriously print such nonsense is difficult to imagine. Some of POAU's own officers are guilty of "hiding" their identity: Paul Blanshard often writes for *The Humanist,* but there is no indication given that he is a Congregational minister.

Other ministers than those associated with POAU must also plead guilty to "hiding" their identities. Dr. Norman Vincent Peale edits a weekly column for a national magazine; yet there is no indication that he is a minister. "Why does he hide his identity?"

Actually Father Keller's column uses two by-lines; "James Keller" and "Father Keller." The choice of by-line is left entirely

---

[1] POAU, *Church and State* (October, 1956), p. 8.

to the newspaper carrying the column. Father Keller himself informs us:

> The Christopher column, "Three Minutes A Day," appears in almost 100 newspapers each day, and we leave it up to each paper to "sign" it as they find suitable for their audience. For instance, here in New York, it appears in the *Mirror* as by "Father Keller."[2]

If, therefore, there is a plot to hide identity, perhaps POAU should look for it among the newspapers which choose the by-line "James Keller." Who knows? Maybe POAU will "discover" that the publishing industry is just one gigantic Catholic propaganda factory "dominated" by "clerical dictators."

"Strict Secrecy Urged On R. C. Chaplains" was the headline over another POAU cloak-and-dagger story:

> Fr. Thomas J. McCarthy, Chancellor of the Military Ordinariate . . . has issued a stern directive reminding his men that memorandums from his office are to be regarded as secret and confidential. . . .
> . . . The nature of material passed to Roman Catholic chaplains which could not stand publicity, can only be surmised. . . . Are there designs here that cannot stand the light of day? Is Roman Catholic action in the armed forces now going underground?[3]

The "stern directive" to which POAU refers is one dated 3 August, 1956. It was written because a prior "directive" (Newsletter) had been discarded "in such a way as to allow [it] to fall into the hands of mischief-makers . . . [who] have an ax to grind against the Church."[4] Monsignor McCarthy was aware that even the most innocent comments can be twisted by anti-Catholic groups into a sinister and mysterious plot by the Church. In the prior Newsletter to the chaplains, Monsignor McCarthy "had hoped that something could be done about the bad literature sold at all the Army, Navy, and Air Force installations."[5] That was the subject which POAU implies "cannot stand the light of day." The "instructions to chaplains" *can* stand "the light of day," but are loath to be surrounded by the dark cloak of mystery that would result from distortion by anti-Catholic groups in this country. As Monsignor McCarthy's "stern directive" relates:

---

[2] James Keller, a letter, 24 March, 1958.
[3] POAU, *Church and State* (October, 1956), p. 7.
[4] Thomas J. McCarthy, a letter to chaplains, 3 August, 1956.
[5] J. F. Marbach (chancellor, Military Ordinariate), a letter, 28 February, 1958.

There are organized groups in the United States whose chief aim is to uncover material which is calculated to embarrass our Church, and the influence of these groups extends into the Armed Forces. One such group which we know of has already had mimeographed thousands of copies of that portion of our last Newsletter which referred to the type of PX literature sold at military sources. . . . [The portion was mimeographed by] one of the most notorious Catholic-baiting organizations in the United States.[6]

POAU exaggerates and distorts this affair to the extent that the Washington group asks, "Is Roman Catholic action in the armed forces now going underground?" Such a gross implication can only be the product of an irresponsible mind. And here again, as usual, we have an instance of POAU acting contrary to its own position. With reference to a POAU statement concerning Stanley Lichtenstein's resignation Mr. Archer declares:

Although I am sending this statement to you for use in our work as you see fit, we prefer to have no public statement made for the press on this subject, unless they go through the national office.[7]

"Are there designs here that cannot stand the light of day?" (See Chapter 13.)

— 2 —

MORE QUESTIONS FOR CANDIDATES

The questions for potential Catholic candidates have been discussed in Chapters 7, 8, and 10. We shall now treat the two remaining POAU queries asked "special" to "every Catholic candidate for president or vice-president of the United States."[8] The very fact that such questions are earmarked "special" falsely implies that there is some inherent factor in Catholicism that is incompatible with the Constitution. POAU declares:

The bishops of your church, in an official statement in November 1948, have denounced the Supreme Court's interpretation of the religion clause of the First Amendment and have urged that the Constitution actually permits the distribution of public money on an equitable basis to sectarian schools and other sectarian institutions. At

[6] McCarthy, op. cit.

[7] Glenn L. Archer, a letter, 25 February, 1958.

[8] POAU, A Ten-Year Balance Sheet (mimeographed, 1958), p. 3.

present the Catholic press and ranking prelates are promoting a plan
. . . for securing grants of federal money to parents to cover the costs
of parochial school tuition by laws which would parallel the G.I.
educational bills. What is your personal attitude toward your bishop's
[*sic*] interpretation of the Constitution, and toward the new plan for
financing parochial schools?[9]

The answer is very simple: the "personal attitude" of a Catholic
candidate is *exactly the same as that of any other candidate*. He
may or may not approve the bishops' interpretation of the Constitution and the plan that parallels the G.I. Bill. His "personal attitude" — whatever it may be — does not, however, determine his
actions as an officeholder. The only "attitude" that determines his
official conduct regarding the interpreting of the Constitution is
that of the various Federal Courts that have ruled or will rule
upon the meaning of the First Amendment. The POAU implication
that a Catholic candidate's official actions in the above instances
must coincide with the interpretation of some bishops, or of all
the bishops, is incorrect. The guiding influence is the "attitude"
of the courts. Catholics know this; POAU will not, and does not
want to, recognize that *fact*.

Now that the question is answered, we may proceed to discuss
the way POAU worded it. First of all, the bishops have *never*
"denounced" the Supreme Court's interpretation of *anything*. In
1948, a bishops' statement *criticized* a Supreme Court decision
which in the opinion of the bishops rested upon faulty history,
logic, and law. That statement echoed a *prior* statement to the
same effect issued by leading *Protestant* churchmen and by a prominent law journal. Could POAU be implying that criticism of the
Supreme Court is disloyalty? If so, POAU itself is disloyal because
it has, and still is, criticizing certain Supreme Court decisions in
sterner language than that used by the bishops.[10] The bishops'
1948 declaration is discussed at length in Chapter 14.

The only schools POAU mentions are "sectarian" and "parochial
schools." This falsely insinuates that the bishops seek special privileges for Catholic schools. Catholic bishops and educators are arguing for private education *in toto*, not simply for their own schools
as POAU would wish us to believe.

The third POAU interrogation is:

---

[9] *Ibid.*, pp. 3–4.
[10] See Chapter 5 for POAU criticism of the Supreme Court.

Many nations recognize your church as both a church and a state, and send official ambassadors to the Holy See. If you became president, what would be your policy concerning the appointment of an American ambassador or a personal representative to the Vatican?[11]

Just as with any other candidate, a Catholic's faith has no bearing whatsoever on the question and, therefore, he may or may not approve of an "American ambassador or a personal representative to the Vatican." He may or may not agree with President Truman's (Baptist and 32nd-degree Mason) desire for a personal ambassador. He may even disapprove of one. As for an "American ambassador," the appointment would have to be ratified by Congress before the ambassador had official status.

Inasmuch as Vatican City does not constitute the Catholic Church and since the Catholic Church does not constitute Vatican City, the fact that many nations "send official ambassadors to the Holy See" does not mean that "many nations recognize your church as both a church and a state." The pope is the temporal ruler over the 109 acres of the State of Vatican City; he is also the spiritual head of the Catholic Church. Such a situation no more constitutes the Catholic Church "both a church and a state" than does the fact that the Queen of England is head of the Anglican Church make that both a Church and a State.

Ambassadors may be sent to the pope in his capacity as spiritual leader of the Catholic Church, or in his role as ruler of Vatican City, or both. However, in no event does this mean that the Catholic Church is "both a church and a state." The temporal aspect of Vatican City is not to be fused with the Catholic Church; there is a clear distinction, POAU notwithstanding.

In reality, POAU terms the pope a "foreign potentate" and "the dictator of the Vatican State in Italy"[12] whenever POAU's purpose is best served by such a description. When POAU wanted to revoke the citizenship of U. S. cardinals (Chapter 10), it, ultimately speaking, would not separate papal spiritual and secular functions, for they reside in "the same person." Thus, the cardinals had "no more right" to vote for the pope, "head of a foreign state," than other Americans for Adenauer.[13] But when POAU opposed

---

[11] POAU, *A Ten-Year Balance Sheet, op. cit.,* p. 4.

[12] C. Stanley Lowell, *Truth Series No. 6* (POAU), p. 4.

[13] POAU, *Church and State* (December, 1958), p. 3. *Because* distinct functions reside in "the same person" is why the papal election is different from others.

President Truman's sending a personal representative to the Vatican, it was necessary to portray the pope as primarily a Church leader:

> "8. How can you reconcile diplomatic recognition of the Pope with the prohibition on [sic] 'an establishment of religion' contained in the First Amendment to the Constitution of the United States? Surely you must realize that the Pope, *whose very title indicates that his function is primarily religious,* is in a different position than the King of England [who] function[s] primarily as [a king] and [is] recognized only as [a king], not a [churchman], by the United States."[14] [Emphasis added.]

POAU, therefore, is able to recognize the distinction between the King (now Queen) of England's dual function as legal head of the Anglican Church, and as ruler of a secular State. But, for POAU, such a distinction is impossible with regard to the pope's dual capacity as ruler of Vatican State and as leader of the Catholic Church. One year the pope is "primarily religious"; the next year he is a "dictator of the Vatican State in Italy." It just depends on what designation will help the current POAU cause.

While on the topic of the Vatican, much has been said about the "tremendous pressure from the Catholic hierarchy which has long sought and lobbied for the recognition of the Holy See by our government."[15] POAU refers to the "Roman Catholic hierarchy" which "is determined to secure the involvement of our government with the papacy and to press its purpose upon the new President and the new Senate."[16] Such insinuations are patently ludicrous. As Archbishop Alter has affirmed, "the American Catholic Hierarchy has not at any time even discussed in its annual meetings, much less requested, the appointment of an Ambassador."[17] And Professor James M. O'Neill reports:

> . . . Mr. Cordell Hull's memoirs, as published in the *New York Times* of May 11, 1948, proved conclusively that no member of the Catholic hierarchy had anything whatever to do with this matter. . . . The Rev. Willard Johnson (a Protestant minister) discusses this

---

[14] *Ibid.* (December, 1951), p. 5. POAU letter to General Clark.

[15] Stated by Dr. C. C. Morrison, former POAU president, in his pamphlet *The Separation of Church and State in America.* Cited by J. M. O'Neill, *Religion and Education under the Constitution* (New York: Harper and Brothers, 1949), p. 32.

[16] POAU, *Church and State* (February, 1953), p. 5.

[17] N.C.W.C. release, 31 March, 1952.

situation in an excellent article in which he specifically mentioned the fact that "there is no evidence that Catholics sought" the sending of Mr. Taylor to the Vatican.[18]

POAU has never produced an iota of valid documentation to substantiate its charges concerning the hierarchy and a Vatican ambassador.

— 3 —

"AMERICAN NAMES BELONG TO AMERICA!"

It is almost impossible not to be genuinely amused when reading this POAU tract:

> One by one the names of American cities are being quietly captured [sic] by Roman Catholic educational institutions while non-Catholic citizens permit the genteel larceny without protest. . . .
> These Americanized labels, of course, are nothing more than a kind of nominative doubletalk. Every Catholic college in America is controlled . . . by the Pope and the hierarchy [see Chapter 8].
> Unhappily, a city's name, once granted to a Catholic college, cannot be recovered. . . .
> Can this be stopped? . . . American higher education is growing at such a miraculous pace that there is not a city in the country which, some day, may not need its own name for its own college. Hands off! American names belong to America![19]

A distinguished non-Catholic historian has written:

> America's first important outburst of political nativism came in the 1840's. Nurtured by the anti-Catholic propaganda which had been so carefully shaped during the preceding decades, thousands of voters . . . had been convinced of the papal designs on the country. . . .
> . . . They admittedly believed that the Catholic Church was grasping for power in America. . . .[20]

The similarity of nineteenth-century and current POAU accusations does not *per se* prove that POAU is to be identified with the past century's crusaders. However, for well over one hundred years Catholics have been accused of possessing "alien" institu-

---

[18] O'Neill, *op. cit.*

[19] POAU, *Church and State* (January, 1957), p. 2.

[20] Ray Allen Billington, *The Protestant Crusade, 1800–1860* (New York: Rinehart and Company, Inc., 1952), pp. 193, 204.

tions and of somehow being less "American" than other Americans; Catholics, therefore, are sick and tired of the same old drivel, such as, "Hands off! American names belong to America." If POAU has any evidence that Catholics and their institutions are somehow not as much of America as others, then it is suggested that the Washington organization should produce evidence instead of words.

The "names of American cities" are not "captured" by anyone. If someone asked you to help him to "capture" the name of Washington, D. C., it is safe to say that you would consider such a person a worthy candidate for psychiatric observation. In addition, the POAU declaration that "a city's name, once granted to a Catholic college, cannot be recovered . . ." is absolutely inane. Boston College is a Catholic institution — Jesuit-run at that — but that does not hinder non-Catholic schools from employing "Boston"; i.e., Boston University. Certainly, if the Jesuits are unable to "capture" the name "Boston" and thereby render it "permanently lost to its citizens," no group can do it.

If POAU really desires to investigate this sinister threat, perhaps the group should ask why the city names of Dubuque and Tulsa have been "captured" by the Presbyterian-affiliated colleges of those localities.[21] Besides, it is well known that the Presbyterian Church is of "foreign" and "alien" origin. Why does that Church use those "Americanized labels"? Truly, this case is worthy of POAU's undivided attention.

— 4 —

THE ELLIS CASE

On 21 February, 1951, a daughter named Hildy was born to an unmarried Catholic mother, Marjorie McCoy. Ten days later the mother consented to an adoption petition of Mr. and Mrs. Melvin Ellis, a Jewish couple. According to a Massachusetts Probate Court, the mother's signature to the petition was given "under strong pressure."[22] A second signature was granted a few days later, but the court determined that the signature was given before

---

[21] *Educational Institutions Affiliated with the United Presbyterian Church in the U. S. A.* (1958).

[22] Joseph McLellan, "The Other Side of the Ellis Case," *Catholic Mind* (September-October, 1957), p. 399. Mr. McLellan's excellent and factual account is highly recommended for those desiring accurate reporting in this case. That account is the basis of this section.

these facts were known to the mother: (1) that both Mr. and Mrs. Ellis had been divorced; (2) that they were both non-Catholic. Although the second signature would carry weight in court, it, in itself, was not conclusive and did not *per se* possess the legal re-requirements that are necessary to lawfully effect the adoption for the Ellises.[23] The Ellises filed an adoption appeal which had to be approved by the Massachusetts courts.

On 27 March, 1951, a few weeks after Hildy's birth and after her mother realized the above facts about the Ellises, Marjorie McCoy filed a counterplea to have her consent to the adoption removed. The Ellises were then told that there was almost no chance of the adoption's being approved by the Massachusetts courts. Thereupon started four years of litigation. Throughout this time, the Ellises kept Hildy despite the fact that they had not secured court approval for her custody in the first place (a required procedure if custody is to be lawful), and despite the fact that there was not a single decision of the courts in which their case was heard (twenty-two appeals were made) that gave *any* justification for their position. Justice Reynolds of the Probate Court affirmed that the Ellises acted in "absolute defiance of the law."[24] A Massachusetts Supreme Court Justice asserted that Mr. and Mrs. Ellis were "wilfully and purposely evading the jurisdiction of this court."[25]

Continually evading the Massachusetts authorities the Ellises finally turned up in Florida where Governor Leroy Collins refused to honor the extradition request of Massachusetts. Mr. Archer of POAU addressed a letter to Governor Collins which grudgingly mentioned that "the technicalities of the law might justify you in returning Hildy. . . ."[26] The "technicalities" to which Mr. Archer refers consist in the fact that the Ellises *never* secured court approval, as legally required, for their custody of Hildy. Apparently, Mr. Archer feels as well qualified to comment on Massachusetts law as he does on the First Amendment which, of course, has no bearing whatsoever on this case.

POAU attempted to use this unfortunate affair to portray "the hierarchy" as some mysterious "moving force" behind the "effort to take Hildy away from the Ellises."[27] Court records demonstrate the falsity of the charge. Those records declare that all the pressure

---

23 *Ibid.*
24 *Ibid.*, p. 400.
25 *Ibid.*

26 POAU, *Church and State* (June, 1957), p. 3.
27 *Ibid.* (May, 1957), p. 7.

or "force" was exerted by those who desired to keep the matter quiet,[28] not *vice versa*.

POAU attempted to describe the case as revolving about the issue of religion: "Clearly, the central issue . . . was one of religion."[29] A Jew-*vs.*-Catholic atmosphere not too subtly pervaded the reports of POAU. The Americans United based its accusation on the assumption that the Massachusetts adoption statute is "the offspring of religious bias and prejudice."[30] But the history of the statute in question belies such a description. Among those who have supported the law are: the four Catholic bishops of Massachusetts; the Episcopal bishop of Massachusetts; the Rabbinical Council of Boston; every leading executive of voluntary Massachusetts child-care agencies — Catholic, Protestant, Jewish, and nonsectarian; the president of the Legal Aid Society; the public welfare organizations of the state; and, of course, the House of Representatives, Senate, and Governor of Massachusetts.[31] In addition, the Massachusetts law is almost identical with those of twenty-four states and the District of Columbia.[32]

Another reason for POAU[33] terming the Hildy affair an issue "of religion" was the fact that the Massachusetts adoption statute asserts that whenever practicable the religion of the adopting party should correspond to that of the child. First of all, that portion of the law is not mandatory.[34] Second, the Massachusetts Supreme Court specifically declared that "the central issue" was *not* "one of religion":

> There has been a good deal of *loose talk* about the difference in the religions of the parties. That *was not* decisive in the disposition of this case previously by the Supreme Court. . . . The full court opinion by Judge Wilkins decided the petitioners *are not entitled* to adopt this child.[35] [Emphasis added.]

Notice the use of the present tense in the last sentence of the

[28] McLellan, *op. cit.*, p. 405.

[29] POAU, *Church and State* (September, 1957), p. 2.

[30] *Ibid.* (September, 1955), p. 6. POAU quoted that description from a statement of a Massachusetts judge. The judge had nothing to do with the case, and obviously was ignorant of the statute's history.

[31] McLellan, *op. cit.*, p. 403.

[32] *Ibid.*

[33] POAU, *Church and State* (September, 1957), p. 2.

[34] McLellan, *op. cit.*, p. 402.

[35] *Ibid.*

court. The Ellises *"are* not entitled to adopt"; i.e., they *never* have had legal custody of Hildy under Massachusetts law. Therefore, it was completely misleading for POAU to refer to the Ellises as "Hildy's foster parents" in May, 1957.[36]

POAU falsely writes:

> At no time has Marjorie McCoy . . . asked for personal custody of her daughter; she only wishes to ensure that Hildy be taken away from the Ellises, who are Jewish, and turned over to Roman Catholic authorities for rearing in that faith.[37]

Actually there was no intention on the part of the mother to give Hildy to Catholic "authorities" or to an institution. The mother, now married, would have kept Hildy with her family, and if that were impossible, Hildy would have been placed in the custody of another Catholic family.[38] Marjorie McCoy has been asking for the return of her daughter ever since Hildy was barely a month old.

POAU claims that the Ellises "would allow Hildy to choose her own religion when she was old enough to decide."[39] But the Ellises have asserted, "We will raise Hildy as a Jew. It will be easier that way."[40]

The "central issue," contrary to POAU-inspired rumors, is whether or not the Ellises can illegally defy duly constituted law and courts. Or stated in a different way, the issue is one of whether or not a mother has the right to determine what shall become of her child. Because of such misinformation as publicized by POAU; because of the illegal evasion of the Ellises; and because of the asylum granted them in Florida by Governor Collins, the duly constituted law and courts have been defied, and the right of a mother to rear her own child has been denied.

In this situation POAU appears as the Jews' best friend. In reality it will fight anyone's battle if it will embarrass the Catholic Church. When President Truman opposed anti-Semitic and anti-Catholic displaced person legislation (see Chapter 10), POAU showed no concern for the Jewish people and went after bigger game, the mysterious Catholic vote.

---

36 POAU, *Church and State* (May, 1957), p. 1.
37 *Ibid.,* p. 7.
38 McLellan, *op. cit.,* p. 404.
39 POAU, *Church and State* (September, 1957), p. 2.
40 McLellan, *op. cit.,* p. 404.

CHAPTER 12

THE BISHOP OF PRATO

BISHOP FIORDELLI OF PRATO, ITALY

LEAVING its "single and only" purpose of maintaining America's First Amendment, POAU sought greener pastures in Italy:

> The facts in the case are undisputed. Mauro Bellandi, a young sausage merchant of Prato, was married to Loriana Nunziati at the City Hall in a civil ceremony. Because they had presumed to be married by someone other than a Roman Catholic priest, the couple aroused the ire of Bishop Fiordelli. He promptly dashed off an open letter. . . .[1]

The letter publicized the fact that the Bellandis, baptized Catholics, had incurred automatic excommunication by marrying in a civil ceremony. It was read in church and described the couple as "public sinners" living in "scandalous concubinage."[2]

For some time Bishop Fiordelli had been confronted with strong communist agitation against Church marriages. He realized the Church would have to take stern measures to combat this influence. In this light he warned Bellandi's fiancée in 1956 that a civil marriage would result in automatic excommunication.[3] The situation was not an isolated one; similar cases had plagued the Bishop for some time; consequently, the Bellandis could not have "aroused" the Bishop to such a degree that he made a snap decision and "promptly dashed off" a letter.

---

[1] POAU, *Church and State* (February, 1958), p. 5.
[2] *New York Times,* 3 March, 1958.
[3] *Ibid.,* 5 March, 1958.

Subsequently, the Bishop was charged in court with defamation of character by Mr. Bellandi. Bishop Fiordelli justified his position as one that strictly pertained to "the spiritual government of the faithful":

> I must prevent my attitude from seeming to be or being interpreted as a recognition that an act which concerns "the spiritual government of the faithful" — the freedom of which is guaranteed by the Lateran Pacts and solemnly proclaimed in Article 7 of the Italian Constitution — could be subjected to the judgment of a civil magistrate.[4]

The Bishop's right to publish and distribute statements on faith and morals is guaranteed in Article Two of the Concordat between Italy and the Vatican:

> Both the Holy See and the Bishops can publish freely, and even display inside and on the outside doors of places of worship and offices connected with their ministry, instructions, orders, pastoral letters, diocesan bulletins and other acts affecting the spiritual government of the faithful which in their judgment should be made public within the limits of their competence.[5]

POAU asserts that the "issue" in the trial of Bishop Fiordelli was "church marriage control."[6] The group refers to the "exclusive control of the Roman Church over marriage."[7] Such accusations are completely erroneous because the Church recognizes as valid (in the case of two non-Catholics) marriages witnessed by non-Catholic ministers, etc. The Church does not "control" non-Catholic marriages. Furthermore, the Catholic Church has no way of even exercising "control" over marriages of Catholics if such individuals do not *voluntarily* wish to heed the Church's teaching. Certainly the Bellandis were not under the "exclusive control" of the Church; they did not heed the Church because they did not wish to do so, and the Church had no way to "control" them and prevent them from incurring a civil marriage. The record of the Bishop's trial clearly asserts that, POAU to the contrary notwithstanding, the issue was something other than "marriage control."

Bishop Fiordelli maintained that his action constituted legitimate execution of the internal discipline of a free and voluntary society,

---

[4] *The Pilot,* 22 March, 1958.
[5] *Ibid.*
[6] POAU, *Church and State* (February, 1958), p. 5.
[7] *Ibid.*

the Church;[8] he also maintained that there was no intention of defaming the character of the Bellandis inasmuch as only their "religious reputation" as Catholics had been denounced by him when they violated a serious teaching of the Church and entered upon a civil marriage.[9] The Bishop contended that the civil courts had no jurisdiction since the affair was purely a religious matter pertaining to the "spiritual government of the faithful."

The Italian court did not agree. It convicted the Bishop of defamation even though the judges affirmed that

> . . . there is no doubt that the accused acted through a highly moral purpose, that of leading the uncertain and bewildered faithful to faith in God and the comforts of religion.[10]

The court did *not* declare that public denunciation *per se* constituted defamation of character; rather, the legal argument turned upon the language used by the Bishop. The court

> eventually decided that a Bishop may call people sinners but may not call them concubines. . . . the law has ruled that this term may not be explicitly used to describe a particular union.[11]

The Americans United disregarded its pious promise of not being concerned with the religious teaching of any faith when Mr. Archer declared that POAU will back any

> bona fide Catholic or ex-Catholic plaintiffs who wish to sue their American bishops or priests for slanders against their moral status arising out of that church's *teaching* that marriage of Catholics not performed by a priest results in "low and abominable concubinage."[12] [Emphasis added.]

Here Mr. Archer betrayed his complete lack of knowledge about Catholic teaching on marriage when he uses the expression "performed by a priest." No priest ever "performs" the sacrament of marriage; in reality a

> . . . priest must be present as her [Church's] official *witness* at the marriages of Catholics. But the priest does *not* administer [perform]

---

[8] *The Pilot*, 8 March, 1958.

[9] *Ibid.*, 12 April, 1958.

[10] *Ibid.*

[11] Quoted from the London *Tablet* by *The Pilot*, 22 March, 1958.

[12] Glenn L. Archer, form letter, Spring, 1958. See also *Church and State* (May, 1958), p. 6.

the Sacrament. The contracting parties minister it mutually by their consent [i.e., those who are to be married marry themselves].[13] [Emphasis added.]

Mr. Archer's offer to bring suit contradicts POAU's goal of "religious liberty." Apparently Archer would ask the court to deny such liberty to Catholic bishops or priests. According to POAU's Bishop Oxnam, "Religious liberty is an absolute right."[14] The Catholic clergy must be an exception.

Mr. Archer's desire to sue also betrays an ignorance of American law. Massachusetts law indicates that the Bishop of Prato would not have been convicted in that state. Cases like Carter *vs*. Papineau, Morasse *vs*. Brochu, and Fitzgerald *vs*. Robinson would make it seem

> clear, then, that in Massachusetts an authorized spokesman for the Church has a privilege to say or write that which injures the reputation of a church member if true, uttered without malice and only to the extent necessary for church discipline. . . .[15]

Furthermore, tradition attributes this position to Protestant Massachusetts and not to "Catholic control" as POAU would probably like all to believe. In 1835 John Quincy Adams (sixth president of the United States) led a committee of Quincy, Massachusetts, citizens who charged the Rev. Mr. W. M. Cornell (Congregationalist) with "impugning the good character of . . ." Quincy citizens. Rev. Cornell had criticized, in a report to his superiors, the ignorance of the Bible and "way of salvation," plus poor church attendance among Quincy citizens. Adams' committee asked Rev. Cornell to come before them and either prove or retract the charges. Rev. Cornell refused and there the matter ended. The minister spoke "without malice" (as had the Bishop of Prato) concerning religion and morals; he recognized no need to defend his remarks before the citizenry let alone the courts.[16]

In the May, 1958, *Church and State* Mr. Archer commented:

> The principle of the Italian court decision should be extended to the United States where the Roman Catholic Church teaches the same

---

[13] Rumble and Carty, *Radio Replies*, Vol. II (Radio Replies Press, 1940), p. 75.

[14] POAU, *Church and State* (April, 1949), p. 3. As our Supreme Court has indicated, Bishop Oxnam is wrong (Chaplinsky *v*. N.H. 315 U.S. 568, 1942).

[15] *The Pilot*, 29 March, 1958. From an article by Mr. Paul V. Powers, a member of the Massachusetts Bar.

[16] *The Quincy Patriot Ledger*, Quincy, Mass., 28 July, 1958.

discriminatory gospel . . . there should be as much freedom from
clerical slander in the United States as in Italy.

But a member of the District of Columbia Bar, who is authorized
to practice before the Supreme Court, deflates the POAU balloon
in the following words:

The POAU statement sheds more light on the position of POAU than
it does on the merits of the Italian decision, particularly since POAU
professes dedication to the "principles of complete separation of Church
and State." It is highly significant that POAU hails a decision rendered in a country where there *is* an official relationship between
Church and State. It is equally significant that American courts have
consistently refused to render the kind of decision which POAU hails
as a "victory for religious tolerance."

American jurisprudence, based on the principles of freedom of
religion in the *First Amendment* and in State Constitutions, has consistently denied to our courts the right to meddle in ecclesiastical
disputes (*Watson v. Jones,* decided in 1872 by the Supreme Court).
. . . In case after case, American courts have applied this principle
to libel actions brought against ecclesiastical authorities for statements
made by them in the course of their ecclesiastical duties, and *such
statements have been held to be privileged.* Thus, for instance, the
Supreme Judicial Court of Massachusetts held in 1850 that "churches
have authority to deal with their members, for immoral and scandalous conduct; and for that purpose, to hear complaints, to take
evidence and to decide; and upon conviction, to administer proper
punishment by way of rebuke, censure, suspension and excommunication" (*Farnsworth v. Storrs*); and this right has been recognized even
after the delinquent ceased to be a member of the church (*Landis v.
Campbell,* decided by the Supreme Court of Missouri in 1883).

The Georgia Court of Appeals, in a parallel case (*Crosby v. Lee,*
1953), recognized that any contrary course of action would "strike
a death blow to the type of religious worship as represented by the
Primitive Baptist Church, and to all other types of religious worship
as contemplated by the provisions of our Constitution. . . ."

The ecclesiastical authorities of every denomination exercise the
right to determine, as did the Bishop of Prato, whether individuals
meet the requirements for good standing in that denomination and
to announce their decision, as was recognized by the Supreme Judicial
Court of Massachusetts in *Carter v. Papineau* (1916). To deny that
right or as Mr. Archer suggests, to force the Church to give ecclesiastical recognition to purely civil marriages contracted contrary to the
law of the Church, would clearly be an infringement of the religious

freedom protected by the First and Fourteenth Amendments and *would not be tolerated by any American court.*[17] [Emphasis added.]

POAU made the most of the affair as long as it could. The February and May, 1958, *Church and State* carried approximately 2000 words of commentary plus pictures, and Mr. Archer published a separate letter on the topic. Then in October, 1958, the balloon burst. An Italian court of appeals reversed the verdict of the first court. *Church and State* courageously handled the reversal in its December issue with a scant 71-word statement in the section "News From Far and Near."

The appeals court's decision, which is more in conformity with American jurisprudence, declared that the Bishop was within his ecclesiastical rights when he opposed the Bellandis' civil marriage. Mr. Bellandi has appealed this latest decision.

---

[17] Joseph M. Snee, "POAU v. Freedom of Religion," *America* (22 March, 1958), p. 714.

CHAPTER 13

POAU MEETS CRITICISM?

WHEN an organization answers criticism by every means other than directly and accurately handling that criticism, one begins to wonder whether (*a*) the group that is criticized can read English sufficiently to understand the complaints against it; (*b*) the group is too ignorant to discuss validly adverse comments leveled at it; (*c*) the group, realizing the cogency of the criticism, deliberately refuses to face it and resorts to discrediting the critic through devious and irrelevant statements. Actually, POAU both knows how to read and is not too ignorant.

— 1 —

MESSRS. SANDERS, STAFFORD, LAWRENCE

In September, 1957, the Protestant publication *Christianity and Crisis* printed an article by Mr. Tom G. Sanders which was highly critical of POAU. The issue of 14 October, 1957, contained two letters: one from POAU's Mr. Archer; the second from Mr. Sanders.

Mr. Archer's letter declared in part:

There is no indication that he [Mr. Sanders] has read even one of the many pamphlets and published speeches which comprise an important part of the organization's [POAU] literary output.

That is a legitimate observation if true. However, Mr. Sanders' letter (in the same issue) specifically denied the charge. Not only had Sanders read many POAU publications in addition to *Church and State,* but he had also talked to Mr. Archer personally some time prior to the appearance of the article. So far nothing seems to be seriously awry. But in December, 1957, POAU editorially referred to the Sanders' article as "astonishingly superficial." Why? Because (*a*) "Mr. Sanders wrote his piece without coming near our national office" and (*b*) "he did not take into consideration many of the most important documents issued by POAU, such as its original *Manifesto* and *Without Fear or Favor. . . .*"[1]

First of all, coming near or not coming near the POAU national office has no essential bearing on the worth of an article about POAU. Second, Mr. Sanders, in his letter published over a month previously, stated that he had talked with Mr. Archer. Third, Mr. Sanders made specific mention of the fact that he had read the pamphlets POAU said he did not read. Again, Sanders made that statement in *Christianity and Crisis,* over a month before the December POAU editorial. It will be remembered that Mr. Sanders' letter in *Christianity and Crisis* appeared in conjunction with Mr. Archer's. Mr. Archer is the editor of *Church and State.* Why did he authorize two false charges about Mr. Sanders when the latter had denied them six weeks earlier in a letter that Mr. Archer could not have failed to notice?

In a letter dated 6 January, 1958, Dr. Russell Henry Stafford told Monsignor John S. Kennedy, editor of *The Catholic Transcript,* that an impending visit to Hartford, Connecticut, by the POAU special counsel Paul Blanshard was "certainly not under the auspices of the Connecticut Council of Churches, of which I have the honour to be President."[2] POAU was forced to indulge in an entirely farcical rebuttal. The Washington group said the "Connecticut Council of Churches offers a classic example of a Protestant organization being used by the Roman Catholic Church for denominational ends."[3] The hierarchy "added new and brilliant chapters to its legend of getting others to do its hatchet work."[4] POAU declared that *The Catholic Transcript* sent "a letter of inquiry" to Dr. Stafford. "Probably the hierarchy had little notion that the ruse would work, but to its unbounded delight the leaders of the Connecticut Council of Churches went for the bait."[5] Dr.

---

[1] POAU, *Church and State* (December, 1957), p. 2.

[2] R. H. Stafford, a letter (copy) to Monsignor Kennedy, 6 January, 1958.

[3] POAU, *Church and State* (April, 1958), p. 2.

[4] *Ibid.*

[5] *Ibid.*

Stafford is included among "Protestant leaders who are willing to be duped."[6]

POAU was, indeed, desperate. The mysterious "hierarchy" has to be employed, and the phrase "hatchet work" implies that POAU was upset over Dr. Stafford's letter. Dr. Stafford has no feeling of being "duped" or doing "hatchet work." He affirms:

> I have not been in touch with any members of the Catholic hierarchy. I am one of the hardest guys on earth to dupe. I need no authorization from the Connecticut Council of Churches or any other body for making officially the statement that the Council had not taken action, which indeed it had not taken [regarding the Blanshard visit], and added thereto [in the letter to Monsignor Kennedy] my personal and private opinion that an out-and-out attack on the Catholic Church or any other institution is a silly and un-Christian form of procedure. . . .
>
> . . . The only connection with the Catholic clergy which was involved [in the "ruse" by the "hierarchy"] was the fact that at a certain meeting a priest asked the Secretary of the Connecticut Council and me in the local group of the National Conference of Christians and Jews if the POAU meeting with Mr. Blanshard as speaker was to be taken as the general and official attitude of the Connecticut Protestant community. Of course it was no such thing, and in the interest of good feeling and courtesy I said so with all possible emphasis.[7]

So much for the "ruse" of the hierarchy that "duped" Dr. Stafford into doing Catholic "hatchet work."

As the reader knows, "William Lawrence" is a joint pen name which is employed by your authors for half a dozen good reasons. In June, 1958, POAU was apparently not aware of that fact when it wrote an editorial captioned "Lawrence Does 'Research' ":

> William Lawrence, a Catholic journalist who spends much of his time doing smear jobs on POAU for the Roman Catholic press, is at it again. He is now conducting "research" for a new piece of hatchet work.
>
> Lawrence is writing certain Protestant publications in long-hand — a scarcely legible scrawl — demanding to know if they "support" POAU. . . .
>
> We predict his article, which will doubtless be featured in the

---

6 *Ibid.*

7 R. H. Stafford, a letter, 20 May, 1958.

Catholic press, will state that Lawrence couldn't find a single responsible Protestant publication or a single responsible Protestant group that supports POAU.

Of what value is such "research" and such writing? About the same value as Lawrence's previous efforts.[8]

We might ask in rebuttal, of what value is such "criticism" and such writing? What is the relation of a "scarcely legible scrawl" to valid criticism of past, present, or future "efforts"? Of what value do the phrases "smear jobs" and "hatchet work" possess without documentation?[9] What is the relevance of false predictions to what is actually written? And why does POAU falsely refer to your authors as "demanding" information? Why does POAU strive to discredit the critic rather than his criticism? Had POAU known that the name "William Lawrence" was a pen name, it is not inconceivable that the group would have described this as part of another "ruse" most likely inspired by the "hierarchy."

— 2 —

DR. WILL HERBERG

POAU will not tolerate disagreement within its own ranks and it lashes back savagely at any other individual or group that disagrees with it. The disagreement need not be aimed directly at POAU at all. As long as one's position is not in accord with POAU's, then one is game for personal assaults originating in the pages of *Church and State*. It does not matter if one be Jew, Protestant, or Catholic; to disagree with POAU is anathema.

Professor Will Herberg of Drew University has been one recipient of POAU calumnies. It happens that Professor Herberg is a Jew who favors public support of parochial schools to the extent of advocating the payment of pupil tuition and teacher salaries. For such heresy Dr. Herberg was the subject of an editorial in *Church and State* where not only his position was ridiculed, but also his personal integrity was questioned. The editorial began by referring to Dr. Herberg as "a Jewish maverick." It then cast aspersions upon his status as a scholar by stating that newspapers have "described" him as a professor of Judaic Studies at Drew University.

---

[8] POAU, *Church and State* (June, 1958), p. 2.

[9] POAU is referring to a series of two articles by William Lawrence about the group. See *The Pilot*, 19, 26 October, 1957.

The use of the word "described" was obviously an attempt to discredit his academic standing.[10]

Further on in the editorial POAU accused Dr. Herberg of exhibiting "a penchant for sweeping generalizations which are almost always false." If true, then Professor Herberg certainly would be violating his sacred trust as a teacher and undoubtedly would not be retained by Drew University. The editorial closes by stating that "Mr. Herberg is a Jew who does not represent the Jewish people."

At first impression, this last statement seems like a very serious accusation to make. On closer scrutiny it turns out that POAU has unwittingly done Dr. Herberg a service — an unintentional one, to be sure. The American Jewish Committee was asked to comment on whether or not Dr. Herberg represented the Jewish people. It replied:

> It needs first to be said that American Jewry is in no sense an autonomous or monolithic unit. And I know of no one — person or agency — who is authorized to speak for all American Jews on any question.[11]

When seen in this light the attempt to discredit Dr. Herberg is not valid at all. No Jew represents all the Jewish people.

In a final effort to discredit him, POAU announced in January, 1958, that the February issue of *Church and State* would carry a reply to Dr. Herberg by a "distinguished rabbi." The February issue carried an eight-line note stating that the reply — by Rabbi Nathan A. Perilman of Congregation Emanu-el in New York City — would be forthcoming in March. The "reply" finally appeared in March — the reprint from the magazine *America* of a letter-to-the-editor written by Rabbi Perilman. Nowhere in its reprint of Rabbi Perilman's letter did POAU divulge that *America* is a Catholic magazine edited by the Jesuits. If the reader were at all interested in who published *America,* he would have to retrieve from his stack of old newspapers the January issue of *Church and State.* Then he would have to turn to page 2, first column, second paragraph and there he would find mentioned once, the words: "Jesuit magazine, *America.*"

Returning to Rabbi Perilman's letter, we find that POAU declares it used the letter from the unidentified *America* in preference to a "statement exclusively written for *Church and State.*" It might

---

[10] POAU, *Church and State* (January, 1958), p. 2.

[11] Philip Jacobson, a letter, 8 June, 1959.

be assumed from this that Rabbi Perilman had actually written the exclusive statement, as it was in February that *Church and State* announced that Rabbi Perilman would author the reply. But the case studies presented in this book have demonstrated how POAU omits many of the "details" of issues reported in *Church and State*. This is another case in point. Rabbi Perilman has kindly clarified the situation. In his words we learn:

> . . . the *only* communication that I had on the subject of the Herberg article was my letter to the publication "America," which very graciously published my letter in full . . . *I did not write an article for POAU*. Until I found a copy of its publication on my desk . . . I did not know of the quotation. . . .
> As to POAU's terming Dr. Herberg "A Jewish Maverick," I do not use the term about anyone.[12] [Emphasis added.]

Rabbi Perilman went on to exonerate Dr. Herberg of his POAU malignment by terming him "a serious and competent scholar."

Just who, if anyone, wrote the unpublished "exclusive" statement in rebuttal to Dr. Herberg is not known.

POAU has used a letter written by a Jewish rabbi to a Catholic weekly in an attempt to discredit another Jew who dared to disagree with its "infallible" utterances. Rabbi Perilman never was a party to maligning Dr. Herberg for simply stating his views. Certainly, Dr. Herberg's position on parochial schools is generally regarded as quite liberal and is not held by the majority in the great body of Judaism; nevertheless, POAU is the only group that found it necessary to blacken the name of Herberg while opposing his views.

— 3 —

POAU RESEARCH DIRECTOR QUITS

"Deafening Silence" was the title given the editorial of the March, 1958, *Church and State*. The "silence" was in reference to the reaction of the Catholic press to the release of POAU's "Questions for a Catholic Candidate." *Church and State* felt the Catholic press had more than adequately denounced POAU for posing the questions but had not taken the time to answer them. It may be that the Catholic press thought its alleged "silence" would allow *Church and State* to hear the "thunderous" answer by one of POAU's high-

---

12 N. A. Perilman, a letter, 25 March, 1958.

ranking national officials. POAU research director Stanley Lichtenstein immediately answered the questions by resigning in protest.

In a press release of 4 February, 1958, Mr. Lichtenstein gave as his immediate cause for resignation the current course of POAU as manifested in the "Questions for a Catholic Candidate." He contended that the "Questions" "actually tend to undermine the constitutional principle which the organization [POAU] professes to uphold."

The Lichtenstein release went on to comment on aspects of POAU's January, 1958, "Ten-Year Balance Sheet," of which the "Questions" were originally part. Mr. Lichtenstein pointed out that the election of a Catholic president would not, as the "Balance Sheet" charged, raise anew ". . . certain social and civic issues which cannot be ignored." The "issues" are government support of sectarian schools and diplomatic relations with the Vatican. The release by Mr. Lichtenstein answered:

> The truth, of course, is that these issues exist independently of the religious affiliation of the President, and would remain whether the people chose a Catholic, a Protestant, a Jewish, an atheistic or any other kind of president.

Mr. Lichtenstein went on to quote from the editorial he wrote for the December, 1951, *Church and State* wherein he criticized voting by religious labels.

The day after Mr. Lichtenstein's resignation was announced in the daily press your authors contacted him via letter in order to further verify some statements with findings. The letter read in part:

> I do not know whether your parting with POAU was on friendly terms or not, but realizing the adverse publicity POAU will receive, I am sure the organization will have to discredit you in some fashion — *probably by minimizing your function while employed by POAU. Or probably the organization will attempt to suggest that your motive for leaving was not the one you publicized;* but rather, a motive arising from "sour grapes" over some irrelevant internal issue.[13] [Emphasis added.]

POAU reacted exactly as anticipated. According to a later statement by Mr. Archer, to be quoted in full, we learn that POAU

---

[13] W. Lawrence, a letter to Mr. Lichtenstein, 5 February, 1958.

did not release a "detailed statement" on Mr. Lichtenstein's resignation because the group believed that it "would be apparent to the public" that he was simply a "disgruntled former employee." Mr. Archer tells us that Mr. Lichtenstein's job was scheduled to be abolished and that Mr. Lichtenstein had lost his usefulness to the organization.

Finally, on 25 February, 1958, Mr. Archer released a "Statement Concerning Stanley Lichtenstein." It was aimed at discrediting the latter's views and minimizing his function at POAU.

February 25, 1958

STATEMENT CONCERNING STANLEY LICHTENSTEIN

Catholic diocesan newspapers, and a few dailies, have recently carried a statement from our former research director, Stanley Lichtenstein, alleging that he "resigned" from this organization over a matter of principle.

We have not issued any detailed statement to the public press, believing that it would be apparent to the public that the Lichtenstein statement was a personal expression by a disgruntled former employee. Mr. Lichtenstein served the organization with reasonable competence for a time, but in recent years his inability to cooperate with other staff members and with newspapermen reduced his usefulness to the organization almost to the vanishing point. He was told last September that his services were no longer desired, but because of past accomplishments and his family needs we gave him time to find employment elsewhere. With our help he finally located a job with the government. He was given a farewell luncheon and a gift from the staff. On the following day he released to the papers a long attack on our organization, centering chiefly upon the questions for a Catholic presidential candidate adopted by our National Council at our last annual meeting in December, and released to the public early in January.

Mr. Lichtenstein was entitled to disagree with his associates concerning the questionnaire for Catholic candidates. He freely expressed his opposition to members of our staff, but he did not choose to raise the issue at our annual meeting when the questionnaire was thoroughly examined and discussed — and adopted in principle — although he heard the reading of the proposed questionnaire, and he could have stated his objections. Because of these circumstances, it is fair to point out that his so-called resignation on a matter of principle was a hoax, designed to cover up his impending dismissal.

As to the substantive objections he has raised to our questionnaire for Catholic candidates, the answer is clearly visible in the original statement of POAU on this subject. We pointed out in that statement that non-Catholic candidates also should be carefully quizzed "whenever they reveal any inclination to favor legislation which would grant public money to sectarian enterprises or which would otherwise threaten our traditional policy of church-state separation." It is quite likely that we will issue some statement in the near future concerning questions which should be addressed to non-Catholic candidates also. We have repeatedly demanded from both Republican and Democratic conventions a clear statement in favor of the separation of church and state for all candidates.

The detailed arguments of Mr. Lichtenstein seem to us quite absurd. We believe that a candidate who endorses the Catholic boycott of the public schools is committing himself to a hostile pre-judgment concerning one of America's free institutions, and that that hostile attitude is relevant to his fitness for the office of the presidency. It is true, as Mr. Lichtenstein points out, that some Protestants have criticized the Supreme Court's decision in the McCollum Case, which forbids the payment of public money to sectarian schools, but we do not know of a single Protestant denomination in the United States which actually favors the payment of public funds to sectarian schools. The very Protestant leaders named by Mr. Lichtenstein in attacking Point 2 of our questionnaire are themselves opposed to the use of public money for the main activities of sectarian schools. As to the question of an ambassador to the Vatican, we have freely and consistently criticized all Protestant as well as Catholic leaders who have advocated this policy. If a Protestant is nominated for the presidency, this will be one of the first questions that POAU will address to him.

Although I am sending this statement to you for use in our work as you see fit, we prefer to have no public statements made for the press on this subject, unless they go through the national office. Further publicity concerning Mr. Lichtenstein might only inflate the importance of an incident which is quite unimportant in our total work.

Cordially yours,
Glenn L. Archer (Signed)
Glenn L. Archer
Executive Director

That statement is saturated with distortions of fact. In the opening sentence Mr. Archer remarks that the news of Mr. Lichtenstein's resignation was carried by only a "few dailies." Mr. Lichtenstein's statement was carried by a great number of dailies. To mention but a few, it was carried by the *Washington Post,*

Cincinnati Enquirer, the *Washington Star,* the *Washington Daily News;* the *Boston Globe,* the *Boston Herald,* and the *Boston Advertiser;* and the UP and AP wire services.

In the second paragraph, Mr. Archer says that Mr. Lichtenstein served POAU with only "reasonable competence." In the very next sentence we read of Lichtenstein's "past accomplishments" while affiliated with POAU. It seems that if Mr. Lichtenstein were only reasonably competent, he would have few "accomplishments" worth considering. On the other hand, if "past accomplishments" warranted POAU continuing him in its employ, then he must have served with more than "reasonable competence."

A close look at the final paragraph completely demolishes POAU criticism of alleged "Catholic censorship." *Church and State* likes to tell its readers that the Catholic people are victims of "cranial rinsing,"[14] whereby they are kept subservient to a "dictatorial-clerical threat" which is foreign to our American way of life.[15] In Mr. Archer's statement we find POAU telling its adherents not to say anything about Mr. Lichtenstein without clearing it with the national office. The national office is functioning as a "censor." Individual chapters are not allowed a separate voice on Church-State matters.[16]

In a letter to Mr. Lichtenstein of 10 May, 1958, your authors quoted segments of Mr. Archer's statement, and asked Mr. Lichtenstein to comment. Without seeing Mr. Archer's full statement Mr. Lichtenstein wrote a lengthy reply based on a few comments that Archer had made in the daily press, and on the segments of the Archer statement forwarded to him by the authors. Mr. Lichtenstein did not see the complete "Statement Concerning Stanley

---

[14] POAU, *Church and State* (February, 1957), p. 2.

[15] *Ibid.* (September, 1956), p. 2.

[16] Article V, section 7 of the POAU bylaws governing the Boston Chapter provides that no one will make any statement that is contrary to the views held by the national organization. This operates in practice as well as theory. Early in January, 1958, a letter was addressed to the president of the Boston Chapter asking if the retainment of a Congregational minister on the White House staff constituted a violation of Church-State separation. The local chapter did not answer until it checked with the national office. The reply came back not as an answer from the Boston Chapter, but as a quote from the "party-line" dictated in Washington. The Boston Chapter president had written to the national organization, "seeking additional information." Either the officials of the Boston Chapter do not know what constitutes a violation of Church-State separation, or the "autocratic power" of the national office is such that local chapters are not permitted to speak at all.

Lichtenstein" until it was sent to him by your authors on 7 June. Well before that date Mr. Lichtenstein's statement, except for his footnote, was in the possession of the authors.

Three other illustrations will show that since Mr. Lichtenstein's resignation POAU has gone to great lengths to place him at the head of the "index" of forbidden subjects for POAU adherents.

Shortly after his resignation, Mr. Lichtenstein forwarded $2 to POAU for a nonmember subscription to *Church and State*. Forthwith he received the two most recent editions of *Church and State* and a receipt. But a week later he received a $2 check from POAU with the unexplained notation his subscription had been canceled. Is his name on an "index" of forbidden subscribers?

On 15 November, 1958, the Boston *Pilot* carried, at your authors' request, an article by Mr. Lichtenstein essentially the same as the one given here. The *Pilot* article was recognized in the Catholic press and was termed by the 29 November, 1958, *America* as a "most telling blow" to POAU. The Americans United completely ignored the article. Is Mr. Lichtenstein's own defense on the "index" of forbidden reading matter for Americans United? In January, 1959, POAU published an index to the 1955–1957 issues of *Church and State*. Mr. Lichtenstein played a prominent role in POAU in those years as managing editor of *Church and State* and then as POAU research director. He authored *Church and State* articles during those years and his photograph appeared in the June, 1955, issue along with pictures of other prominent national leaders. However in the 1955–1957 index the name Lichtenstein does not appear once. POAU members have been subjected to a thorough "brainwashing" and elimination of Stanley Lichtenstein. His name cannot even be found in the index. Mr. Lichtenstein's self-vindication is now quoted in full for those who are "permitted" to read it.

HOW MR. ARCHER BECAME 'DISGRUNTLED'
by Stanley Lichtenstein

Glenn L. Archer, executive director of . . . POAU, made a number of comments (published on February 4 in the *Washington Daily News*, p. 2; the *Washington Star*, p. A-15; the *Washington Post*, p. A-18; and Religious News Service, Domestic Service, p. 14) about the press release which I had issued for release on February 4, 1958, concerning my resignation from POAU's staff. Archer's remarks were fundamentally false, although here and there he dropped a scrap of distorted truth in amongst the fabrications.

I was, he said, an obviously "disgruntled former employee" who had been fired. Well, not exactly fired, he said in another version of the statement, but "advised last fall that [my] position would be abolished in a pending staff reorganization and . . . [that I] should seek new employment." Also, that he and the office staff had given me "a party and an $18 brief case," and he had helped me to find a government job. And, further, that the firing or reorganization "had no connection with our [POAU's] questionnaire for political candidates or other policy matters." Archer did not say what the alleged actual reasons were, but complained that I had "made no mention of [my] policy disagreement until [I] sent out a mimeographed press release to newspapers attacking [my] former employers." [See below, footnote by Mr. Lichtenstein.]

The facts are these:

Archer knew nothing of my new job until I told him about it on January 21, advising him that I would leave his staff on January 31 to start work for my new employer on February 3. I had been hired strictly on my merits by the government agency after being interviewed by seven different persons, none of whom was acquainted with Glenn L. Archer. Two years earlier, I had filed a standard Form 57 job application with the government, answering "yes" to the question, "May inquiry be made of your present employer regarding your character, qualifications, etc.?" When Archer received the government inquiry, he answered in so many words that I was an effective editor and writer who had served him well for many years. A number of other persons who had known me professionally also expressed their good opinion of me on the government forms. The fact that when I actually did leave Archer's employ I made public my strong conviction of the wrongness of POAU's "Challenge to Catholic Candidates," made Archer regret that he had told the truth about my competence and character on that earlier occasion. He had become a "disgruntled" former employer.

During nine years of service on POAU's staff I had fought a long and, ultimately, a losing fight to make the organization live up to the affirmations in its original *Manifesto* that it would concern itself solely with the constitutional principle of church-state separation, that it would be non-sectarian and inter-denominational, and that it would not make war against the religious doctrines of any church nor on behalf of the religious doctrines of any other church. I could not have lasted as long as I did except for the circumstance that for some seven of the nine years I was Archer's chief ghost writer (and he is a man who needs ghost writers very badly). The organization's published statements of policy embodied my views to a very considerable extent. Thus, not only had I told Archer — and later, Associate Director C. Stanley Lowell and Special Counsel Paul Blanshard — on many occasions that I regarded Article 6 of the Constitution, barring any religious test for public office, as equally important with the First Amendment in establishing the meaning of church-state separation, but I had also succeeded in making my view POAU's official view in a number of editorials and stories I had written for its official organ, *Church and State,* in earlier years.

As time progressed, I had become increasingly disturbed by what I considered to be errors of omission — principally, the organization's failure to take direct issue with influential Protestant leaders who in my judgment were competing with Catholic leaders in campaigns to obtain government sanction and support for religion — their religion, of course. But it was not until Senator John F. Kennedy began to loom large as vice-presidential or presidential timber that POAU moved towards making the positive error, the error of commission, that I had dreaded most of all — the application of a systematic religious test to candidates for the highest political offices in the land. That was the last straw, as far as I was concerned, and I knew it was time to leave. In the later years, Archer had threatened to fire me on a number of occasions — in particular, when I had ventured to send letters to the editors of various publications expressing my views on this and related questions. (See, for instance, my exchanges with Paul Blanshard in *The Humanist,* 1956, No. 5, pp. 253–254, and in *The New York Times,* August 21, 1957.) But he did not actually let me go, largely, I suppose, because he still found my technical services useful.

The fact that POAU has failed to reply to my detailed arguments on the merits of the case seems to me to be a vindication of my position. Aside from expressing his own disgruntlement, Archer's reaction has been entirely defensive. He has said, belatedly, that POAU would also issue a questionnaire for Protestant candidates. That, in my judgement, would be compounding the felony. I believe deeply that all legitimate political questions — including questions of church-state relations — are the same for all candidates, and are not to be put separately to hyphenated Catholic-American, Protestant-American, Jewish-American or Free-Thinking-American candidates. That sort of approach could mark the beginning of the end for this Republic.

Stanley Lichtenstein (Signed)

Lichtenstein footnote:

Archer, in his February 25 mimeographed letter, contradicted his own earlier assertion to the press that I had made no mention of my policy disagreement before leaving POAU. Now he changed his story and said that I had "freely expressed [my] opposition to members of our staff. . . ." He then added: ". . . but [I] did not choose to raise the issue at our annual meeting when the questionnaire was thoroughly examined and discussed — and adopted in principle — although [I] heard the reading of the proposed questionnaire, and [I] could have stated [my] objections." This revised Archer story is really ludicrous, in view of the facts:

The annual meeting referred to was held on December 3, 1957, and Archer had deliberately withheld the draft of the "Ten-Year Balance Sheet" statement from me before that meeting. (It had been written by Paul Blanshard.) In fact, I was not even in the room when the draft statement was read to the trustees and national advisors. My only part in the proceedings (which were held in the large front room on the second floor of POAU's national headquarters building) was to deliver, as requested, a brief and routine report on the work of the research and press relations department in 1957. This report was accepted with acclaim. I then left the room and went into the room next door, where my desk was located, to attend to some office matters which had to be taken care of immediately. As it happened, my room and the big front room were connected by a door, and through that door I was able to hear the muffled sounds of the reading aloud of Paul Blanshard's draft "Questions for a Catholic Candidate." That was my first acquaintance with the text, and there had been no opportunity for me to "raise the issue at [POAU's] annual meeting. . . ." It was not that I "did not choose to raise the issue," but, rather, that Archer did not choose to give me any opportunity to raise the issue in any free discussion with the national officers of POAU. The questionnaire was not "thoroughly examined and discussed," as he asserts, by those officers. It was simply accepted with uncritical enthusiasm. The only dissenter — POAU's "disgruntled" research director — had been excluded from the discussion.

— 4 —

POAU AND PROFESSOR JAMES M. O'NEILL

Professor O'Neill is probably best known for his *Catholicism and American Freedom,* a definitive, validly documented, accurate reply to Mr. Blanshard's volume, *American Freedom and Catholic Power.* Inasmuch as POAU embodies the views of Mr. Blanshard, its special counsel, an exposure by Professor O'Neill of Mr. Blanshard's gross errors was indirectly a refutation of the POAU program. Therefore, both POAU (in *Church and State*) and Mr. Blanshard (in his POAU-endorsed *My Catholic Critics*) felt obliged to discredit Professor O'Neill in their customary manner.

The following article by Professor O'Neill was especially written for inclusion in this volume. This article merely skims the surface of a multitude of POAU-Blanshard inaccuracies:

P O A U   and   J M O ' N

J. M. O'Neill

POAU is an organization of necessarily uninformed or partially informed Americans apparently united in efforts to spread misinformation about Catholicism, their American Catholic fellow citizens, and the Constitution of the United States. Their publications are absurdly lacking in the most elementary evidence of scholarship in dealing with historical facts, in competent reasoning and interpreting, and even in accurate reporting. Since I have spent some time in exposing the shoddy scholarship of one of the high priests of POAU, Paul Blanshard, the publications of this society frequently comment on my writings with little regard for completely accurate and factual reporting, or the decencies of controversy.

The POAU *Church and State Newsletter,* April 1952, p. 2, has this item: "It's unfair to quote the popes, says layman O'Neill in new Book" — in a large headline. This is false and of course wholly without any substantiation. As a substitute for proof there appears under this headline the statement that I "maintain" that Blanshard's book is "unscholarly, untruthful — and where it tells the truth — is unfair." I am quoted (from p. 216 of my *Catholicism and American Freedom*): "Papal encyclicals are not *per se ex cathedra* utterances. . . ." This, in my book, is a whole sentence, not part of a sentence as given in the *Newsletter,* and I attached three excellent references to my statement. No well-informed person would think of questioning the complete accuracy of what I wrote. POAU goes on to remark that my position is that: "The good that popes do is 'official' and the evil that popes do is 'unofficial.' " This is not a quotation from my books or an honest interpretation of anything I wrote. In the context of this article, this probably represents a desire (possibly due to ignorance) to give the idea that "official" and "*ex cathedra*" are synonyms.

Since the writer (or printer) for POAU inserted an ellipsis in a quotation from me that was not accurate quoting, it is interesting that in the *Newsletter* I am charged with having, "in direct quotations" from Blanshard, "actually omitted parts of sentences and paragraphs without indicating the omissions." It is true that the three little dots indicating something left out were omitted in two or three places in my book. I know one omission was an error by the typist. I do not know who was responsible for the others. But I trust that interested readers will check Blanshard's references (my pages 263, 264 and Blanshard's 47 and 50) to see how completely without value these omissions were in reporting the essence of Blanshard's statements. The closing paragraph of this article totally misrepresents the *Imprimatur* — I suppose not surprising when one knows that Glenn Archer, Executive Director of POAU, signed his name to a statement that "Nihil obstat" means "disapproved" and "Imprimatur" means "approved."

The POAU *Newsletter of* July, 1952, p. 7, gives the substance of the David Dempsey story in the *N.Y. Times* (Dec. 2, 1951) of how Mr. Blanshard got a copy of the proof of my book *Catholicism and American Freedom* (Harper's 1952), and made a protest to Harper's which resulted in a long delay of the publication of my book exposing Blanshard's lapses in scholarship. Dempsey's story, says the *Newsletter*, "bears little resemblance to the facts as stated by Paul Blanshard" in his pamphlet, *My Catholic Critics,* and reprinted in the *Newsletter.* According to POAU's report of "the Dempsey version," Harper's initiated the affair by showing part of my manuscript to Blanshard, and after some exchange of letters, sent him the whole proof for his opinion. As Blanshard tells it, after I had "made a number of widely irresponsible charges before Catholic forums" [which I had not done], he wrote to Harper's in *July, 1950,* asking that he be allowed "to read the manuscript before it went to press. This was not granted, but I finally secured . . . a copy of the book in page proof in October 1951. . . ." Then he protested, and Harper's gave the proofs to a law firm to see if the book contained libelous matter.

The law firm took three months to do what should have been done in three days. They, of course, found no libelous matter. In my conferences with the lawyer in charge, it became quite evident to me that I was dealing with an attorney who was definitely pro-Blanshard and anti-O'Neill, but still a good enough lawyer to make judgments on the law involved — *after a delay of three months!* The Blanshard statement that Harper's "cut out the most vulnerable portions from the text" is false; Harper's cut out *nothing*. No changes were made at the suggestion of the lawyers except a few insignificant ones, and those *with my approval*. The most definite item of the sort I can recall was to change my statement that something was "false reporting" to "inaccurate reporting." This concerned nothing written by Blanshard but a passage in a monthly magazine commenting on his book. Not a single exposé of Blanshard's errors in his book was "cut out" by anyone after his protests. Many were never mentioned by me; space considerations made a complete treatment impossible.

However, neither the story in the *N.Y. Times,* nor that of Blanshard in his pamphlet, *My Catholic Critics* (p. 4), is in most vital aspects the same story Harper's gave me. I was in the West when I read the tale in the *Times.* I at once wired Harper's saying I hoped they would quickly publish a denial in the *Times.* As soon as I returned East, I found out why Harper's preferred to ignore the matter. The Harper version agrees with relevant facts as I know them concerning the Harper person who accommodated the Beacon Press and Mr. Blanshard to the detriment of Harper's and Mr. O'Neill. As I received the explanation in the Harper office, it was as follows.

Dr. Tead, my editor at Harper's, and I had agreed, when the book was about to be put into type, on the persons who were to be asked to write advance comments on the proofs, and we further agreed that neither of us would send the proofs to anyone without the other's approval. We wanted to avoid the distortions and misrepresentations which we expected (and got) until the book was published and any interested readers could check the attacks on it with the book itself, and so decide the merits of the criticism. This program was, of course, carried out when Dr. Tead was in the office. However, when Dr. Tead was away for a time, a strongly pro-Blanshard member of the Harper household, whose attitude was apparently known to the Beacon Press, and who had received a request from the Beacon Press to let it have a copy of the proofs, sent Beacon a full set.

Note that Blanshard writes "I finally secured, with the consent of the publisher [*sic*], a copy of the book in page proof in October 1951" (p. 4). The Beacon Press, in a "Publisher's note" on *My Catholic Critics* gives no explanation other than: "Proofs of the O'Neill book reached us from Harper's last October. . . ." I think that Mr. Blanshard's statement, and the note of the Beacon Press are quite significant as indicating that neither wishes to divulge who among the Harper personnel is responsible for this service to the Beacon Press and disservice to Harper's.

In June, 1958, I wrote to Mr. Dempsey (with whom I had been closely associated when I was Chairman of the National Committee on Academic Freedom of the American Civil Liberties Union) and asked him for his version of the origin of the sending of my proofs to the Beacon Press. He graciously sent me the following information, with permission to use it, emphasizing that it was reconstructed from memory: Someone from the Beacon Press stopped in at the *Times Book Review* office, on a sort of good will visit. The subject of Blanshard's book and the O'Neill rejoinder came up in the conversation. The visitor from the Beacon Press mentioned that Harper's had sent either my manuscript or the proofs to Beacon presumably for uncovering any inaccuracies in my work. Mr. Dempsey checked with someone in the "editorial department at Harper's" and received confirmation of the report that a set of proofs of my book had been sent to Beacon. It seems a fair guess that Mr. Dempsey talked with the same person in Harper's editorial staff who had already obliged the Beacon Press in this matter.

Mr. Dempsey's memory of this affair seems to agree (as one should expect) with the report I received from Harper's: The Beacon Press initiated the getting of the proofs by asking a member of the Harper staff (whose relevant attitude was doubtless well-known to the Beacon staff) to send them the proofs. Dr. Tead's absence from his office made this pro-Beacon anti-Harper action possible.

Mr. Blanshard's pamphlet, *My Catholic Critics,* is largely a repetition of the misrepresentations he had in his book. It is replete with inaccuracies, and particularly with answering something other than the exact exposure of his failure as a scholar which he pretends to be answering.

Probably a good preparation for estimating Blanshard's technique for misguiding the uninformed and uncritical reader, would be to read my chapter 12 on "The Blanshard Documentation" in *Catholicism and American Freedom.* On page 4 of his pamphlet (the second page of text) Blanshard prepares his readers by introducing me with the phrase "barefaced literary fraud" and in substance accuses Harper's of publishing deliberately "false statements."

A few examples of his favorite technique of invalid documentation to bolster a pretense of scholarship will have to suffice. This Blanshard habit led Mr. David Rome to write the best single sentence estimate of Blanshard workmanship which I have ever seen. In his scathing review of the Blanshard book, Mr. Rome in the *Congress Bulletin* (Canadian Jewish Congress, Montreal, July, 1949): "Mr. Blanshard confuses documentation with validity. . . ."

Here are some instances: I quoted Blanshard (from p. 280): "When an American Catholic Bishop says fervently that he accepts the doctrine of the separation of church and state, the skeptical inquirer may turn his eyes southward and see what the bishop means by this profession of an American doctrine." My comment was (*Catholicism and American Freedom,* p. 91), "He offers no evidence, no documentation to support this." My statement was, and still is, absolutely accurate. This inaccurate statement about American Catholic bishops is essentially an expression of his whole absurd thesis. On page 19 of his pamphlet he tries to answer my criticism with the following: ". . . the whole section from p. 279 to p. 284 is a heavily documented summary of facts which support the sentence that O'Neill quotes." This is not true; there is not a single reference given here (or elsewhere in his book) that supports his insult to the Catholic bishops. This Blanshard section (pp. 279–284) has 10 numbers referring to notes in the back of the book. If any reader will look up Mr. Blanshard's references to three Catholic weekly publications (*Catholic Register, America,* and *Commonweal*) he will find, I believe, truthful comments on *conditions in South America,* which so far as I know have never been endorsed by any American, Catholic or other. Then, if he will read some seven or eight books referred to, he will perhaps find something about these same conditions. There is not even a suggestion in the notes that any of these references support Blanshard's attack on the American bishops. He has documentation all right, but it is totally invalid.

We find in this *Newsletter,* once again, Blanshard's ridiculous attempt at mind reading in saying that . . . "the American Catholic bishops who praise democracy always [*sic*] utter their praises with an important mental reservation. . . ." This is, apparently, a slight variation of his position that our type of constitutional democracy is contrary to Catholic *doctrine* and that the American hierarchy is planning to destroy it whenever they get the power. Blanshard's total attitude toward the over 500 American Catholic bishops in our history seems to be that the whole line is a line of hypocrites or heretics or both. Neither Blanshard nor other agents of POAU have ever offered a single item of valid evidence in an attempt to prove the truth of this position, or to refute the two centuries of voluminous evidence to the contrary.

In his book, Mr. Blanshard quotes at length (p. 80) from a pamphlet by Father Paul L. Blakely, S.J. (1937) "Our first duty to the public school is not to pay taxes for its maintenance." "The first duty of every Catholic father to the public school is to keep his children out of it." In my answer (p. 209) I say: "Finally Mr. Blanshard refers again to Father Blakely's much quoted statement which never apparently expressed the opinion of anyone but Father Blakely." I have seen and heard a number of opinions or comments on this pamphlet by Catholics, clerical and lay, but never one of approval. Now 21 years after it appeared the great majority of young Catholics in education are in non-Catholic education — most of them of course in public education. In the last few years in the elementary grades Catholic schools have caught up with public schools and have approximately one-half (or one or two percent over one-half) of the Catholic children. On the high school level, according to the latest figures from

Catholic sources about 70% are in non-Catholic schools, and on the college and university level, about two out of three. (See my *The Catholic in Secular Education,* Chapter 1, Longmans, Green, 1956.)

In his *My Catholic Critics* Blanshard writes (p. 35): ". . . and his [O'Neill's] repudiation of Blakely is wholly specious, since Blakely was one of the top leaders of the NCWC who wrote his pamphlet under the Imprimatur of Cardinal Hayes, and the pamphlet has never been repudiated by top officials." This reference to the Imprimatur indicates that Mr. Blanshard still believes when he wrote this pamphlet that all Catholics are supposed to agree with whatever is published with an *Imprimatur.* If he believed that, it is because he has rejected conclusive and unvarying evidence to the contrary; and has never taken a few minutes to find out for himself what the *imprimatur* means — if he did not believe this, then this passage is dishonest writing. *The Imprimatur by Cardinal Hayes does not even imply that Cardinal Hayes or anyone else agreed with what Father Blakely wrote.*

On this same page, Blanshard mentions "support of both Catholic schools and churches by public taxation" as "the Catholic policy" and mentions Quebec as an example of it. If he were interested in getting and giving accurate information, he would know and report that in Quebec Protestant and Catholic schools receive public assistance on a program of equality, and non-Catholic countries, as England and the Netherlands, have the same policy. Further competent scholarship would necessarily have revealed that whatever policy any country has in regard to the use of public money in education is a policy of the government, not of any church. Even when one church has special privileges not granted to other churches, as the Lutheran in Norway, Sweden and Denmark, the Presbyterian in Scotland, the Anglican (Episcopalian) in England, the Catholic in Spain and Italy, this status is granted by the government, not appropriated by the Church. Belgium, which is said to be 94% Catholic, and Israel, which is approximately 96% Jewish, give government financial aid to all religious bodies. Mr. Blanshard (presumably in the hope that careless readers will accept his statement about *the* Catholic policy as the truth instead of the total misrepresentation which it is) offers one quotation from the Brooklyn *Tablet* about the McCollum case — which does *not* support his position.

Mr. Blanshard repeats in his pamphlet (p. 40) that "a well-known Catholic author" was a member of the "panel of distinguished scholars who combed the various versions of the manuscript [and] made it almost, but not quite, error-proof." The unidentified Catholic author was Thomas Sugrue, who in a detailed letter to me denied Mr. Blanshard's claim to Sugrue's endorsement of the Blanshard work, and to any participation in producing, or any responsibility for, the "accuracy" of its content. With Mr. Sugrue's permission I published his letter in full (pp. 183–184 of my book, *Catholicism and American Freedom*). I submit that it is unbelievable that Mr. Blanshard did not read this letter when he was going through the proofs or the published book; of course he had known all along what Mr. Sugrue was engaged to do and did. Any slightly informed Catholic, or anyone else with ordinary knowledge of Catholicism and American history (author, editor, publisher, critic or advertiser) would necessarily know that no honest scholar who had taken the trouble to use his scholarship on the Blanshard manuscript could endorse or approve Mr. Blanshard's work. His totally unsupported claim that his book had Catholic endorsement or support is a most revealing indication of the sort of audience for which he wrote.

On p. 6 of his pamphlet Mr. Blanshard writes that I "ignore the chief sources of Catholic authority, the papal encyclicals, the canon law, and the utterances of Catholic rulers in Catholic countries." He closes this paragraph with this sentence: "It is an acknowledged fact that the Vatican permits its representatives temporarily to favor separation of church and state and freedom of thought in non-Catholic countries when such liberalism can be useful in building ecclesiastical power." I estimate that it would take about sixty pages the size of those in the Blanshard pamphlet fully to explain and correct the thirteen errors in these two passages. There is not a single factual statement or implication in either of them that is true or legitimate. Those who are sufficiently ignorant or emotionally immature to believe the nonsense here expressed or implied, would doubtless never heed the correction, or would refuse to believe it regardless of the evidence.

That there are some people who are willing to sell this sort of "false witness" against Catholic neighbors is not surprising; but it is almost incredible that a man of Paul Blanshard's training — a university graduate, Phi Beta Kappa, a minister, and a lawyer would engage in such enterprise, or that any publishing house with editors who could read would consent to publish such stuff, or that an organization having as some of its leaders men who hold positions of responsibility and respectability (as POAU has) would consent to spend time, money, and energy to promote the sale of such inaccurate and insulting attacks on their Catholic fellow citizens.

PART III

ANALYSIS OF A COMPLETE
POAU ARTICLE

CHAPTER 14

"RISING TEMPO OF ROME'S DEMANDS"

THIS section of the book will be devoted to an analysis of an entire POAU article entitled "Rising Tempo of Rome's Demands" by C. Stanley Lowell, associate director of POAU. Mr. Lowell's article originally appeared in the 7 January, 1957, issue of *Christianity Today*. After its publication in that magazine, the article was reprinted in pamphlet form by POAU and is currently being distributed by the organization.

According to a POAU announcement, "Rising Tempo of Rome's Demands," together with another Lowell article, has reached a combined circulation of one million copies.[1]

By treating only a single article of approximately nineteen hundred words two points will be illustrated: first, the amount of error POAU is able to compress into so short a space; second, that it is easy for a group such as POAU to produce undocumented criticism concerning a multitude of issues, whereas to answer such criticism requires a good deal of research and explanation.

As will be shown, Mr. Lowell in particular and POAU in general employ a literary device that may be termed caricaturization. By this is meant the construction of conclusions based on evidence that is either greatly distorted or simply nonexistent. When speaking of evidence as nonexistent, it is meant that the evidence is simply assumed either because there is no evidence available or because available evidence tends to discredit the conclusion the author wishes to make. Upon arriving at a false conclusion about the Catho-

---

[1] POAU advance announcement of the 23–24 September, 1957, religious freedom meetings held in Boston, Massachusetts.

lic Church by these means, the Church is then criticized for teaching or doing whatever has just been erroneously concluded that the Catholic Church teaches or does.

After "Rising Tempo of Rome's Demands" appeared in *Christianity Today,* two readers commented as follows:

> One of the most important articles I have ever read. It should be published very widely. . . . The most thorough analysis of the growing menace to religious freedom I have ever read.[2]

Queried concerning the accuracy of his article, Mr. Lowell replied, "As to my 'Rising Tempo' I am not in the habit of putting out lies. The facts are accurate."[3] Facts, indeed, are accurate but the question remains: Have POAU and Mr. Lowell reported the facts? Furthermore, have they reported *all* the facts or has only one set of events been treated, thereby creating a distorted and highly misleading presentation.

The author respectfully urges the reader to carefully examine "Rising Tempo of Rome's Demands" before reading the following analysis. Mr. Lowell's article appears in its entirety in the Appendix.

Unless otherwise indicated all quotations from POAU sources will be from "Rising Tempo of Rome's Demands."

— 1 —

THE BISHOPS AND THE CONSTITUTION

A good example of what has been just stated concerning caricaturization occurs in the first two paragraphs of Mr. Lowell's article. The author begins by writing that in November, 1948, Catholic leaders of that

> . . . powerful church undertook a drastic reorientation of their attitude toward the United States government. . . . The statement of the Bishops issued at that time will repay thoughtful reading by every American. These men serve notice that the vast power of their organization will henceforth be devoted to destroying the principle of Church-State separation.
>
> . . . They say plainly that "Separation of Church and State has become the shibboleth of doctrinaire secularism." They pledge them-

---

[2] "Letters to the Editor," *Christianity Today,* 4 February, 1957, p. 24.
[3] C. Stanley Lowell, a letter, 12 September, 1957.

selves to "work peacefully, patiently and perseveringly" for its destruction. Thus, with a bold announcement supported by the cleverest of propaganda, this powerful church has set out to destroy the free position of the American churches.

That serious charge means that the Catholic Church in the United States seeks to undermine the American principle of separation of Church and State as definitively expressed in the First Amendment. "Congress shall make no law respecting an establishment of religion, or prohibiting the free exercise thereof . . ." reads the pertinent portion of the First Amendment.

Now, there are two ways of distorting what someone else has written — by omitting certain words that form an integral portion of the passage quoted; by placing the quotation in a setting entirely foreign to the context in which the quoted passage originally appeared. This latter is called "quoting out of context." Mr. Lowell's reference to the bishops' statement of November, 1948, is an example of both methods of distortion.

The source from which Mr. Lowell inaccurately quotes is a statement issued by the hierarchy entitled "The Christian in Action" (21 November, 1948).[4] Mr. Lowell's first quotation from the bishops' statement is: "Separation of Church and State has become the shibboleth of doctrinaire secularism." But in the original statement those words are only a section of a sentence, and two words of that section have been omitted by Mr. Lowell. Besides, it is necessary to read the four sentences immediately prior to the one in question in order to preserve the proper context. Those four sentences are:[5]

> The meaning [of the First Amendment] is even clearer in the records of the Congress that enacted it. Then, and throughout English and Colonial history, an "establishment of religion" meant the setting up by law of an official Church which would receive from the government favors not equally accorded to others in the co-operation between government and religion — which was simply taken for granted in our country at that time and has, in many ways, continued to this day. Under the First Amendment, the federal government could not extend this type of preferential treatment to one religion as against another, nor could it compel or forbid any State to do so. If this practical policy be described by the loose metaphor "a wall of separation be-

---

[4] Raphael M. Huber, O.F.M.Conv. (ed.), "The Christian in Action," *Our Bishops Speak* (Milwaukee: Bruce Publishing Company, 1952), pp. 145–153.

[5] *Ibid.*, pp. 150–151.

tween Church and State," that term must be understood in a definite and typically American sense.

Immediately following is this sentence, only the italicized portion of which Mr. Lowell quotes:

> It would be an utter distortion of American history and law to make that practical policy involve the indifference to religion and the exclusion of co-operation between religion and government implied in the term *"separation of Church and State"* as it *has become the shibboleth of doctrinaire secularism.*

It is obvious that Mr. Lowell: (1) cites only a section of a sentence without so indicating; (2) omits the two vital words "as it" without informing the reader; (3) omits two quotation marks found in the original; (4) unjustifiably capitalizes the first word to help create the false impression that the sentence fragment is a complete sentence; (5) places the mangled fragment in a context which obviates any remaining chance for even a semiaccurate understanding.

It is equally clear that the bishops are not serving notice, as Mr. Lowell states, "that the vast power of their organization will henceforth be devoted to destroying the principle of Church-State separation." The bishops were not criticizing the true American sense of "separation of Church and State," but rather the implication of the term "separation of Church and State" *as it has become* the shibboleth (watchword) of doctrinaire secularism. "The failure to center life in God is secularism . . ." state the bishops.[6] It is not our original American tradition of "separation of Church and State" that is criticized, for the bishops say:

> We feel with deep conviction that for the sake of both good citizenship and religion there should be a re-affirmation of our original American tradition of free co-operation between government and religious bodies — co-operation involving no special privilege to any group and no restriction on the religious liberty of any citizen. We solemnly disclaim any intent or desire to alter this prudent and fair American policy of government in dealing with the delicate problems that have their source in the divided religious allegiance of our citizens.[7]

Mr. Lowell's second quotation from the bishops' statement is interwoven in this sentence of his: "They pledge themselves to

---

[6] *Ibid.,* p. 145.   [7] *Ibid.,* p. 153.

'work peacefully, patiently and perseveringly' for its destruction."
"They" obviously refers to the bishops, and "its" obviously refers
to the American principle of separation of Church and State. The
portion from the bishops' statement ("work peacefully, patiently
and perseveringly") is misquoted and is quoted out of context.

The sentence immediately prior to the one to which Mr. Lowell
refers reads: "We, therefore, hope and pray that the novel interpretation of the First Amendment recently adopted by the Supreme
Court will in due process be revised." Following that sentence is the
one from which Mr. Lowell quoted: "To that end we shall *peacefully, patiently and perseveringly* work."[8] It will be noticed that
the italicized portion is quoted in the correct order by Mr. Lowell,
although the word "work" is somewhat relocated. While the reloca-
tion of "work" does no violence to the meaning of the text, to put it
in within quote marks does indicate a lack of regard for accuracy
and scholarship.

However the new context in which Mr. Lowell places the quotation quite clearly leads the reader to believe that the Catholic
bishops have pledged themselves to "work peacefully, patiently and
perseveringly" for the destruction of the American principle of
separation of Church and State. But, when we refer to the bishops'
original document, it is then obvious that the end to which the
bishops shall "peacefully, patiently and perseveringly work" is the
revision of a *novel* interpretation by the Supreme Court concerning
the First Amendment, *not* the destruction of the *traditional* American principle of separation of Church and State.

The novel interpretation referred to is the Court's interpretation
which "would bar any co-operation between government and organized religion, even where no discrimination between religious bodies
is in question."[9] It is the same interpretation that "a group of non-
Catholic religious leaders recently noted, will endanger 'forms of
cooperation between Church and State which have been taken for
granted by the American people' and 'greatly accelerate the trend
toward the secularization of our culture.'" It is the same interpretation concerning which "The Journal of the American Bar Association ... pertinently remarks: 'the traditionally religious sanctions
of our law, life, and government are challenged by a judicial pro-
pensity which deserves the careful thought and study of lawyers and

8 *Ibid.*
9 *Ibid.,* p. 151.

people.' "[10] The full statement of the non-Catholic religious leaders just referred to may be found in James M. O'Neill's *Catholicism and American Freedom,* page 56 (Harper and Brothers). The statement of *The American Bar Association Journal* is in the June, 1948, issue.

Neither of Mr. Lowell's references to the 1948 bishops' statement supports his conclusion that the hierarchy seek to destroy the principle of Church-State separation or the free position of the American Churches. On the contrary, the full text of the bishops' statement illustrates that the bishops are defending the traditional American policy of separation of Church and State against any efforts to distort that policy as embodied in the First Amendment. The Catholic bishops do not stand alone in this defense.

That the American Catholic hierarchy have always given unqualified approval to the Constitution is best illustrated by the fact that no statement can be produced in which the bishops declare otherwise, whereas a multitude of statements by Catholic bishops can be found expressing unqualified praise of American democracy and the Constitution.[11]

Mr. Lowell's treatment of the bishops' statement has illustrated what has been termed literary caricaturization. His conclusion is based upon evidence that is either greatly distorted or simply nonexistent. He constructs a fictitious position and then proceeds to criticize that position as though it were a real one.[12]

— 2 —

EDUCATION AND THE BIBLE

According to Mr. Lowell's next few paragraphs, the hierarchy in nineteenth-century America "was concerned to eliminate from the

---

[10] *Ibid.*

[11] J. M. O'Neill, *Catholicism and American Freedom* (New York: Harper and Brothers, 1952), Chap. 3.

[12] In addition to "Rising Tempo of Rome's Demands" POAU similarly "reports" the 1948 statement in the following pamphlets: *My Reply to the Archbishop, Wake Up America, Truth Series No. 1, Separation and Spirituality, The Free Pulpit, Separation and Religion, Facing a Common Peril, A Summons to Americans, Religious Liberty, Reality or Illusion?* and *Out of Bounds.* After "quoting" the two portions of the bishops' statement that Mr. Lowell above refers to, *Wake Up America* announces, "THIS ACT MADE POAU ABSOLUTELY NECESSARY." Thus, POAU has staked the reason for its existence upon two highly distorted quotations.

public schools every reference to God, the Bible and religion and to make the schools strictly secular institutions. . . . Roman Catholics undertook to drive religion out of the schools not because they were atheistic or secularistic people, but because they were not powerful enough to determine the kind of religion to be taught. They preferred no religious teaching at all if they could not have Roman Catholic dogma."

Professor Ray A. Billington's well-documented book concerning American Nativism of the nineteenth century tells a different story.[13]

> The clash between Catholics and Protestants over the use of the Bible in the public schools took its most dramatic form in New York City where the controversy was intensified by the nature of the school system in 1840 when Catholic citizens first began their complaints. New York schools at this time were under the control of the Public School Society. . . . One of the avowed purposes of this society was "to inculcate the sublime truths of religion and morality contained in the Holy Scripture" so that Bible reading was given a prominent place in the curriculum of the schools under its jurisdiction. . . .
>
> The King James version of the Scriptures was read daily in all of the schools of the society and the regular prayers, singing, and religious instruction were not in accord with Catholic belief. Particular grounds for complaint existed in the textbooks used in the society's schools; all were blatantly Protestant in sympathy and many were disrespectful of Catholicism. . . .
>
> The presence of these books in a public school system receiving support from the state certainly gave Catholics the right to demand more just treatment.[14]

He continues:

> Opposed as he was to Godless schools, Hughes [Catholic bishop of New York] nevertheless believed that they alone could do away with sectarian influences in instruction.[15]

Professor Billington goes on to say that Bishop Hughes's failure

---

[13] Ray Allen Billington, *The Protestant Crusade, 1800–1860* (New York: Rinehart and Company, Inc., 1952). This is an excellent study of nineteenth-century anti-Catholicism. Blanshard referred to it in *American Freedom and Catholic Power* (1958), and Mr. Lichtenstein (while with POAU) referred to it as "generally accurate" and to Billington as "a man of high reputation" (a letter, 5 August, 1957). But in a letter of 21 August, 1958, Mr. Lowell said he was not familiar with *The Protestant Crusade* by Billington. How can Lowell speak as an authority on the subject and admit ignorance of the most outstanding work on it?

[14] *Ibid.*, pp. 143–145.   [15] *Ibid.*, p. 149.

to eliminate compulsory Protestant sectarian instruction from the public schools led him to concentrate "his efforts on building parochial schools for the education of Catholic children."[16]

A similar situation existed in Philadelphia, as Professor Billington relates:

> . . . Bishop Francis Patrick Kenrick of the Philadelphia diocese had, on November 14, 1842, addressed a letter to the Board of Controllers of the public schools complaining that the Protestant Bible was being read to Catholic children and that religious exercises were being made a daily part of the instruction. He respectfully asked that the Catholic children be allowed to use their own version of the Bible and that they be excused from other religious instruction. In January, 1843, the school board complied with this request, allowing children to read from any version of the Bible which their parents selected.
>
> Dissatisfaction with this action developed slowly during the following year, stirred by the American Protestant Association which promptly seized upon the issue as one worthy of its undivided efforts. Pamphleteers and the local religious press were unrestrained in their condemnation of the Controllers' action and demanded that Protestants throw every obstacle in the path of Catholics who sought to introduce un-Christian education.[17]

Professor Billington illustrates how the request of Bishop Kenrick was looked upon as a plot to banish the Bible from public institutions.

> In vain did Bishop Kenrick publish a second letter to the Controllers [1844] . . . stating that he "did not object to the use of the Bible, providing Catholic children be allowed to use their own version."[18]

The following footnote by Professor Billington refers to a decision by the Maine supreme Court regarding Protestant-version Bible reading in public schools:

> Donahoe v. Richards, 38 Maine, 379. The arguments before the court were intensely anti-Catholic in tone. They are printed in the New York *Observer* August 31, 1854. This decision, making it possible for school authorities to force the reading of the King James version of the Scriptures, remained the leading case on the subject for many years, despite Catholic objections. Students were expelled from Boston and New York schools as late as 1858 and 1859 for

---

[16] *Ibid.*, p. 155.   [17] *Ibid.*, p. 221.   [18] *Ibid.*, p. 222.

refusing to read the Protestant Bible. It was not until 1890 that the Egerton Bible Case, tried in the Wisconsin courts, reversed the decision in Donahoe v. Richards and made it possible for Catholic children to attend public schools without having their religious beliefs interfered with.[19]

Catholic authorities did not want Godless schools, neither did they want compulsory attendance of Catholic children at classes in Protestant religious instruction. Mr. Lowell clearly ascribes other motives to the hierarchy. Intentionally or not, he implies that the hierarchy objected to religious instruction (Bible reading, etc.) in the public schools because the Catholic Church desired, but was not able to monopolize, the religious instruction in those schools. Actually, however, the desire of the hierarchy was merely for an even break regarding sectarian instruction in public schools. Bishop Kenrick of Philadelphia, for one, felt that the fairest procedure would be to allow Catholic students to use the Catholic version of the Bible, and to be excused from religious instruction of a Protestant nature. He did not object to Bible reading, etc., on those conditions, nor did he try "to eliminate from public schools every reference to God, the Bible and religion and to make the schools strictly secular institutions," as Mr. Lowell writes with reference to the hierarchy.

To document his assertions Mr. Lowell refers to one out of "more than one hundred cases" that Catholics brought before the courts:

> I cite here but one of the hundred — that of *People ex rel. Ring v. Board of Education in Illinois*. In this case Roman Catholics sought to eliminate Bible reading and devotional exercises from the public-school program. The court agreed with their contention that these practices did violate Church-State separation as expressed in the Constitution and ordered them discontinued.

Mr. Lowell has spelled "Constitution" with a capital "C" and has not modified it with an adjective; consequently, he must be referring to the Constitution of the U. S. In so doing he is being misleading. The traditional American policy of Church-State relations is expressed in the First Amendment. This amendment is directed only against Congress, prohibiting Congress from enacting laws either for or against an establishment of religion (national church) and from legislating against the free exercise of religion.

---

[19] *Ibid.*, p. 315, n. 19.

"This left the states free to establish and maintain state churches as some New England States did for a generation after the adoption of the First Amendment."[20] More will be said on this subject in Chapter 17. However, the point at hand is this: 1925 is the earliest date anyone may cite as the time when the States were first bound by the First Amendment.[21] It was *1910* when the Supreme Court of Illinois rendered its decision in *People ex rel. Ring*.

Hence, neither the case cited by Mr. Lowell, nor any of the "more than one hundred cases," if prior to 1925, had any relation to the First Amendment.

The Supreme Court of Illinois explicitly states that only the constitution of Illinois is involved: "The question, therefore, to be decided in this case is, is the reading of the Bible in the public schools of this State prohibited by our State constitution?"[22]

A reading of the Illinois Supreme Court's opinion makes it clear that the complaint stemmed from the use of the King James version in public school Bible reading, and that Catholic children were required to participate without their consent and against the wishes of their parents. In addition, there were the singing of Protestant hymns and the recitation of Protestant orientated prayer. The following is the conclusion of the court:

> The exercises mentioned in the petition [of Catholic parents] constitute worship. They are the ordinary forms of worship usually practiced by Protestant Christian denominations.[23]

Hence, the Catholic parents in this case *sought to eliminate* exclusive Protestant *Bible reading and* compulsory Protestant *devotional exercises from the public school program.* The italicized portion contains the words of Mr. Lowell's reporting of the case. Why did the parents seek the above action? Because their children were required to participate, against their own and their parents' wishes, in Protestant acts of worship. This case certainly does not support Mr. Lowell's conclusion that ". . . Catholics undertook to drive

---

[20] W. E. Binkley and M. C. Moos, *A Grammar of American Politics* (New York: Alfred A. Knopf, 1950), p. 116.

[21] *Ibid.,* p. 124. Actually there has never been a U. S. Supreme Court *decision* that declared that states are bound by the First Amendment; there has been such loose talk in the *dicta* and opinions but not before 1925.

[22] V. L. Nickell (ed.), "The People ex rel. Jeremiah Ring *et al. vs.* The Board of Education of District 24," *Supreme Court Decisions Concerning Reading of the Bible and Religious Education in the Public Schools* (State of Illinois, 1956), p. 16.

[23] *Ibid.,* p. 8.

religion out of the schools . . . because they were not powerful enough to determine the kind of religion to be taught." As the Rev. John A. Hardon states:

> Unfortunately the decision of 1910, which is still in effect, went beyond the intent of those who brought suit. They were not against the Bible as such, but against the use of a Protestant version with additional comment imposed without discrimination on all the children.[24]

Even Mr. Lowell must see some difference between trying "to drive religion out of the schools" and seeking to eliminate an exclusive situation whereby one group of religious tenets is taught to persons of other faiths combined with the fact that those persons are required to receive such instruction against their will.

Now Mr. Lowell turns to an erroneous discussion of the Baltimore Council of 1840:

> The provincial council of the Roman Catholic Church in Baltimore, 1840, imposed on priests the responsibility of seeing to it that Catholic children attending public schools did not participate in any religious exercises there. They were also to use their influence to prevent any such practices in the public schools.

Here is what P. Guilday has to say about the 1840 Council of Baltimore:[25]

> The sixth decree called attention again to the grave risks the public or common school held for the Faith of Catholic boys and girls who were obliged to listen to the Protestant Bible, sing Protestant hymns, and hear sermons against the Church. The clergy and Catholic parents were advised to assert their civic rights in this grave question for it could not be denied at the time that the common schools were being used as annexes to the Protestant churches. . . . But the bishops considered it prudent only to direct the pastors to prevent Catholic pupils in these schools from being forced to join in Protestant religious services. . . .
> Parents were solemnly warned of the dangers their children encountered in non-Catholic educational institutions. "Long and melancholy experience" had proven the truth of this attitude, as well as that shown by the prelates of former Councils on the question of the textbooks in

---

[24] J. A. Hardon, "Cooperation of Church and State," in *Homiletic and Pastoral Review*, March, 1957, p. 524.

[25] P. Guilday, *A History of the Councils of Baltimore* (New York: Macmillan Co., 1932), pp. 125–129.

use in those schools and colleges. "We can scarcely point out a book in general use in the ordinary schools, or even in higher seminaries, wherein covert and insidious efforts are not made to misrepresent our principles, to distort our tenets, to vilify our practices and to bring contempt upon our Church and its members."

Thus it is clear that: (1) The Council did not, as Mr. Lowell relates, direct priests to prevent Catholic students attending public schools from participating "in *any* religious exercises there" (emphasis added) but rather directed "the pastors to prevent Catholic pupils in those schools from being forced to join *Protestant* religious services" (emphasis added) as the history of the Council reports; and (2) Mr. Lowell is not accurate when he states that priests "were also to use their influence to prevent any such practices in the public schools" (i.e., any religious exercises), for the history of the Council reports no such decree. The sixth decree of the Council was not directed to eliminate all religious exercises in public schools but to prevent Catholic students from being forced to participate in exercises insofar as those exercises were non-Catholic.

Mr. Lowell next comments:

> The "secular public school" was in substantial part the achievement of the Roman Catholic Church. Today, however, this church has about-faced. Today it denounces the secular public school as "godless" and argues loudly for the return of religion to education.

The Catholic Church in America has not "about-faced." The hierarchy still opposes any system of public education wherein Catholic students are forced to receive Protestant religious instruction or to participate in Protestant worship. By the same token, Protestants would certainly have the right to protest the practice of any public school system wherein Protestant students are required to receive non-Protestant religious instruction and to participate in non-Protestant worship without their own and their parents' consent. Should a Protestant group protest against such a situation, it would hardly be logical to say that therefore Protestantism is attempting "to eliminate from the public schools every reference to God, the Bible, and religion and to make the schools strictly secular institutions," as Mr. Lowell concludes with reference to the Catholic Church. On the contrary, both Protestant and Catholic (Jewish also) leaders favor those released-time programs whereby each faith is afforded an equal opportunity to give religious instruction to those students who desire it.

Mr. Lowell affirms that the Catholic Church has denounced the public schools as "godless." It is true that *some* Catholics, both lay and clerical, have criticized the public schools in such a fashion. Those individuals in the majority of cases have simply called attention to the fact that the teaching of positive religion in public schools is illegal; i.e., the public school is "godless." But is such an opinion meant to imply that public education is not doing a good job under the circumstances and is therefore something to be destroyed? Suppose, for the sake of argument, that that is the implication. A further question is now in order: does such a rare and extreme opinion therefore commit the American hierarchy and the Catholic Church to the same attitude? Definitely not. In Chapter 8 we have already seen that the American hierarchy in 1955 termed the plain physical fact of the public school system "a matter for unanimous congratulation." We have also seen papal declarations asserting the right of the State to conduct education insofar as no State monopoly was involved. Finally, a Catholic source was quoted as declaring that Catholics have a moral obligation to support public education regardless of whether or not positive religion is taught therein.

It is true that education without positive religion is considered inadequate by the hierarchy and, indeed, by all true Catholics. This does not mean, however, that public schools are therefore denounced as "godless." The fact that *some* Catholics have attacked public schools does not mean that the Catholic Church holds the same opinion any more than do the Protestant denominations because a few Protestants have voiced substantially identical attacks.[26]

The National Catholic Educational Association says, "At no time has the Catholic hierarchy ever taken the stand that public schools are 'godless.' "[27]

Mr. Lowell and POAU continue:

> Today movements for the teaching of "moral and spiritual values" in the public schools, like the recent one in New York City, find the hierarchy in hearty endorsement.

---

[26] For such criticism by a Protestant see: R. H. Martin, "Fourth R in American Education," in *Christianity Today*, 2 September, 1957, p. 11.

[27] O'Neil D'Amour, a letter, 28 February, 1958.

This endorsement is evidently not approved nor thought genuine by Mr. Lowell. It, among other things, is termed a "change of front" on the hierarchy's part.

Need it be repeated that the hierarchy has not changed "front" by endorsing the importance of teaching spiritual and moral values to children — whether in New York City or elsewhere? The hierarchy has objected to the exclusive practice of one faith being taught in a positive manner to children within the public system regardless of parental consent. The New York program is not of that type. No specific faith is taught. The rights of neither Protestant, Jew, Catholic, nor atheist are violated.

Briefly, just what is the New York program about which Mr. Lowell seems so apprehensive?

First, the program of teaching moral and spiritual values is not regarded as synonymous with the program of released time. The program referred to by Mr. Lowell represents a reaffirmation of principles that have for a long time been implicit in the public school curriculum of New York City. Those principles have always been *supported by leaders of the Protestant, Jewish, and Catholic faiths.* This information has been derived from correspondence with the New York City Board of Education.[28] This Board has published a pamphlet called "The Development of Moral and Spiritual Ideals in the Public Schools."[29]

The pamphlet states that it is a function of the school to build good character in its students. It goes on to say that the policy of inculcating spiritual and moral values

> recognizes that most children come to school with a belief in God, and that the schools must not teach for or against the religious beliefs or disbeliefs of any group.[30]

The program does not involve the formation of a special class in "moral and spiritual values." Rather these values are treated within the framework of the normal curriculum of social studies, science, home economics, etc. For example, in social studies the students learn that

> The underlying philosophy of American Democracy is based upon the premise that the individual possesses God-given rights which the

---

[28] Ethel P. Huggard, a letter, 17 October, 1957.
[29] New York City Board of Education, 4 October, 1956.
[30] *Ibid.,* p. 5.

state can neither give nor take away. This, too, is the basis of the American concept of civil rights and religious liberties . . . and of the worth and dignity of each individual, regardless of his race, creed, color, talents or station in life. Even those who may question the validity of the concept that God is the source of the inalienable rights of the individual admit that this ideal was basic in the thinking of our forebears.[31]

Why POAU should endorse Mr. Lowell's apparent objection against a religious group favoring such a fair, nondiscriminatory, and worthwhile program is best known to POAU itself.

In the entire section concerning education, POAU and Mr. Lowell have not given readers an accurate or factual account. Some inaccuracies may seem trivial, but a series of trivial inaccuracies, or even one, may be the basis of a major point which otherwise would be seen as obviously untrue.

— 3 —

THE CATHOLIC VOTE

In the next two paragraphs Mr. Lowell discusses what he terms the "Catholic vote." The first paragraph is dedicated to a reiteration of the assertions made at the beginning of his article with reference to the 1948 bishops' statement: "As far as Rome was concerned, this pronouncement marked the end of the line for Church-State separation." This conclusion has already been shown to be utterly false.

The following paragraph of Mr. Lowell's is extremely interesting, for it exemplifies what may be termed a "heads I win, tails you lose" type of criticism. It also illustrates a man presenting evidence which, if anything, contradicts his conclusion.

> The Roman Church claims a membership of 33 million in the United States, which has become in the hands of the hierarchy a gigantic battering ram to breach the wall of separation. The adults in this membership comprise the "Catholic vote" of which we hear so much. There are, comparatively, not many Catholics holding high public office. This is actually a source of strength to the hierarchy since it is able to keep in perpetual intimidation the Protestant officeholders who fear nothing more than that the "Catholic vote" might be turned against them.

---

[31] *Ibid.*, p. 10.

Whether or not high officeholders are all Catholics or all Protestants, the bishops will be accused by Mr. Lowell and POAU of wielding the "Catholic vote." Let's be sensible; either there is a "Catholic vote" or there is not. If there is, then Mr. Lowell should produce the evidence.

The term "Catholic vote" may have several meanings. It may simply refer to the fact that Catholics vote. Mr. Lowell does not seem to object to that. The term may refer to the probability that some Catholics vote for certain candidates simply because the candidates are Catholic, just as it is equally true to say that some non-Catholics vote for candidates simply because the candidates belong to a particular non-Catholic faith. Such a voting criterion is unreasonable as Monsignor John A. Ryan has indicated:

> The Catholic citizen is also obliged to vote intelligently and honestly. He does wrong when he casts his ballot for incompetent or corrupt candidates on the lazy assumption that their opponents are just as bad, or because he desires to put a friend or a fellow Catholic into office.[32]

However, Mr. Lowell does not have such a situation in mind. What he and POAU criticize is clear, namely, the Catholic bishops allegedly are able to, and in fact successfully do, tell Catholics for whom and for what to vote, and thereby "keep in perpetual intimidation the Protestant officeholders."

We are told of the influential and ominous "Catholic vote" and yet we are also told that "there are, comparatively, not many Catholics holding high public office." How strange that evidence of the "Catholic vote" is not to be found in the religious affiliation of those holding high public office. But, declares Mr. Lowell, such a situation "is actually a source of strength to the hierarchy since it is able to keep in perpetual intimidation the Protestant officeholders." Besides the fact that no evidence is produced to support that charge, it is certainly insulting to Protestant officeholders. Mr. Lowell and POAU seem to be saying that high Protestant officeholders are spineless gentlemen capable of subverting the best interests of the country because of perpetual "intimidation."

If the hierarchy is going to "intimidate" anyone, Massachusetts with a Catholic population of over 50 per cent would be the place

---

[32] John A. Ryan, *Christian Democracy Series No. 1* (New York: Paulist Press, 1941), p. 24.

to investigate. But regarding "intimidation" Senator John F. Kennedy of Massachusetts states:

> . . . it is unfair and illogical to assume that the enactment of this legislation [referred to by Mr. Lowell — see below] was not in accord with public policy or that it resulted from the "intimidation" or pressure from Catholic clerical or other sources. For my own part I can honestly say that never in my public life have I been approached by a representative of the Catholic Church or for that matter any other church to perform an official act which was not consistent with the public interest as I saw it. I think this probably represents the experience of most of my colleagues both in the House and in the Senate.[33]

Congressman Edward P. Boland, Second District, Massachusetts, was also queried about Congressional "intimidation" by church groups, Catholic or otherwise. He knew nothing about the subject and he sent the question to the Legislative Reference Service of the Library of Congress for investigation. The Service replied to Congressman Boland, "We have no information on this point."[34] Neither, it is safe to say, does Mr. Lowell.

Even if there were a relatively large percentage of Catholic officeholders, would that prove that the bishops tell Catholics how to vote or that Catholics would be required to obey them if they did? There were more Methodist officeholders (102; see *Time*, 4 February, 1957) in the 85th Congress than those of any other religious faith. Does that fact mean there is a "Methodist vote" in the sense that Methodists are told how to vote by their bishops or that they must obey their bishops in such a matter?[35] Of course not.

Ecclesiastical authorities of all faiths have the right and the responsibility at times to bring to the attention of their faithful certain legislative measures under consideration that may significantly affect the moral well-being of, or unjustly discriminate against, the faithful. However the final decision is left to the individual's own conscience. (This subject is more thoroughly discussed in Chapter 15.) The exercise of this right and responsibility by the Catholic hierarchy does not entail the subversion or illegal by-passing of any portion of our Constitution.

---

[33] John F. Kennedy, a letter, 3 July, 1957.

[34] A letter, 13 August, 1957.

[35] It is paradoxical that POAU fears a mythical "Catholic vote" while urging a "Protestant vote" in Congress. See Chapter 10 in this relation. See also 15 May, 1948, p. 2, *Church and State Newsletter*.

Mr. Lowell next describes a few legislative acts of Congress that allegedly were approved simply because the Congress feared to offend the "Catholic vote." Still, he has not provided any evidence that there is actually a "Catholic vote." The evidence he provides, i.e., that there are few Catholics in high public office compared to the percentage of the population that is Catholic, indicates, if anything, the *lack* of a "Catholic vote."

Regarding the vote of religious groups in the past two presidential elections, the American Institute for Public Opinion (Gallup Poll) published the following data:[36]

	1952 Catholic	Protestant	Jewish
Republican	44%	63%	23%
Democratic	56%	37%	77%

	1956 Catholic	Protestant	Jewish
Republican	49%	63%	25%
Democratic	51%	37%	75%

Hardly evidence of a Catholic vote.

Professor J. M. O'Neill in his *Catholicism and American Freedom* reports that the results of a few studies regarding the voting records of Catholic Congressmen shows no evidence of a "Catholic vote." Catholics did not all vote one way, for their votes ranged anywhere from the liberal side to the antiprogressive side. The majority of Catholics were classified as liberals, and they voted not as Catholics but as Republicans and Democrats, just as their non-Catholic colleagues did.

The evidence available regarding a "Catholic vote," then, certainly does not support Mr. Lowell's undocumented assumption. Once again POAU has endorsed a false conclusion.

There are some indications that Mr. Lowell has recognized his mistake. At a Boston lecture delivered in September, 1957, he stated that he did not believe that there was a Catholic vote, and that he hated to think that there ever had been one. He further stated that voting patterns are explained more accurately by sociological reasons than by religious affiliation.[37] Nonetheless, there is

---

[36] Press release, 23 January, 1957.

[37] Lecture delivered at Arlington Street Church Parish Hall, 23 September, 1957, 2 p.m.

no doubt that his presentation of the subject in "Rising Tempo of Rome's Demands" is definitely pointed toward convincing the reader that there is, indeed, a Catholic vote wielded at will by the hierarchy. This is evident from such references as "the unveiled threat of reprisal at the polls"; the hierarchy "is able to keep in perpetual intimidation the Protestant officeholders"; etc.

It is true that Mr. Lowell writes "Catholic vote" as opposed to Catholic vote. Quotation marks are supplied by Mr. Lowell, and it is correct to say that quotation marks are often used to imply doubt or to imply that the contrary is true with reference to the word or phrase included between the quotation marks. But the context surrounding "Catholic vote" clearly indicates that for Mr. Lowell there is in reality a Catholic vote which is directed by the bishops.

Other POAU-endorsed information supports Mr. Lowell's myth. In the last half of 1956, Mr. Archer, executive director of POAU, wrote as follows:

> Protestants . . . did not desire to offend the Roman Catholic vote . . . Congressmen know that if they oppose, their political life will be endangered. . . . Roman Catholic political pressure . . . Roman Catholic political action is on the march.[38]

—4—

CATHOLIC "POLITICAL POWER" IN ACTION

Mr. Lowell continues in his "Rising Tempo" article:

> This political power is skillfully wielded to secure preferential treatment for the Roman Church. A good example is the nearly $1 million voted by the Eighty-fourth Congress to refurbish the Pope's summer palace. The payment was for damages allegedly inflicted by American bombs upon a neutral power in World War II. The summer palace was not located in Vatican City, however, and the damage, according to impartial observers, was negligible.

Here are the facts as recorded in Report Number 2251 (84th Congress, 2nd Session) that accompanied the legislation (H.R. 10766) to which POAU and Mr. Lowell refer:

> In the course of hostilities against German armed forces during World War II the papal domain Castel Gandolfo was accidentally

---

[38] Glenn L. Archer, *My Reply to the Archbishop* (POAU, 1956), pp. 9–10.

damaged . . . by bombs dropped from United States planes. . . . The United States Army Claims Service has determined through a survey of the damage that a reasonable assessment . . . would be $964,199.35.

The money was not to "refurbish" the papal domain as Mr. Lowell reports, but for "losses and damages" as Report 2251 declares. Although he later mentions "damages," it comes as a sort of anticlimax to the misleading "refurbish."

POAU refers to "damages allegedly inflicted," and says that "the damage, according to impartial observers, was negligible." However, the report cited clearly indicates that the United States Army Claims Service surveyed the damage. Does POAU mean to say that the Army falsely reported damages when the damages were only "allegedly inflicted"? And does POAU mean to say that the Army was not impartial when it reported the damage as $964,-199.35? Mr. Lowell does not forward any proof for these serious implications.

Mr. Lowell correctly states that Castel Gandolfo is located outside of Vatican City. But this does not mean that Castel Gandolfo is not neutral territory or not part of the papal domain. The Congressional Report states the Castel Gandolfo is part of the papal domain, and the Lateran Treaty of 1929 between the Holy See and Italy declares in Articles 14 and 15:

> Italy recognizes the full ownership of the Holy See over the Papal Palace of Castel Gandolfo . . . [and that it] shall enjoy the immunities recognized by International Law to the seats of diplomatic agents of foreign States.[39]

Castel Gandolfo is geographically within Italian territory, yet actually belongs to the Holy See and not to Italy. Mr. Lowell is intelligent enough to know the truth in this matter.

In his entire discussion Mr. Lowell supplies no documentation to indicate how and when the Church's "political power" was exerted in this case. He writes, "No one would have thought of voting against it. To do so might have offended the 'Catholic vote.' " If Mr. Lowell was not present or did not have a representative present at Congress, he could not know whether or not anyone voted against the bill; much less could he know the thoughts of

---

[39] Sidney Z. Ehler and John B. Morrall (eds.), *Church and State Through the Centuries* (Westminster, Md.: The Newman Press, 1954), pp. 389–390.

the various legislators. This is true because the bill "passed both houses without a record vote."[40] No evidence whatsoever is given to support his claim of a "Catholic vote."

POAU, via Mr. Lowell, now directs its attention to the War Claims Act of 1948, as amended.[41]

Sections 7 (a) and (b) of that Act provide reimbursement for expenditures incurred by religious organizations in the Philippines for relief supplied to members of the United States armed forces or to American citizens during World War II. The sections also provide compensation to religious organizations for loss or damage sustained as a consequence of the war to property or facilities connected with educational, medical, or welfare work.

Mr. Lowell once again implies that the Catholic Church received money for nonexistent war damages or services: "The church collected for services [sic] allegedly suffered to [sic] its installations." (Emphasis added.)

Apparently POAU believes that the War Claims Commission did not adequately investigate the damages. However, Section 7 (d) of the Act affirms:

> In making such determinations the Commission shall utilize but not be limited to the factual information contained in the records of the Philippine War Damage Commission; the technical advice of experts in the field; the substantiating evidence submitted by the claimants; and any other technical and legal means by which fair and equitable postwar replacement costs shall be determined.

Therefore, the War Claims Act specifically orders the Commission to accurately assess the dollar value of the various claims. Mr. Lowell produces no evidence that the Commission did not do precisely that.

In an apparent effort to create the impression that for some ominous reason payments under the Act were strictly hush-hush Mr. Lowell writes, "How many millions were paid is difficult for an outsider to determine." Accurately speaking, anyone who desires to know the precise cash outlays may do so, for the payments are public record. Program awards under subsections 7 (a) and 7

---

[40] Library of Congress (Legislative Reference Service), a letter to the Honorable Edward P. Boland, 6 September, 1957.

[41] Public Law 896 (80th Congress, 2nd Session). Principal amendments: Public Law 303 (82nd Congress, 2nd Session); Public Law 997 (84th Congress, 2nd Session).

(b) of the Act have aggregated $20,097,157.16.[42] Approximately 80 per cent has accrued to organizations affiliated with the Catholic Church,[43] which is not surprising since the Philippines are predominantly Catholic (1957 : 82 per cent). The large percentage paid to the Catholic groups results not from any discrimination in the Act nor from biased application of the Act, but simply from the fact that more Catholic than non-Catholic facilities rendered services or were damaged during the war. POAU neither does nor can produce valid evidence that indicates another explanation.

House Resolution 6586 (Public Law 997) is next discussed. H.R. 6586 is the most recent amendment to the War Claims Act of 1948. Mr. Lowell informs us:

> . . . House Bill 6568 [sic] . . . was smuggled through the Senate in the confusion before adjournment of the Eighty-fourth Congress [Mr. Lowell means House Bill 6586].

The iota of truth in this statement is that H.R. 6586 passed the Senate on 27 July, 1956, the last day before the recess. However, the Legislative Reference Service of the Library of Congress has ascertained that "Senate Majority Leader Lyndon Johnson asked and received unanimous consent for its consideration. Senator Johnson made a brief statement as to the bill's purpose."[44] Thus, H.R. 6586 certainly cannot be said to have been "smuggled through the Senate." Senator Johnson, a non-Catholic, is from solidly Protestant Texas and therefore is not open to the charge of being kept in "perpetual intimidation" by the phantom "Catholic vote."

Mr. Lowell continues by declaring that H.R. 6586 ". . . merely amended the law so that Archbishop Santos of Manila, whose 'claims' had been rejected by the Commission, could get his millions along with the millions that had gone to his colleagues."

It is correct that H.R. 6586 "amended the law," i.e., the War Claims Act of 1948. Essentially, H.R. 6586 now enables religious organizations in the Philippines to qualify for payments if the organizations are of the same denomination as a religious organization functioning in the United States; whereas prior to this amend-

---

[42] Foreign Claims Settlement Commission of the United States, *Awards on Section 7 (b) Property Claims; Awards on Religious Relief Claims Filed Pursuant to Section 7 (a) of the War Claims Act of 1948, as Amended.*

[43] Foreign Claims Settlement Commission, *Decision on Rehearing* (Claim No. R-2099-2, Docket No. 8484), p. 8.

[44] Frederick B. Arner, a letter, 20 September, 1957.

ment the law required affiliation with a religious organization in the United States.

Contrary to Mr. Lowell's explanation that H.R. 6586 was adopted "so that Archbishop Santos of Manila . . . could get his millions . . . ," the Foreign Claims Settlement Commission writes:

> This change [H.R. 6586] appears to have established eligibility in a number of organizations both *Protestant* and Catholic which had previously been considered ineligible.[45] [Emphasis added.]

Mr. Lowell informs us that ". . . there is a chance that the Protestants may qualify for about $30,000 under H.R. 6586." But another POAU publication quotes a 2 April, 1957, Religious News Service dispatch stating that Protestants have submitted claims for $3,508,000 of which $2,466,000 is asked by the Methodist Church, Mr. Lowell's denomination.[46]

Regarding the sum claimed by Archbishop Santos of Manila, Mr. Lowell reports:

> Although the sum was "only $8 million," it should be recalled that the Archbishop's claims originally ran to $30 million.

Concerning the original sum of "$30 million," the Foreign Claims Settlement Commission does not substantiate such a figure. It appears that Mr. Lowell's facts are approximately $28.3 million in error, for the Archbishop's original claims prior to H.R. 6586 were in the amount of $1,732,666.32; another claim was in no stated amount according to the Commission.[47]

The "$8 million" that Mr. Lowell states as the amount claimed by the Archbishop under H.R. 6586 is also somewhat in error. But the difference between fact and fiction in this case is only about $6.2 million. The Archbishop submitted two claims: one for $58,879; another for $1,732,666.[48] Referring to various Catholic claims, Mr. Lowell declared that "All will be paid in time." In the Archbishop's case, the claims were not completely paid: the respective amounts were $18,003 and $1,227,319.[49]

The Foreign Claims Settlement Commission made this cogent

---

[45] Andrew T. McGuire (general counsel for the Commission), a letter, 20 September, 1957.

[46] POAU, *Church and State* (May, 1957), p. 6.

[47] Andrew T. McGuire, a letter, 18 December, 1957.

[48] *Ibid.*

[49] *Ibid.*

remark: "The article which prompted your inquiries evidently contained misstatements of fact."[50] That article is, of course, the one that is being analyzed, Mr. Lowell's and POAU's "Rising Tempo of Rome's Demands."

Throughout Mr. Lowell's treatment of the War Claims Act, he does not mention the source of the funds that are awarded to the various religious groups. It is reasonable to assert that an average reader would assume such funds were derived from public taxes. The national director of POAU, Mr. Glenn L. Archer, whose articles rival those of Mr. Lowell's for the greatest number of errors per paragraph, does not leave the reader to assume that the grants are from public taxes — he says so definitely.[51] But the Claims Commission, on the contrary, reports that "The source of monies in the War Claims Fund is certain liquidated German and Japanese assets."[52]

Before passing on to perhaps the greatest blunder of them all, it might be worthwhile to indicate briefly the various motives that may have prompted Congress to legislate the War Claims Act in general, and the amendment H.R. 6586 in particular. Mr. Lowell of course, indicates that the motive was fear of the Catholic Church's "political power."

In the mid-thirties Congress passed the Tydings-McDuffie Act which granted the Philippines full independence as of 4 July, 1946. Under the terms of this Act the United States was responsible for the defense of the Philippines until independence was effected. Therefore, Congress possibly felt obligated to restore those facilities of the Philippines that were destroyed or damaged by a war in a period when the United States was directly responsible for the defense of the Philippines. The War Claims Act of 1948 helped to accomplish such restoration.

The foreign Claims Settlement Commission also throws some light on this question:

> The educational, medical and welfare work carried on by religious organizations in the Philippines unquestionably has been, and is, of great value and merit. . . . The work not only has its substantial intrinsic worth, but it has tended to strengthen bonds of common ideals between the peoples of our nation and the peoples of the Republic of

---

[50] *Ibid.*

[51] Glenn L. Archer, *The Ramparts We Watch* (POAU), p. 10.

[52] Andrew T. McGuire, a letter, 18 December, 1957.

the Philippines to the extent that they can never be broken. We have here, indeed, a bulwark against the spread of communism, in all probability the strongest in the Far East.

The Congress undoubtedly had these considerations in mind at the time of enactment of subsection 7 (b) [compensation for damage sustained as a result of the war] of the War Claims Act of 1948, as amended.[53]

So much for the Act as a whole. Why was H.R. 6586 enacted? It will be recalled that this amendment merely requires that a Philippine group be of the same denomination as one in the United States whereas previously direct affiliation had to be shown. The Commission declares in a claims' case prior to H.R. 6586:

> In the administration of the Act, in some instances, it has occurred to us that determinations in exact accord with what we believed to be the expressed will of Congress did not produce what we might otherwise have considered to be an even distribution of justice. . . . Nevertheless, the question of the correction of any inequities which may exist would, in our judgment, be a question for the Congress. . . .
>
> The only word that leads us to difficulty, and this certainly is not a novel or new problem for the Commission, is the definition of the word "affiliation.". . . The law itself gives us little succulence in this problem. . . .
>
> Had the Congress given us a more precise bench-mark within which to interpret the meaning of the word "affiliated". . .[54]

Perhaps Congress provided this "bench-mark" in H.R. 6586 and thus produced "an even distribution of justice." Mr. Lowell prefers to see the motive of Congress as stemming from a fear of Catholic "political power." Of course, no documentation supports such a charge.

Finally, we come to an almost inexcusable blunder by POAU and Mr. Lowell. Apparently the Catholic Church must be portrayed as an enemy of public education even in the Philippines. Mr. Lowell asserts in connection with H.R. 6586:

> The public schools of the Philippines received not one cent. Nor will they, because they lack a high-powered lobby and the unveiled threat of reprisal at the polls.

It is true the H.R. 6586 did not provide "one cent" to the Philip-

[53] *Decision on Rehearing, op. cit.,* p. 1.
[54] *Ibid.,* pp. 4, 7, 9.

pine public schools. But Mr. Lowell's statement leads one to believe that the Philippine schools had *never* received aid because "they lack a high-powered lobby. . . ." Once again the Legislative Reference Service of the Library of Congress aids us:

> The Foreign Claims Settlement Comission has stated:
>
> "It may also be of interest to you that, contrary to certain press comments in regard to this legislation [H.R. 6586], Philippine public schools and hospitals which sustained war damages have been aided. Under the provisions of the Philippine Rehabilitation Act of 1946 . . . more than $34 million was awarded to public educational institutions."[55]

Just what opinions the Baptists, Methodists, Presbyterians, Congregationalists, Seventh Day Adventists, Episcopalians, various Jewish groups, and other religious organizations, aided by the Acts described above, hold regarding the POAU article under discussion are not known by these writers. How Mr. Lowell could make such a flagrant error is unimaginable. Furthermore, he has compounded this and the numerous other errors therein by affirming: "The facts are accurate."[56]

—5—

THE HILL-BURTON ACT

In 1946 Congress approved the Hospital Survey and Construction Act, popularly termed the Hill-Burton Act. As its name indicates, the measure is directed toward alleviating the hospital shortage in this country by means of financial and other forms of aid.

It is difficult to understand just what Mr. Lowell and POAU have in mind when they refer to the "absurd inequities of the Hill-Burton grants." Mr. Lowell declares, "Under it [Hill-Burton Act] the Roman Catholics have collected $112,039,000 for their institutions. Protestant institutions have received $23,118,000. Even the disparity of these figures does not tell the story."

Apparently, POAU feels that the Act unconstitutionally or otherwise discriminates against non-Catholics, and the disparity between Catholic and Protestant grants is cited as proof. A brief examination of the Hill-Burton Act will show that it is not discriminatory

---

[55] Frederick B. Arner, a letter, 20 September, 1957.
[56] C. Stanley Lowell, a letter, 12 September, 1957.

at all, but rather most impartial regarding who may receive the grants. Such an examination will not only illustrate that "even the disparity of these figures does not tell the story," but that the disparity tells no story at all in explaining or substantiating Mr. Lowell's reference to the "absurd inequities of the Hill-Burton grants."

Title VI of the Public Health Service Act is what has been termed the Hill-Burton Act; Part A, "Declaration of Purpose," is partially quoted as follows:

> . . . to assist the several States to inventory their existing hospitals . . . , to survey the need for construction of hospitals, and to develop programs for construction of such public and *other non-profit hospitals* as will . . . afford the necessary physical facilities for furnishing adequate hospital, clinic, and similar services to all their people . . . to assist in the construction of public and *other non-profit hospitals* in accordance with such programs. . . .[57] [Emphasis added.]

Obviously, no pro-Catholic bias exists in that portion of the Act. Section 625 of the Act is entitled, "Approval of Projects and Payments for Construction." It affirms in part:

> . . . For each project for construction pursuant to a State plan approved under this part, there shall be submitted to the Surgeon General through the State agency an application by the State or a political subdivision thereof or by a public or *other non-profit agency*.[58] [Emphasis added.]

One government pamphlet has this to say about the eligibility for Hill-Burton aid:

> To be eligible, the facility must fill a community need and be sponsored either by a non-profit organization or by a city, county or State.[59]

Therefore, if Mr. Lowell believes that there is an inequity insofar as those eligible to receive Hill-Burton aid are concerned, he is obviously in error. No such discrimination between religious groups exists. To further emphasize that point, the following is quoted from a letter received from the U. S. Department of Health, Education and Welfare (HEW):

[57] U. S. Department of Health, Education and Welfare, "Public Health Service Act, Title VI," *Public Health Service Manual Laws and Regulations,* July, 1956.

[58] *Ibid.*

[59] U. S. Department of Health, Education and Welfare, *Meeting Community Health Needs* (Washington, D. C.: U. S. Government Printing Office, 1957), p. 2.

The application submitted [for Hill-Burton aid] by project sponsors requires no indication of religious affiliation in those cases where the institution is a sectarian hospital.[60]

It is obvious, then, that the Hill-Burton Act not only authorizes "Federal grants to sectarian hospitals," which is the only description given by POAU, but also authorizes Federal aid to any nonprofit organization, or to any city, county, or state. This latter authorization accounts for approximately 80 per cent of the Hill-Burton grants.[61] Hence the Act does not primarily benefit sectarian hospitals as Mr. Lowell's treatment would indicate.

Mr. Lowell does not mention that the Federal aid does not pay for the entire project. Federal funds may pay between one third and two thirds of the project cost. Dr. John W. Cronin, chief, Bureau of Medical Services, Public Health Service, declares that "This assistance has averaged about one-third of the cost of projects aided."[62]

A careful analysis of all Hill-Burton grants shows Mr. Lowell's figure of $23,118,000 for Protestant hospitals to be grossly inaccurate. Although the Act itself makes no provision for recording the religious affiliation of applicant hospitals, the Department of HEW does make an attempt to record the religious affiliation, if it can be determined from the name of the hospital (i.e., Baptist Hospital, Pensacola, Florida). However, the names of many denominational hospitals give no indication of religious affiliation (i.e., Baton Rouge General Hospital, Baton Rouge, Louisiana). Both of these hospitals are Baptist affiliated and have received Federal aid amounting to $2,245,339.[63]

The most accurate way of determining the amount of money granted Protestant hospitals is to compare the names and locations of all hospitals listed in the *Hospital and Medical Facilities Project Register* with those listed in the *Directory of Protestant Hospitals and Institutions.* A comparison of these two listings shows that as of 30 June, 1957, Protestant affiliated hospitals had received over

---

[60] Hoge, V. M., a letter, 9 August, 1957.

[61] *Ibid.*, enclosure.

[62] John W. Cronin, *Hospital Construction, Progress and Prospects,* 1957 (reprinted from *Hospitals,* 1 January, 1957), p. 2.

[63] U. S. Department of Health, Education, and Welfare, *Hospital and Medical Facilities Project Register,* December 31, 1957.

$62,500,000 in Hill-Burton funds.[64] Mr. Lowell's figure was $23,118,000.

Mr. Lowell compounded his error by asserting, "In Alabama alone . . . this church [Catholic] has obtained $6 million for its hospitals. Baptist churches . . . have a conscientious objection to taking Federal Funds. Only a pittance therefore has gone to this group." He continues by stating, "What is worse, businessmen have begun to refuse to contribute to Baptist hospital campaigns asking, 'Why don't you get your money from the government the way the Catholics do?' "

Unfortunately, Mr. Lowell gives no indication as to what he terms a "pittance," nor does he identify the "businessmen" and the hospitals referred to. A comparison of the sources just cited shows that as of 30 June, 1957, 20 per cent of the fifty-six Baptist-affiliated hospitals listed in the *Directory of Protestant Hospitals and Institutions* had received Hill-Burton money totaling $8,282,-455. As of 30 December, 1958, the figure stood at $9,451,808.[65]

If eight or nine million dollars is a "pittance" by Mr. Lowell's standards, then why does he object to the six million dollars that were granted to Catholic hospitals in Alabama? Even if we assume Mr. Lowell's six million dollars figure as accurate, he has not shown any "discrimination" or "absurd inequities." What Mr. Lowell has failed to mention is that while there are 128 hospitals in Alabama,[66] the American Protestant Hospital Association lists only four Protestant-affiliated hospitals and the HEW Project Register adds but one other. Of the five, two are Baptist, and one each for Episcopal, Methodist, and the Salvation Army. As of 30 June, 1957, the Episcopal and Methodist hospitals had received Hill-

---

64 *The Hospital and Medical Facilities Project Register* of the Department of HEW is published monthly with cumulative listings published in June and December. The cumulative listing of 30 June, 1957, has been used in order to approximate the publication of *Rising Tempo of Rome's Demands*. The *Directory of Protestant Hospitals and Institutions* (January, 1959), is distributed by the American Protestant Hospital Association, Chicago, Illinois. These two sources have been used in computing all Hill-Burton data cited.

65 Baptist hospitals in the following areas have accepted Hill-Burton aid. *Florida* — Miami, Pensacola, and Plant City; *Louisiana* — Baton Rouge, Homer, and De Ridder; *North Carolina* — Durham; *Oklahoma* — Oklahoma City, Pryor, Stillwater, and Tulsa; *Pennsylvania* — Philadelphia; *South Dakota* — Madison; *Texas* — El Paso; *West Virginia* — Philippi.

66 *Information Please, 1959 Almanac* (New York: The Macmillan Company), p. 430.

Burton aid amounting to $329,381.[67] By the same date, over 34 million dollars in Hill-Burton money had gone to the state's non-sectarian hospitals.

The premise of Mr. Lowell's charge seems to be that non-existent Protestant hospitals in Alabama have been discriminated against in favor of existing Catholic institutions. It is illogical to conclude that legislation aimed at helping all hospitals is "discriminatory" in favor of Catholic institutions simply because there are few Protestant institutions available to take advantage of the legislation.

Ironically Mr. Lowell has never found it necessary to question the fact that in Illinois 42 per cent of all Protestant-affiliated hospitals have received Hill-Burton aid totaling $7,091,651. Also in North Carolina Protestant hospitals received nearly five million dollars, while Catholic hospitals received less than one million dollars. However, it must be recognized that these and Mr. Lowell's figures are statistics taken out of context and do not show "absurd inequities" nor "discrimination." Each hospital that has received Hill-Burton aid has done so in full accordance with the law. Religious affiliation is not a factor.

While developing his own statistics on Hill-Burton aid and attacking the Catholic Church Mr. Lowell conveniently overlooked the position of his and POAU vice-president Oxnam's own denomination (Methodist). As early as 15 June, 1951, the then president of the Board of Hospitals and Homes of the Methodist Church, Bishop William T. Watkins, wrote to Dr. Karl P. Meister, executive secretary of the Board that:

> For whatever use it may have, the following is my conviction on the matter of church institutions accepting appropriations from the Federal Government for hospital use. . . .
> . . . I am in favor of the ministry of healing [that] the church will be able to carry to numerous sufferers by the aid of government funds. . . .

Whether or not Bishop Watkins' thinking has guided his church is not known, but by 30 June, 1957, grants to Methodist hospitals amounted to $13,607,648. As of 30 December, 1958, more than 55 per cent of all Methodist hospitals listed in the directory of the American Protestant Hospital Association had accepted Federal aid totaling an excess of $21,000,000. Mr. Lowell and POAU have said nothing.

---

[67] As of 31 December, 1958, the same institutions had received $424,815.

POAU attacks upon Hill-Burton aid to Catholic hospitals has taken on a perpetual character. Periodically *Church and State* carries an analysis of the amount of money awarded Catholic hospitals as opposed to Protestant hospitals. In March, 1959, *Church and State* reported that according to figures released by HEW, Catholic hospitals had received $168,634,000 as opposed to $58,854,000 for Protestant institutions. Certainly the *Americans United* know that these figures are only rough estimates of the actual amounts awarded sectarian institutions. When your authors received the same tabulation from HEW they were so advised. However, a comparison of the HEW Project Register and the Protestant hospital directory showed that as of 31 December, 1958, 38 per cent of the 508 listed Protestant hospitals listed in the directory had received aid amounting to $78,500,000.

Oddly enough, especially in view of past comments by Mr. Lowell and others, the March *Church and State* concluded that "Little or no discrimination is possible at the Federal level, where the allocations are made to States on a strictly scientific formula, involving population and per-capita income averages."

After years of falsely charging "discrimination" and "absurd inequities" in the Hill-Burton Act, POAU has now absolved the Federal government of wrongdoing and has turned its attention toward state health agencies. Whereas HEW offered POAU the opportunity to construct but one "straw man," switching the emphasis to the state level now offers no less than 49 states against which POAU can hurl charges of discrimination. Alabama, the fiftieth state, is by virtue of its consideration in this book disqualified.

Organized discrimination on such a level of government cannot exist unless there is (1) a group to be discriminated against (2) another group strong enough to force its will upon the government against the first group. In Alabama neither of these conditions exists. Two of its five listed Protestant hospitals have received Federal aid and according to Mr. Lowell Baptist hospitals have a "conscientious objection to taking Federal funds." Hence there is no one to be discriminated against. Second, the Catholic population of Alabama is less than 3 per cent of the total population.[68] In a democratic society it is unrealistic to assume that 3 per cent of the population can comprise a pressure group capable

[68] *The 1957 National Catholic Almanac* (Paterson: St. Anthony's Guild, 1956).

of forcing its will upon the other 97 per cent. The question might be asked: If there is no discrimination within the terms of the Act, why have Catholic institutions been allotted approximately twice as much money as all other church-affiliated groups combined? The answer is found in a letter from the Department of HEW stating that:

> . . . approximately seventy-five percent of sectarian hospitals in the United States are owned and operated by the Roman Catholic Church. For that reason more projects are sponsored by the Catholic Church than by other groups.[69]

If POAU is simply objecting to the fact that Catholics contribute more money to hospital programs than any other religious group, and therefore qualify for more Federal aid than any other religious group, it is submitted that such an objection to that type of "inequity" is indeed "absurd." Unequal payments certainly are not always the result of inequitable legislation.

Nor is it reasonable to assume that Mr. Lowell is criticizing Federal grants to sectarian hospitals on the ground that such aid is unconstitutional. In 1899 the Supreme Court "unanimously rejected a claim that a contract between the District of Columbia and Providence Hospital (conducted by the Sisters of Charity), providing government funds for the construction of a new isolation wing, was a violation of the First Amendment. . . ."[70]

Then again Mr. Lowell's objection possibly may be found in these two sentences:

> The Roman Church has found the Hill-Burton Act a marvelous means for penetrating the hitherto impervious Protestantism of the South. Handsome healing centers serve as strong means for propagation of this faith.

No one will deny that Catholic hospitals are religion-orientated. Such institutions are regarded by the Church as performing one of the corporal works of mercy and as performing fraternal charity. Did not Christ declare, ". . . I say to you, as long as you did it to one of these my least brethren, you did it to me" (Mt. 25:40–41)?

Mr. Lowell's description might lead one to assume that Catholic hospitals are immediately interested in converting patients rather

---

[69] Hoge, V. M., *op. cit.*

[70] Joseph H. Brady, *Confusion Twice Confounded* (South Orange: Seton Hall University Press, 1955), p. 42.

than curing them. This is not the case. Catholic ethical directives state that any such "odious proselytism" should be avoided. Assuming that the mere presence of the hospitals and religious personnel have a considerable indirect effect on the patients and locality, would that be a rational basis for labeling Hill-Burton grants "absurd inequities"? Obviously not. Mr. Lowell cannot be objecting to the possibility that Catholicism may increase throughout the South, for POAU has expressly affirmed, "Our controversy is not with any church, Roman Catholic or any other."[71]

As we remarked at the beginning of this section, it is difficult to understand just what "absurd inequities" Mr. Lowell and POAU have in mind. Two letters of inquiry have not helped to clarify the issue. The first letter dated 10 September, 1957, received a reply from Mr. Lowell, but he did not touch upon the Hill-Burton question that had been asked. Another letter (30 April, 1958) was addressed to the POAU Executive Committee. This letter contained 86 questions, one of which asked about the "inequities" of the Hill-Burton Act (Question 70). POAU replied that it could not answer the questions because of staff limitations.

It is indeed unfortunate from the standpoint of replying to Mr. Lowell's assertion that he did not illustrate at least one inequity that may validly be termed "absurd." His and POAU's only "evidence" has been of the assumed variety and has not been and cannot be supported by accurate reporting.

—6—

BISHOPS' STATEMENT, 1955

Mr. Lowell writes, "The campaign to shift the cost of Roman Catholic sectarian schools to the American taxpayer bids fair to be as successful as the hospital program." He continues:

> The campaign began easily as fringe benefits were sought from the government — bus transportation, textbooks, health benefits, lunches and the like. More recently, as for example in the Bishops' statement issued in November, 1955, there is insistence upon the "full right to be considered and dealt with as components of the American educational system." This statement also claims for parochial-school pupils the same government aid that goes to public-school pupils.

---

[71] *A Manifesto* (POAU, revised edition, January, 1957), pp. 9–10.

As Mr. Lowell well knows, the Supreme Court, in the Everson case (1947), upheld the validity of a New Jersey law providing free bus transportation for all school children irrespective of school attended. He is also undoubtedly aware of the Supreme Court decision in the Cochran case (1930) that "held valid a state law authorizing the use of public funds to supply 'school books to the school children of the state' including not only public school children but also children in parochial and private non-sectarian schools."[72] Thus, two of four "fringe benefits" that Mr. Lowell enumerates have been declared constitutional by the Supreme Court. However, in other literature POAU makes the point that such decisions were only permissive; i.e., the states are not *required* by the Constitution to provide textbooks and bus transportation. That appears to be quite true. But it must be remembered that POAU was "set up solely for the purpose of *maintaining* the American Constitutional doctrine of separation between church and state."[73] (Emphasis added.) Thus, inasmuch as both the Everson and Cochran decisions were rendered prior to the founding of POAU, it would follow that POAU should defend those benefits that were declared constitutional rather than to refer suspiciously to them as a part of a "campaign to shift the cost of Roman Catholic sectarian schools to the American taxpayer," or to seek the eradication of such benefits as POAU has done in other literature.

Why the opposition by POAU to such constitutional measures? And why does POAU charge the hierarchy with subverting the Constitution because the bishops criticized a Supreme Court decision, when POAU itself has attacked and is attacking the Cochran and Everson decisions of the Court? At this juncture the reader should be able to supply an appropriate answer.

Regarding the other two "fringe benefits" (school lunches and medical care) that Mr. Lowell mentions, POAU does not object to them on any grounds.[74] With this background we are now able to proceed to a discussion of Mr. Lowell's conclusion that in the *1955 statement* the bishops seek something *more* than the welfare benefits, inasmuch as the hierarchy insisted upon "the full right

---

[72] R. E. Cushman, *Leading Constitutional Decisions* (New York: Appleton-Century-Crofts, Inc., 1958), p. 145.

[73] POAU, *Church and State* (October, 1948), p. 3.

[74] *Ibid.* (May, 1956), p. 4. See also Glenn L. Archer, *Without Fear or Favor* (POAU, 1955), p. 20.

to be considered and dealt with as components of the American educational system."

Mr. Lowell has quoted accurately from the 1955 statement. However, the context in which he places the quotation does not correspond to the context of the statement from which it was extracted. The full text of the 1955 bishops' statement is entitled *The Place of the Private and Church-Related Schools in American Education.*[75] As may be correctly deduced from its title, the statement did not pertain to *Catholic* schools alone, but to all church-related schools and to all private schools. Mr. Lowell does not mention those facts.

Did the 1955 statement demand support other than "fringe benefits"? The following extract from the pronouncement will answer that question (italicized portion is the section Mr. Lowell has quoted):

> Their [private and Church-related schools] place is one dictated by nothing more than justice and equity, and accorded the recognition of their worth. They have, we repeat, *full right to be considered and dealt with as components of the American educational system.* They protest against the kind of thinking that would reduce them to a secondary level and against unfair and discriminatory treatment which would in effect, write them off as less wholly dedicated to the public welfare than the state-supported schools. The students of these schools have the right to benefit from those measures, grants, or aids, which are manifestly designed for health, safety and welfare of American youth, irrespective of the school attended.

Probably one of the most logical and concise statements issued by any court regarding aid to private education was a portion of the Mississippi Supreme Court's opinion rendered in Chance *vs.* Mississippi (1941). This decision upheld a Mississippi law providing the loan of textbooks to students in *all* qualified elementary schools. The Court in part stated:

> If the pupil may fulfill its duty to the state by attending a parochial school, it is difficult to see why the state may not fulfill its duty to the pupil by encouraging it "by all suitable means." The state is under a duty to ignore the child's creed but not its need. . . . The state which allows the pupil to subscribe to any religious creed should not, because of his exercise of this right, proscribe him from benefits common to all.[76]

---

[75] *The 1956 National Catholic Almanac* (Paterson, N. J.: St. Anthony's Guild, 1956), p. 518 ff.

[76] Quoted from John A. Hardon, "Co-operation of Church and State," in *Homiletic and Pastoral Review*, March, 1957, p. 527.

Is not this what the bishops were saying? The bishops' 1955 declaration asked for nothing more than "fringe benefits." Mr. Lowell incorrectly implies otherwise.

The fringe benefits have been a part of a "campaign" to shift parochial school costs to the American taxpayer, declares Mr. Lowell. He seems to fear that the constitutional fringe benefit portion of the "campaign" will lead to unconstitutional enactments. But any measure could be opposed on the ground that it *might* lead to something unconstitutional. Democracy might lead to anarchy. The criterion is an inadequate one.

It is not to be denied that individual Catholics, both clerical and lay, have thought and said that justice demands public support for private schools on the same basis as for public schools. Such pronouncements obviously go beyond the justice requested in the 1955 statement. But should those pronouncements be looked upon as a Catholic plot to obtain illegal support? Disagreements should be rationally and factually discussed. Only those who desire to becloud the issue would have any reason to inject highly charged and emotion-provoking accusations into the debate.

— 7 —

CONNECTICUT EDUCATION STUDY

According to Mr. Lowell:

> A useful gimmick in softening the public for sectarian subsidies is the so-called "study" of education. Proposals for a "study" were slipped through the Connecticut legislature as a "noncontroversial" item.

Mr. Lowell goes on to say that Catholic leaders subsequently appealed for state subsidies and that these "demands were based on the commission's 'scientific study.' "

The picture is now complete: pro-Catholics (if not Catholics themselves) devised a "gimmick" to soften the public for sectarian subsidies. Such a gimmick, a "scientific study" of education, was slipped through the Connecticut legislature. And sure enough, this "so-called 'study' " was used as a basis by Catholic leaders to appeal for "state subsidies." The plot is exposed as another Catholic scheme. But let us look at the facts in the case.

Fact Number 1: the study was not "slipped through the Connecticut legislature" for the best of all reasons — the proposal for the study was not presented to the legislature. As a letter from an official of the Connecticut State Department of Education explains:

> The study was not requested by the Connecticut legislature; indeed, the legislature did not meet until 1957, one year after the study outline was approved by representatives of the schools to be studied.[77]

Fact Number 2: the study was not "slipped through" anyone. It was known to all interested groups. This is evident from the study itself, entitled *The Relationship of Public and Non-Public Schools in Connecticut*:

> In accordance with long standing practice, the Commissioner of Education invited representatives of the agencies concerned to discuss the proposed study and the data gathering forms to be used. Representatives from the Connecticut Council of Churches, the Catholic dioceses of Bridgeport, Hartford and Norwich, the Connecticut Association of Independent Schools, the Jewish rabbinate, the Connecticut Association of Public School Superintendents and the Connecticut State Department of Education met on January 3, 1956, and approved the study outline and inquiry forms.[78]

Fact Number 3: the study does not contain the phrase "parochial schools" in connection with any statistical breakdowns contained within the study. Indeed, the phrase "parochial schools" occurs only once (p. 2) with reference to a decision of the Administrative Council of the Department of Education in 1950. The phrase "parochial high school" (p. 7) also occurs once in an insignificant fashion. All breakdowns are designated as "Non-public," e.g., "Percent of Children 7–15 Years Enrolled in Connecticut Non-Public Schools, 1955–56." Hence, no accurate evaluation of the contribution of Catholic schools can be made from the material contained in the study.

Fact Number 4: the responsibility for the initiation of this study was not that of the Catholic Church as POAU effectively implies. The letter from the State Department of Education states:

> The plans for this study, the gathering of the data, and the writing of the report were entirely my responsibility as Chief of the Bureau of

[77] Maurice J. Ross (chief, Bureau of Research and Statistics), a letter, 10 October, 1957.

[78] Connecticut State Board of Education, *The Relationship of Public and Non-Public Schools in Connecticut* (May, 1956), p. v.

Research and Statistics of the Connecticut State Department of Education. The study purports to be nothing more than a status study.[79]

And the study itself declares, "At its meeting of December 7, 1955, the State Board of Education directed that a status study be made. . . ."[80]

Fact Number 5: POAU presents no valid reason for its disparaging term "so-called 'study.' " Has POAU seen and read the study? If so, why does not Mr. Lowell refer to those sections of the 57-page report that cause him to regard it as merely a "so-called 'study' "?

Fact Number 6: the "spate of press releases about how many children were in parochial schools" could not have been based on the education study inasmuch as the study did not have a parochial-school breakdown. Nor, for the same reason, could the "demands" of the "well-directed chorus" of "Roman Catholic leaders" be based on the study.

Fact Number 7: Catholic leaders in Connecticut have never (either before or after Mr. Lowell's article) appealed for "state subsidies," if by "subsidies" preferential and/or unconstitutional aid is meant.

Fact Number 8: although Mr. Lowell does not identify the precise Connecticut "gimmick" in his article, he is referring to the 1955 study. In a letter Mr. Lowell affirms, "I believe the 'Educational Study' authorized in 1955, to which you refer is the one also mentioned in my article, *Rising Tempo.*"[81] A state education official declares, "As far as I know, this department has made no previous studies regarding non-public schools in Connecticut."[82]

— 8 —

BACK DOOR, FRONT DOOR

Mr. Lowell's remarkable article continues:

. . . the drive for tax support has developed yet a new twist. This is a demand that tuition payments to parochial schools be allowable income tax deductions. The . . . Knights of St. John . . . and the

[79] Ross, *op. cit.*
[80] Connecticut State Board of Education, *op. cit.*
[81] C. Stanley Lowell, a letter, 12 December, 1957.
[82] Maurice J. Ross, a letter, 3 December, 1957.

Central Catholic Verein . . . are among the many Roman Catholic groups that have appealed to Congress for this kind of "relief." Thus a back-door assault on the public treasury keeps pace with the front-door demand.

The following "demand" constitutes the "assault on the public treasury" by the Knights of St. John:

Resolved, that the Knights of St. John do *respectfully urge* that the Congress of the United States and the legislatures of the several States exempt from income tax tuition paid to *private* elementary and high schools.[83] [Emphasis added.]

The "demand" and "assault" of the Catholic Central Union (Verein) of America is as follows:

. . . we *respectfully suggest,* for example . . . the extension — by the Federal as well as the state governments — of the accepted principle of income tax deductions for charitable and educational purposes to apply also to payments made by parents to accredited *private and parochial* schools for the education of their own children.[84] [Emphasis added.]

Two conclusions are evident: (1) the semantic technique of using such emotion-provoking words as "demand" and "assault" is wholly unwarranted; (2) the resolutions of the two Catholic groups did not, as Mr. Lowell reports, pertain only to Catholic schools but to all private schools. Mr. Lowell apparently wished to convey the idea that the Catholic associations desired a preferential status for Catholic schools regarding government aid.

It is not clear just why the two groups are classified as assaulting the back door. Apparently, the bishops have monopolized the front door. If there are any more "assaults," Mr. Lowell will have to install a revolving door.

— 9 —

TROUBLE SPOTS

Continuing his discussion of education, Mr. Lowell injects this remark:

In many communities where they are in the majority Roman Cath-

---

[83] Knights of St. John, *Resolutions* (Dayton, Ohio: Fiftieth Convention, 9–12 July, 1956), p. 7.
[84] Catholic Central Union (Verein) of America, *Declaration of Principles* (Wichita, Kans.: 28 July–1 August, 1956), p. 13.

olics have simply taken over the public schools. They have staffed them with nuns and priests whose salaries, paid from state funds, go directly to their superior, without deductions. It took long and expensive litigations to clear up situations of this kind in Missouri, New Mexico, and Kentucky.

His reference to Catholics having "taken over the public schools" in certain communities has been discussed in detail in Chapter 8 (Franklin County, Missouri; Dixon, New Mexico; Bradfordsville, Kentucky). While it seems hardly necessary at this point, let us repeat that there is nothing in Catholic doctrine that even remotely obligates a Catholic to take over or undermine public schools. Mr. Lowell's treatment implies that there is such an obligation. The implication is absurd.

We are more concerned with Mr. Lowell's statement that the salaries of priests and nuns "paid from state funds, go directly to their superior, without deductions." He then immediately mentions Missouri, New Mexico, and Kentucky.

First of all, what is the Federal law on this matter of taxing members of religious orders? According to a letter received from the Internal Revenue Service, "You are advised that salaries paid to members of a religious order constitutes taxable income unless such member has taken a vow of poverty."[85] That, of course, pertains to Federal taxation. It will be noticed that *any* religious order, Catholic or Protestant, can qualify for such tax treatment. Episcopalian and Lutheran groups comprise the major portion of Protestant religious orders. However, Mr. Lowell and POAU direct their efforts against Catholic orders.

So much for the Federal tax situation. What is the ruling for state taxes to be paid by members of religious orders?

The Department of Revenue in Missouri declares:

> We wish to advise you that any salary or income received by any individual regardless of their connection with religious orders is taxable for income tax purposes to the State of Missouri.[86]

What if the money was paid directly to the order and not by way of a member? Again, the Missouri Department writes that such

[85] Frank J. Cavanagh (Treasury Department, Boston Office), a letter, 14 March, 1958.
[86] Bryan Ornburn, a letter, 11 December, 1957.

a situation "might definitely affect their [religious orders] tax exempt status."[87]

Thus, in Missouri, salaries do *not* "go directly to their superior, without deductions."

The Bureau of Revenue of New Mexico replies to a letter, "Please be advised that under our state income tax law and regulations, all salaries are taxable on our state tax returns since the beginning of our income tax law in 1933."[88] However, with reference to members of religious orders, "I am sure that very few receive $1,500.00 a year, which is the minimum requirement for filing of state income tax return by single persons."[89]

The Kentucky Revenue Department informs us that "The income received by Roman Catholic nuns or Episcopalian sisters for teaching in Kentucky Public Schools is not taxable if the money received is turned over to their religious order because of the vow of poverty."[90] Mr. Lowell's statement, therefore, applies only to the state of Kentucky which follows the Federal procedure.

Mr. Lowell continues:

> There are still numerous "trouble spots" all around the country. Last year in Indiana, for example, more than $2 million in tax funds went to "public schools" that were in effect parochial schools of the Roman Church.

The State Superintendent of Public Instruction in Indiana refutes such a charge:

> The schools referred to in your letter of June 14 are public schools and not parochial schools.
>
> The two million dollars referred to in your letter went to public schools.
>
> May I advise that no money is distributed on a state level to private or parochial schools.[91]

While on the subject of Indiana, what is the tax status of members of religious orders in that state?

> There is no personal exemption allowed any individual except the flat amount of $1,000 per year which is provided to every taxpayer.

---

[87] *Ibid.*, 22 January, 1958.
[88] F. E. McCulloch, a letter, 10 December, 1957.
[89] *Ibid.*, 23 January, 1958.
[90] Clayton Stewart, a letter, 16 December, 1957.
[91] Wilbur Young, a letter, 20 June, 1957.

The income referred to above [of "Roman Catholic Nuns or Episcopalian Sisters"], therefore has been subject to Indiana Gross Income Tax since the law became effective May 1, 1933.[92]

According to POAU and Mr. Lowell, one of the "numerous 'trouble spots' " is Kansas: "There are 152 garbed nuns teaching in the public schools of Kansas with their salaries going to their church." Does Mr. Lowell mean to imply that "garbed nuns" cannot legally teach in Kansas public schools? If he does, he is wrong according to a letter of the Superintendent of Public Instruction:

> I might, however, point out that Kansas courts have not ruled that it is illegal for teachers dressed in garb peculiar to a given church to teach in public schools provided such teachers are certified.[93]

If Mr. Lowell is not referring to an illegality, why mention "garbed nuns" in the first place?

Just how does Mr. Lowell arrive at the precise figure of "152 garbed nuns"? The question is asked because the Kansas State Superintendent writes: ". . . there are no official records that would give such information."[94] Although there are no official records, what would be the Superintendent's guess as to the number of Protestant ministers serving as public school teachers? "It would be my guess that there are quite a number of teachers who have at one time or another served as ministers in Protestant churches."[95]

The Kansas Revenue Department writes that if members of religious orders receive salaries from the state and the income belongs to them, "it would be taxable to them under the Kansas law." However, "if their salaries become the property of the organization to which they belonged . . . it would not be taxable to the teachers under the Kansas law."[96] Thus, under certain circumstances such income is taxable. Mr. Lowell does not mention those circumstances. Nor has he mentioned any favoritism toward Catholic orders by any law in any case that he has cited. One gets the impression that POAU and Mr. Lowell just do not like Catholics, notwithstanding the POAU statement that the organization is "the Roman Catholic's best friend."[97]

---

[92] Claude Ware (Indiana State Revenue Department), a letter, 5 December, 1957.

[93] Adel F. Throckmorton (Superintendent of Public Instruction), a letter, 14 August, 1957.

[94] *Ibid.*, 4 October, 1957.   [95] *Ibid.*

[96] R. A. Dalquest, a letter, 9 December, 1957.

[97] Glenn L. Archer, *Separation and Spirituality* (POAU, 1956), p. 12.

— 10 —

WELFARE PROGRAMS

Mr. Lowell warns that "In simple justice it must be said that the Roman Catholic hierarchy is now within sight of its goal." Just what is this "goal" that apparently will subvert the Constitution and thereby deprive America of its freedoms? Mr. Lowell has not proved that any such goal exists. He states, "Many activities of this church are already receiving tax support. Hospitals, schools, orphanages and other 'welfare programs' are in this category." Some activities of the Catholic Church receive some tax support just as some non-Catholic activities receive some tax support. Such support has existed from the era of James Madison and other Founding Fathers (see Chapter 17) — a fact which makes Mr. Lowell's "are already receiving" absurd. There is no preference or illegality involved in those measures that provide funds for certain religious enterprises.

Church-related activities, Catholic and non-Catholic, that have received some tax money are engaged in what may be properly termed welfare programs that benefit society as a whole. Mr. Lowell, however, uses the term "welfare programs," in quotation marks, thus implying that hospitals, orphanages, schools, and the like, are not welfare programs at all, especially, we suppose, when conducted under Catholic auspices. No evidence is or can be presented to substantiate the implication.

Mr. Lowell says, "Other activities receive sizable grants from community chests." Assuming this statement to be true, what of it? If certain Catholic activities, or non-Catholic programs, receive Community Chest support, what better proof is there that those activities truly benefit the community and are, indeed, welfare programs?

According to Mr. Lowell, "The time is in sight when all the so-called 'social service' activities of the Roman Church will be supported by tax funds collected by compulsion from citizens of all faiths." Notice the quotes surrounding social service; in addition, the adjective "so-called" is now employed. Now it is the "so-called 'social service' activities." Once again it is quite obvious that Mr. Lowell does not believe that hospitals, orphanages, and the like, are indeed social services, especially when Catholics administer them.

Mr. Lowell offers no evidence for his conclusion that "the time is in sight when all the so-called 'social service' activities of the Roman Church will be supported by tax funds collected by compulsion from citizens of all faiths." At the *present time* all taxes are "collected by compulsion from citizens of all faiths." If someone doubts that, just try omitting next year's tax payments. Furthermore, that very same tax money is being used to partially support church-related activities, both Protestant and non-Protestant. Christian Scientists do not like to see their taxes being used to construct hospitals of all kinds. Atheists do not relish the thought of their tax money helping to provide chaplains for the armed services. Obviously, the common good is prior to any personal objections to such expenditures. The Supreme Court concurs in this viewpoint.[98] Finally, Mr. Lowell presents no compelling evidence that "all" social service activities of the Catholic Church will receive any more tax support than all the social service activities of Protestant churches will receive.

Mr. Lowell has been leveling serious charges. He is calling attention to what he considers an alarming situation. But he has not illustrated that the situation even exists, whereas it has been illustrated in preceding sections (bishops' statements, legislative acts, etc.) that Mr. Lowell has no logical basis for his conclusions.

— 11 —

PLURAL ESTABLISHMENT

The next few paragraphs of "Rising Tempo" regarding "plural establishment" represent examples of enlightened confusion. Our first task is to discover just what Mr. Lowell means by the term "plural establishment." He writes:

> The Protestants, if they are realistic, will see but two alternatives before them. One, they must accept the principle of government subsidies to churches — that is, the principle of plural establishment. . . .

Thus, "plural establishment" is equated with church subsidies. What subsidies have been presented by Mr. Lowell? The Vatican War Damage Bill and the War Claims Act of 1948 were mentioned. Those measures, however, were not "subsidies," but compensation to various denominations for the actual value of damaged facilities.

---

[98] W. E. Binkley and C. M. Moos, *A Grammar of American Politics* (New York: Alfred A. Knopf, 1950), p. 117.

A subsidy includes the notion of payment in excess of current market value, or a direct gift with no tangible service received in return. Nor is the Hill-Burton Act a *church* subsidy. It is a subsidy to agencies which desire to construct hospitals. Churches comprise the minority in this group. To call the Act a church subsidy is on a level with calling the G.I. Bill a John Brown subsidy because Brown happens to be one of the thousands who receive benefits from the Bill. Just what is Mr. Lowell talking about? The closest measure to a church subsidy is tax exemption for church property. And even this is not strictly a church subsidy, for many other non-profit organizations, POAU included, receive the same exemption.

Further on, Mr. Lowell describes "plural establishment" as a change "from the principle of voluntarism to the principle of official compulsion. . . ." Just how Mr. Lowell defines these two new principles is not clear. The reader may grapple with this problem.

Definition aside, we do receive this penetrating insight: "The worst feature of plural establishment, however, would be the extremity of its pluralism." He continues, "Our culture would be hopelessly enclaved as 250 religious establishments or more threw themselves into the wild scramble for tax funds." If our culture is going to be "hopelessly enclaved" religion-wise, will such enclavement be caused by the "scramble for tax funds" or by the fact there are over 250 ideologically diverse religious organizations in the United States? If a "wild scramble for tax funds" is a cause of cultural enclavement, why is not this country already "hopelessly enclaved" inasmuch as thousands of individuals and groups (not necessarily religious) are currently in the "wild scramble"? The answer is that the "scramble" is not a factor at all.

The most serious element of Mr. Lowell's discussion of "plural establishment" is his attempt to associate that phrase with the "establishment of religion" clause of the First Amendment. He states that Protestants

> . . . must stop kidding themselves with the false tolerance that plays into Rome's hands, and battle to hold the line for Church-State separation. . . .
>
> We shall have . . . a religious establishment in a country whose Constitution forbids it. That establishment will be pluralistic — or otherwise.

The First Amendment of the Constitution affirms in part that

"Congress shall make no law respecting an establishment of religion. . . ." This clause was adopted to allay the fear of some Founding Fathers that ". . . a national church might be established."[99] The phrase "establishment of religion" means *"an* established church."[100] (Emphasis added.) Chapter 17 will discuss that point in greater detail.

When Mr. Lowell equates "plural establishment" with "an establishment of religion" a contradiction is involved. Professor James M. O'Neill pinpoints this contradiction as follows when he writes that a

> . . . most original contribution to the attempt to make the First Amendment mean something that it clearly never meant to Madison or Jefferson or the members of the First Congress is the invention of the phrase "multiple establishment" [synonymous with "plural establishment"]. To talk of a "multiple establishment" of religion . . . is contrary to the centuries-old usage of the term "establishment" by scholars, lay and religious, Catholic and Protestant. If this constant historical use of the term, and the term as defined and explained in such places as encyclopedias and dictionaries, has any legitimate meaning, it is about as absurd to use the phrase "multiple establishment" as it would be to use the phrase "multiple monopoly" to indicate a monopoly of the soap industry that could be given equally to all soap manufacturers who desired it.[101]

How would it be possible for a particular Church (an established, national Church) to have a monopoly of government aid or to receive preferential treatment when the term "plural establishment" ("250 religious establishments or more") is made synonymous with "an establishment of religion"? How can there be 250 or more churches each possessing a monopoly of government aid or receiving preferential treatment?

Closely related to this topic is Mr. Lowell's reference to "religious establishments." Here again he is apparently attempting to give the impression that "religious establishments" or "religious establishment" can be used interchangeably with "an establishment of religion" as expressed in our Constitution. Professor O'Neill writes that in the Supreme Court case of Bradfield *vs.* Roberts (1899), Justice Peckham,

---

99 *Ibid.*, p. 116.

100 *Ibid.*

101 James M. O'Neill, *Catholics in Controversy* (New York: Farrar, Straus and Cudahy, Inc., 1954), pp. 62–63.

. . . in an opinion delivered for a unanimous court, said that "a religious establishment" was "a phrase which is not synonymous with that used in the Constitution which prohibits the passage of a law respecting an establishment of religion." In other words, the First Amendment did not prohibit a law about a religious establishment, such as a hospital, church, school, orphan asylum conducted under religious auspices, but a law about a monopolistic position of favor to one religious group and so discriminating against all other religious groups.[102]

WESTERLY, RHODE ISLAND

The following quotation from "Rising Tempo" is a prime example of grossly distorted reporting — a distortion that POAU has obviously endorsed:

> Westerly, Rhode Island, is a tiny community that offers a good example of the sort of thing we might expect under plural establishment. The Roman Catholics of Westerly, having developed their own schools to the point where certain public school buildings were no longer needed, proceeded to take them over for their own use. The town council voted them to the Roman Church at a purchase price of $1. The Methodists of Westerly were resentful as they saw these valuable properties falling to the Roman Catholics, one by one. They decided to get one for themselves. After working some wheels within wheels and getting help from Catholic citizens who believed in "fair play" — they were able to get one of the buildings for $1.

An inquiry was addressed to the town of Westerly; the following reply was received from a town official:

> Whoever was the author [Mr. Lowell] of the article mentioned *certainly was misinformed or was making an attempt to distort facts.*
> . . . Although the Roman Catholics have a school in Westerly, the Public Schools are at the present time crowded. A public school building program . . . produced two elementary schools to replace two very old buildings that were *too old and in need of so much repair that they could no longer be used for public school purposes.*
> . . . It was not the Roman Catholics' developing school program that made certain public buildings no longer needed, but the need for new, modern, and larger facilities located at better sites.
> When these old school buildings *became obsolete* . . . many groups

102 James M. O'Neill, *Catholicism and American Freedom* (New York: Harper and Brothers, 1952), p. 50.

filed requests to be considered when and if the Town Council decided
to dispose of them.

The Roman Catholic Bishop of R. I. requested an opportunity to
obtain *one* of these Old School sites for "School Purposes." His plans
were to repair the first floor and equip it for the first three or four
grades. In considering this request the Town Council considered the
annual saving of educating grade pupils at a cost of close to $400.00
per pupil, and this school [of the Bishop] would lessen the public
school burden by approximately $40,000 per year. Therefore they de-
cided to give this particular property to the Roman Catholic Bishop,
to be used for "School Purposes" only.

. . . Now as for the Methodists, they requested consideration on
another school site — but for "Church Purposes" which would not save
the town money but would put into tax exempt [status] valuable town
property.

From the above you can see the logical reasoning of the Town Council to entertain one request and not the other.

. . . Much was said and written by people who did not know the facts.

Subsequently the directors of the Methodist Church sat down calmly
with the Town fathers and agreed that they would change their request
to include "educational purposes" in their request for this school site.
With this change in the request the Council voted to give to the Methodists the same consideration given the Roman Catholic Bishop. . . .

The erection of a new Catholic Church has just begun near the site
of the school given to the Catholic Bishop, but it is being erected on
lands acquired privately by the Catholic Bishop.[103] [Emphasis added.]

A Methodist clergyman has confirmed the substance of the above
facts.[104] However, in fairness it must be mentioned that the clergyman did not like what happened and disagreed with the logic of
the Town Council's decision, especially concerning the relevancy
of the $40,000 per year saving to the town. Such a viewpoint should
be respected, just as the Town Council's opinion should be respected. Disagreement is one thing; inaccurate and biased reporting
is something else.

— 12 —

CONCLUSIONS

Mr. Lowell now proceeds to draw a number of conclusions, which,
of course, are invalid because the theses on which they are based

---

[103] Arthur B. Gervasini (Town and Probate Clerk), a letter, 12 June, 1957.
[104] Howard Love, a letter, 19 August, 1957.

lack supporting evidence. As a matter of fact, documentation has been provided in our analysis that contradicts every Lowell thesis.

He writes, "The alternative is clear. Protestants must face this challenge frankly at the political level." This is strange advice from one who four paragraphs previously urged Protestants to "battle to hold the line for Church-State separation." Now he is urging them to act at "the political level." Protestants, of course, as well as any other group, lay or religious, have the right to face challenges (whatever they may be) "at the political level." But it would be wise first to make certain that there is a "challenge" to be faced. Mr. Lowell provides no valid evidence that "challenge" actually exists. A false position is attributed to the Catholic Church and the position is then treated as a reality. Has Mr. Lowell demonstrated that the Catholic Church "has set out to destroy the free position of the American churches"?

"As the Roman Church moves toward state financing and toward those favors which are the precursor of establishment, Protestants must stand in resolute opposition." Just what "favors" are precursors of establishment? Mr. Lowell mentions none in his article unless the payment by Congress to Vatican City for bomb damage qualifies as such. That this "favor" will be a "precursor," however, is doubtful since the prerequisite for such a "favor" is to have property undergo TNT treatment.

"The Roman Catholic propaganda that softens the nation for official favors must be dispassionately exposed." By "official favors" Mr. Lowell apparently means legislation preferring one Church over all others. Such legislation has not been "exposed" by him, "dispassionately" or otherwise. Nor have he and POAU produced any "Catholic propaganda" directly or indirectly advocating that type of legislation. On the contrary, we have seen the bishops advocate "cooperation involving no special privilege to any group and no restriction on the religious liberty of any citizens."[105] Do Mr. Lowell and POAU object to this co-operation which the bishops recommend between Church and State? Or do they object to any co-operation? If the latter is true, Mr. Lowell and POAU should say so explicitly and should specifically object to tax-exempt church property, chaplains in the armed forces, and the like.

"Protestants must recognize that they are not promoting secularism when they insist that the Roman Catholic Church shall raise

[105] See note 4.

its funds the way other churches do, or when they insist that there shall be no official favors or preferments for any church." There has not been one instance cited by Mr. Lowell that the Catholic Church has ever in its entire United States history raised its funds in a less honorable manner than any other Church.

"At first, as a feeble minority it [Catholic Church] accepted Church-State separation. The principle seemed best in the circumstances." Where have the bishops ever conditioned their acceptance of the First Amendment (or entire Constitution) on special circumstances? Mr. Lowell presents no such statement of the bishops, nor can he, for there is none.

"Now . . . it calls for the end of Church-State separation." Where does the Catholic Church call for the end of the traditional American policy of "Church-State separation"? Aside from misquoting the bishops, Mr. Lowell produces no documentation.

"It intimidates Congress. . . ." When has the Catholic Church intimidated Congress? It is strange that no member of Congress has exposed such intimidation. "It . . . censors and silences opposition." This charge has not even been discussed in Mr. Lowell's article; hence, it is rather surprising to see it appear in his concluding paragraph. From what evidence has he concluded?

"It . . . collects vast sums from the public treasury." If one reflects that annual budgets are in excess of 70 billion dollars, he will realize that the "vast sums" collected by *all* faiths represent a figure well below 1 per cent of annual Federal expenditures.

As the Attorney General's list of subversive organizations is perused, one does not find the Catholic Church mentioned. That is quite a strange fact if Mr. Lowell and POAU are correct in declaring that the Catholic Church "intimidates Congress," has "taken over the public schools" in certain communities, has "set out to destroy the free position of the American churches," is "devoted to destroying the principle of Church-State separation," and "censors and silences opposition."

Here ends our discussion of "Rising Tempo of Rome's Demands." More could be written but it is believed that the reader requires no additional evidence from which to judge the worth of the POAU pamphlet.

Although Mr. Lowell is the author of "Rising Tempo," the pamphlet is an authentic piece of POAU literature inasmuch as that organization has printed, advertised, and distributed it. The tract is also representative of POAU literature as a whole. Almost every statement that Mr. Lowell makes in "Rising Tempo" has appeared in several other POAU publications. For example, POAU has incorrectly reported the bishop's 1948 statement in at least ten other pamphlets. Thus, this chapter is not merely an indictment of Mr. Lowell's form of reporting but also a general charge against POAU as a whole.

It is left to the reader to draw his own conclusion concerning Mr. Lowell's evaluation of his article: "As to my 'Rising Tempo' I am not in the habit of putting out lies. The facts are accurate."[106]

---

[106] C. Stanley Lowell, a letter, 12 September, 1957.

PART IV

THE CHURCH AND THE STATE

CHAPTER 15

FORMS OF GOVERNMENT AND TEMPORAL INFLUENCE

— 1 —

FORMS

BY THIS time — especially after reading the first portion of Chapter 4 — it should be apparent that POAU is attempting to spread the impression that Catholicism favors dictatorships and monarchial regimes in preference to, and to the detriment of, democratic systems. For example:

> A discussion of "Democracy" does not occur in the Catholic Encyclopedia. . . . This is not to say that there are no democratic Catholics in America or elsewhere. It is simply to say that democracy is an idea foreign to the essential political ideology of the Roman Catholic Church-State.[1]

The general impression received from such an account is that democracy is incompatible with and opposed by Catholicism. That is completely without foundation in fact. Pius XI in 1931 reiterated the long-standing Catholic position that with respect to forms of government

> . . . men are free to choose whatever form they please, provided that proper regard is had for the requirements of justice and of the common good. . . .[2]

---

[1] POAU, *Church and State* (February, 1951), p. 2.

[2] *Quadragesimo Anno*, 15 May, 1931. Cited in Anne Freemantle, *The Papal Encyclicals in Their Historical Context* (New York: The New American Library, 1956), p. 232.

And in 1944 Pope Pius XII said:

> It is hardly necessary to recall the teaching of the Church, that "it is not forbidden to prefer temperate, popular forms of government, without prejudice, however, to Catholic teaching on the origin and use of authority," and that "the Church does not disapprove of *any* of the various *forms* of government, provided they be by themselves capable of securing the good of the citizens" (Leo XIII, Encyclical "Libertas," June 20, 1888).
>
> . . . democracy, in the broad sense, admits of various forms, and can be realized in monarchies as well as in republics. . . .
>
> . . . the democratic form of government appears to many a postulate of nature imposed by reason itself. . . .
>
> . . . State absolutism, which is not to be confused, as such, with an absolute monarchy, which is not now under discussion, consists in fact in the *false principle* that the authority of the State is unlimited and that even when it gives free rein to despotic aims, and goes beyond the confines between good and evil, there is no right of appeal against it to a higher law which binds in conscience.[3] [Emphasis added.]

Typical of the reaction of the American press to the message from which the above is quoted was the response of the *Washington Post:*

> There are two immensely significant elements in the Pope's message. One is his explicit condemnation of dictatorship. The other is his implicit endorsement of democracy. He did not, of course, go so far as to make this endorsement absolute and universal. Rather he reiterated the traditional Catholic idea that the content of government is much more important than form, and on this he quoted his predecessor, Leo XIII.[4]

St. Thomas Aquinas, generally considered to be the greatest of Catholic philosophers, declared (thirteenth century):

> The best arrangement of rulers in any city or kingdom is had when one man is, according to merit, set at the head to preside over all, and

---

[3] Christmas message, 24 December, 1944. Cited by John B. Harney, *Pius XII and Democracy* (New York: Paulist Press, 1945), pp. 7, 8, 13. Regarding "Catholic teaching on the origin . . . of authority": that teaching is not to be confused with the theory of the "divine rights of kings" which declares that the right to rule is conferred upon the ruler directly by God. The Catholic teaching is that the source of all civil authority is from God Who alone has the authority to impose moral obligations upon human beings. However, the authority is indirectly conferred on the ruler by God via (*a*) the explicit consent (e.g., an election) of the people who designate who is to exercise authority or (*b*) the implicit consent of the people (e.g., continuation of tradition of hereditary monarchy). See Ryan and Boland, *Catholic Principles of Politics* (New York: Macmillan, 1940), pp. 308–309.

[4] Cited by John B. Harney, *op. cit.*, p. 32.

under him are others ruling according to merit; yet such a regime is the concern of all because the rulers are not only elected from all but also elected by all.[5]

The official attitude of the Church concerning forms of government is best summarized by saying that

> None of the three classical forms of government (monarchy, aristocracy, democracy) nor any of their modifications or combinations, is morally unlawful or unfavorably regarded by the Church. It is true that many Catholic writers [and non-Catholic writers] have defended the monarchial as superior to the other forms, but the Church has never officially sanctioned such a view, nor formally expressed a preference for any of the other polities.[6]

Therefore, no *form* of government is preferred over any other by the Church. But that is quite different from the POAU implication contained in its assertion that "democracy is an idea foreign to the essential political ideology" of Catholicism. Millions of Catholics approve of democracy; the Church does not by any means condemn that approval. POAU has sought to imply that Catholics believe in democracy despite their Church.

One argument that attempts to prove the POAU thesis is to point to the hierarchic structure of the Church:

> The Roman Catholic Church . . . is an authoritarian government. . . . The people have no responsibility toward the selection of their rulers nor any right to depose them or limit their action. . . .
> . . . the *concept of absolute power*, implicit in all Roman Catholic ideology. . . .[7]

> To put it bluntly, the government of this Holy See is a one-man, absolute dictatorship exercised by a non-American.
> . . . So, while professing to be American democrats, they continue to be ruled as Catholics from outside the United States by an authoritarian machine. . . .[8]

An unavoidable — but erroneous — impression is received that there is at least an implicit condemnation of democracy by the very nature of the Church's organization — even after the spurious

---

[5] Cited by Ryan and Boland, *op. cit.*, p. 73.

[6] See *ibid.*, p. 310.

[7] POAU, *Church and State* (February, 1951), pp. 2, 4.

[8] Paul Blanshard, *Truth Series No. 5* (POAU), pp. 3, 4.

terms of "absolute power," "dictatorship," etc., are disregarded. Concerning the government of the Church Pope Pius XII said:

> In the Church, *otherwise than in the State,* the primordial subject of power, the highest instance of appeal, is never the community of the faithful. Therefore, there does not nor can there exist in the Church, *as she was founded by Christ,* a popular tribunal or a judicial power emanating from the people.[9] [Emphasis added.]

Thus, the hierarchic form ("authoritarian," POAU calls it) of the Church is maintained because that is the way Catholics believe Christ founded her; and since Catholics believe Christ to be God, who is to be so presumptuous as to change what God has ordered? One may argue, of course, that Christ did not found the Church this way or that He did not found any church, but such argument must be based on theological grounds to which POAU's "single and only purpose," the First Amendment, has absolutely no relevance. There is no "popular tribunal . . . emanating from the people" because Christ so decreed. However, the fact that the "highest instance of appeal" in the spiritual order does not reside in the community of the faithful is *not* to imply that there can be no "popular tribunal . . . emanating from the people" in the temporal order; the Pope said as much when declaring that the functioning of the Church in this matter is "otherwise than in the State." The Church recognizes and endorses the distinction between the structural-jurisdictional nature of the State and Church. But POAU attempts to change this distinction of thought into a continuum (see note 3 regarding how the State structural-jurisdictional nature emanates from the people).

The fallacious "Concordat argument" is a favorite ruse whereby POAU tries to associate Catholicism with unpopular political regimes.

> The concordat between Mussolini and the Pope is well known [*sic*]. Within six months of Hitler's accession to power in 1933 Pope Pius XI had negotiated and signed a concordat with that dictator.[10]

POAU loses no time in quoting sources that attempt to imply that the pope is morally responsible for or approves all the actions performed by a nation with which a concordat has been effected:

---

[9] Allocution, 2 October, 1945. Cited by Michael Chinigo (ed.), *The Pope Speaks* (New York: Pantheon, 1957), p. 283.

[10] C. Stanley Lowell, *A Summons to Americans* (POAU), p. 3.

We Jews will not soon forget the official concordat between Rome and the Nazi regime, between the official spokesman of Catholicism and the most brutal, bestial mass murderers in history.[11]

But the truth is that concordats (*a*) do not imply a preference for the form of government the contracting country may possess; (*b*) do not imply approbation of all the contracting nation may do in the future; (*c*) do not transfer all moral responsibility to the pope for what a contracting government may do.[12]

What *is* a concordat? "A Concordat is an agreement or treaty between the Holy See and a civil government concerning rights of the Church and matters of common concern to the Church and state. . . . These treaties have been diplomatic attempts by the Holy See to safeguard the freedom of the Church against infringement by civil rulers."[13] Actually, concordats with totalitarian regimes have often been attempts "to avoid religious conflicts with totalitarian States, giving way wherever this has been possible, to remove the motives or pretexts for persecutions."[14]

Despite all this, POAU would convince us that some unworthy or sinister motive lies behind each concordat or "unholy alliance."[15]

The concordat between Hitler and the Vatican was signed on 20 July, 1933, despite fear that the Nazis would not observe their promises.[16] Later in the same year, the Church condemned the racial theory of Nazism.[17] On 14 March, 1937, Pope Pius XI issued the encyclical *Mit brennender Sorge,* a message addressed to the bishops in Germany. The encyclical was a severe denunciation of Nazi totalitarianism:

> Whoever transposes Race or People, the State . . . from the scale of earthly values and makes them the ultimate norm of all things, even of religious values, and deifies them with an idolatrous cult, perverts and falsifies the divinely created and appointed order of things.[18]

---

[11] POAU, *Church and State* (March, 1950), p. 4. Dr. Maurice N. Eisendrath is quoted. Apparently, the time sequence of concordat signing and mass murders is forgotten; also subsequent denunciations by the Papacy.

[12] Kane, *op. cit.,* p. 183.

[13] F. A. Foy (ed.), *The 1958 National Catholic Almanac* (Washington: St. Anthony's Guild, 1957), p. 346.

[14] L. Sturzo, *Church and State* (New York: Longmans, Green and Company, 1939), p. 536.

[15] POAU, *Unholy Alliance.*

[16] S. Z. Ehler and J. B. Morrall, *Church and State through the Centuries* (Westminster, Md.: The Newman Press, 1954), pp. 484–486, 520.

[17] *Ibid.,* p. 517.   [18] *Ibid.,* p. 522.

The 1929 Concordat with Mussolini had a similar aftermath. Soon after it was signed a violent contest flamed up as the result of the conflict between fascist totalitarian ideology and the basic principles of the Catholic Church.[19] Therefore, the encyclical condemning fascist totalitarianism was issued on 29 June, 1931. The encyclical bitterly denounces the Mussolini rule as a "regime based on an ideology which clearly resolves itself into a true, a real pagan worship of the State, the 'Statolatry.' . . ."[20]

It should be clear that the POAU attempt to accuse the Catholic Church of supporting or tacitly approving the Hitler-Mussolini regimes because of concordats with them is inexcusable. Quite significant is the fact that both the German and Italian concordats are honored by the postwar republics of those two countries (Germany now being West Germany).

In Chapter 4 we saw that POAU implied that the Church gets along with Red totalitarianism. It was on 19 March, 1937, that Pius XI issued his encyclical denouncing atheistic and totalitarian communism. He quoted Pius IX who had declared in 1846 that the doctrine of communism was "infamous" and "utterly opposed to the natural law itself, the adoption of which would completely destroy all men's rights, their property and fortune, and even human society itself."[21]

Certainly POAU must be familiar with the papal decree of 1949 regarding automatic excommunication of communists, even of those who are not Party members. As one commentator explained, "excommunication is independent from the organization of the Communist political Party; any Catholic who professes the fundamental articles of Communist theory [regardless of whether or not he puts them into practice] contracts excommunication irrespective of whether he is a member of the Communist Party or not. . . ."[22] Knowingly contributing to communist propaganda (writing, reading, printing, selling, distributing it) means exclusion from the sacraments.[23]

---

[19] *Ibid.*, p. 458.

[20] *Ibid.*, p. 475. From *Non abbiamo bisogno.*

[21] *Ibid.*, p. 546. *Divini Redemptoris.* Pius IX uttered his condemnation in his *Syllabus.*

[22] *Ibid.*, p. 609.

[23] *Ibid.*

Other POAU efforts to "prove" that the Church is totalitarian-minded are equally fallacious as well as calumnious.[24]

— 2 —

TEMPORAL INFLUENCE OF THE CHURCH

POAU constantly declares and implies that the Catholic Church considers herself supreme not only in the spiritual sphere but also in the temporal. A special effort is made by the Americans United to insinuate that the Church's jurisdiction in the realm of faith and morals extends to strictly secular activities:

> This ["power" of the Church], to be sure is said to be limited to the control of faith and morals, but since there is empirically nothing in human experience that lies outside the domain of thought and action — which is coterminus with the domain of faith and morals — its claim is sovereign over all life. This concept of absolute authority. . . .[25]

The immediate fallacy of the POAU statement is the equating of "thought and action" and "faith and morals." To be sure, "faith and morals" always involve thought or action or both, but certainly not all "thought and action" pertains to faith and morals, for if it did, then all true Catholics would always agree about everything, a truly absurd situation.

POAU asserts that "basic Catholic theory puts [the] Church into [the] political arena."[26] In view of previous POAU declarations, the group's meaning of "political" renders the assertion completely false. POAU intends to create the impression that "basic Catholic theory" places the Church directly into purely political affairs. The Church does not, and claims no authority to, enter the purely political sphere.

This is certainly not to say that all "thought and action" in the political area is without relation to faith and morals. Not everything in the political sphere is immune from moral regulation. In

---

[24] POAU constantly publishes pictures in which a bishop or priest and a totalitarian leader are present; i.e., the fallacious guilt-by-association routine (see Chapter 4). If the Church condemns Communism, then isn't there a contradiction when it also teaches that it is not opposed to any form of government? No, because what is condemned is not the form *per se* of communism, i.e., the *structure* of government. It is the philosophical *content* of communism that is denounced. There is a clear distinction.

[25] POAU, *Church and State* (February, 1951), p. 2.

[26] *Ibid.* (November, 1952), p. 6.

the words of Bishop John King Mussio, "People say that the Bishop
is in politics. Let me say simply that I am and shall continue to be
wherever a *moral question* is involved."[27] (Emphasis added.) The
Bishop refers to "petty thieveries" and "incessant graft" as facets
of political life that will be condemned by him whenever they
appear. How is he going to help eradicate such practices? The
mission will be accomplished primarily through the *shaping of the
laity's conscience* by means of sermons, formation of Catholic Action
(a sinister title to POAU) groups, and the like, in order to deal with
moral issues involved.

Protestant action groups legitimately employ the same procedure.
The 500 delegates of the Fifth World Order Study Conference of
the National Council of Churches has advocated U. S. recognition
of Communist China, its admission into the UN, and closer ties
with communist countries in general.[28] Surely if the NCC can call
for closer co-operation with communist states, the Catholic Church
may call upon her faithful to combat communism. The World Order
Conference is by its name alone entering the "political" field and
undoubtedly hopes to influence and help mold the temporal thinking
of American Protestantism.

Another instance of legitimate Protestant Action is contained in
this news report:

> The social action committees of Protestant churches in this city will
> organize at a fall conference for a war against gambling, timed to coin-
> cide with the next city political campaign. One minister said last night
> he hopes for "an upheaval in the city government" as a result of the
> committees' efforts.[29]

Clearly, the only way the Church can influence anybody is
through the shaping of that person's conscience. To the degree that
an individual's conscience is voluntarily in conformity with the
thinking of the Church, to that degree the Church is able indirectly
to affect moral issues in temporal affairs, be they political, social,
economic, or whatever.

> In the light of the foregoing discussion, the pretended menace to
> civil authority from the allegiance of Catholic citizens to the Church
> vanishes into thin air. The Church has no authority . . . over the acts

---

[27] *The Pilot,* 2 November, 1957.
[28] *Time,* 5 January, 1959, p. 60.
[29] *Springfield (Mass.) Republican,* 14 April, 1957.

of the State, so long as these are not in conflict with religion or morality. If any Church official, priest, bishop, or pope, were to command Catholics to vote a certain way on free trade, or on income tax, or a bonus for ex-soldiers, or any other political issue that involves no clear moral or religious question, the injunction would properly be disregarded by substantially all to whom it was addressed. *Even in regard to political matters that have a distinct moral aspect, the authorities of the Church never issue instructions, or even advice, unless the question is one of very grave importance and its moral or religious implications are evident to all.* Those who profess to believe [e.g., POAU] that any modern state is threatened by the claim of the Church to pronounce judgment on the moral phases of civil affairs, *are ignorant alike of the principle and the manner in which it is customarily applied.*[30] [Emphasis added.]

It is clearly impossible to discuss in this chapter all the examples wherein POAU attempts to "document" its absurd assertion that the Church considers her authority as "absolute" and "sovereign over all life." We shall, however, analyze one of these.

A prime example is a POAU story with the headline "Decide Cases According To Church Dogma, Pope Tells Catholic Judges."[31] This news report declares that

> Catholic judges are asked by the Pope to study means by which they may violate their oaths of office without being caught at it and thrown off the bench. Unless all American judges of Catholic persuasion . . . reject the Pope's instructions . . . all non-Catholics can expect to have their rights violated whenever they appear in court before Catholic judges who are willing to prostitute their offices upon directives from Rome.

A recollection of our discussion of oaths (conclusion of Chapter 10) will immediately make the reader suspicious of any claim that the late Pope Pius XII has instructed jurists to seek means to violate their oaths of office. As usual, the POAU "report" about what Pope Pius said is a complete misrepresentation. The Most Rev. Eric F. Mackenzie, a canon law expert, referred to the POAU comment about the Pope's speech by affirming that

> Actually there was no occasion for such a reaction. The Pope was *not* considering American Catholic judges. He rather had in mind an entirely different situation: the procedures of courts in countries where

---

30 Ryan and Boland, *op. cit.*, pp. 329–330.
31 POAU, *Church and State* (November, 1949), p. 4.

totalitarian, despotic governments are ruthlessly slaying and imprisoning all opponents of their doctrines and practices. He condemned — as all right-thinking men must condemn — not merely tyrannical leaders, but also the judges and lawyers who degrade courts of justice into machines of persecution.[32]

It is unfortunate that there is an organization such as POAU. Under the guise of protecting America against nonexistent civil and political threats by the Catholic Church, POAU attacks its primary target, Catholicism *per se*.[33]

---

[32] *The Pilot,* 19 November, 1949.

[33] Many other POAU "reports" about judges could be cited. In the story under discussion, POAU implies that Catholic justices can never grant divorces, but must follow "Church dogma." That is false. Where civil law requires a judge to grant a divorce, he is allowed to do so by the Church. See *The Pilot* (Msgr. Riley's column), 26 April, 1958. Also, F. J. Connell, *Morals in Politics and Professions* (Westminster: The Newman Press, 1955), pp. 29–31.

CHAPTER 16

CHURCH-STATE UNION AND RELIGIOUS LIBERTY

ONE of POAU's most frequently stated contentions is that when-ever Catholics form a controlling majority their faith requires them to make the Catholic Church the State Church and to restrict non-Catholic religions. The following POAU statements demonstrate that position:

[1] Where the Roman Catholics are a minority the hierarchy piously requests religious freedom; where they are a strong majority it arro-gantly demands the end of others' freedom.[1]

[2] We're [Catholics] for religious liberty, until we become a major-ity in a country.[2]

[3] . . . the ideal of the Roman Catholic Church is *church-state union* wherever that policy results in the establishment of the Roman Catholic religion, while in areas where that is not possible it pursues a purely opportunistic policy. . . .[3]

[The Catholic Church believes] that the state has a duty to support the "one true church," and repress the "heretics."[4]

[4] [POAU quotes a source which refers to] the demand that Catholics anticipate the establishment of Catholicism as our national religion.[5]

[5] . . . the power seeking [Catholic] prelate who would undermine our form of government and mold us all through legislation in an ulti-mate goal of uniting Church and State.[6]

---

[1] Glenn L. Archer, *Separation and Spirituality* (POAU, 1956), p. 6.
[2] POAU, *Church and State* (July, 1952), p. 8.
[3] *Ibid.* (March, 1954), p. 6.
[4] *Ibid.* (February, 1954), p. 1.
[5] *Ibid.* (April, 1951), p. 3.
[6] *Ibid.* (January, 1949), p. 3.

Regardless of the Catholic percentage of a nation; regardless of Church-State arrangements that are or have been employed by any country; regardless of what POAU or any other group has "interpreted" as Catholic doctrine, there is no Catholic teaching which requires Catholics to institute the Catholic Church as a State Church, or to restrict non-Catholic forms of worship, or to grant the Church favors not afforded other faiths under the law.

Testimony of prominent members of the Catholic clergy support this position.

1. Cardinal Cushing of Boston:

> I have never met any ecclesiastical leader who desired the union of Church and State in this country. . . . I for one want absolutely no part of anything of the kind.[7]
>
> It is ridiculous to assert that, were Catholics ever to gain the balance of political power in the United States, they would be obliged by their principles to impose restrictions on the religious activities of their non-Catholic fellow-citizens.[8]

2. Most Rev. John T. McNicholas, former Archbishop of Cincinnati:

> Whatever may be said to the contrary, we declare without qualification that Catholic men pledge their first civic loyalty to their own country; they owe no civic allegiance to any other civil power or government on earth. If Catholics constituted 90 per cent of the men of America tomorrow, they would change no provision of their Federal Constitution [which renders impossible a national Church]. . . . They would defend it at the sacrifice of their lives.[9]
>
> We deny *absolutely and without any qualification* that the Catholic Bishops of the United States are seeking a union of Church and State *by any endeavors* whatsoever, either proximate or remote. If tomorrow Catholics constituted a majority in our country they would then, as now, uphold the Constitution and all its Amendments. . . .[10] [Emphasis added.]

3. Archbishop Karl Alter of Cincinnati:

> I can categorically state that there is no doctrine of the Catholic

---

[7] *The Pilot*, 17 May, 1958.

[8] *Ibid.*, 31 May, 1958 ("News-Notes" column).

[9] Cited by John A. O'Brien, *The Truth about the Inquisition* (New York: Paulist Press, 1950), p. 59.

[10] Cited by James A. Corbett, *The Church, the Constitution and Education* (Notre Dame: Ave Maria Press, 1953), inside front cover.

Church which places upon its members the obligation to work for a change in respect to that religious freedom which is guaranteed to all of us by the Constitution of the United States.[11]

[If Catholics ever became a majority, they would stand by the Constitution] and never undertake to change its guarantee of religious freedom.[12]

4. Cardinal Gibbons, the then ranking Catholic prelate in the United States (1909):

> . . . American Catholics rejoice in our separation of church and state. . . . For my part, I would be sorry to see the relations of Church and State any closer than they are at present. . . . I thank God we have religious liberty.[13]

5. Rev. Francis J. Connell, C.SS.R., former dean of the School of Sacred Theology of the Catholic University of America, is reported to have said that it is "utterly false" that Catholics would be obliged by the principles of their faith to establish the Catholic Church as the State Church of the nation if they ever obtained the balance of voting power.[14]

6. Rev. John A. O'Brien, Ph.D., LL.D., of the University of Notre Dame:

> Thus the charge is made that Catholics, being a minority group in this country, are in favor of religious freedom for all groups; but if they once obtained the ascendancy they would deprive other citizens of their legal right to freedom of conscience and worship. *We can't imagine anything farther from the mind of the Church or more repugnant to the Catholics of America.* . . .
>
> We want *no favored position* for the Catholic Church in America, as is often alleged; we have *no secret dreams* of union of Church and State. . . .[15] [Emphasis added.]

These declarations could not have been made if there were anything in Catholic doctrine that required the formation of a State Church, the enactment of laws bestowing preferential benefits upon the Church, or the restriction of non-Catholic minorities.

POAU often quotes formidable appearing documents which at

---

[11] *The Pilot*, 9 February, 1957.
[12] *The Catholic World* (August, 1958), p. 321.
[13] Cited by O'Brien, *op. cit.*, p. 58.
[14] *The Pilot*, 25 January, 1958.
[15] O'Brien, *op. cit.*, pp. 57–58.

first glance directly contradict all that has been just stated. Probably the sternest assertion that POAU has quoted is one that was published in the Jesuit *Civilta Cattolica:*

> The Roman Catholic Church . . . must demand the right of freedom for herself alone, because such [a] right can only be possessed by truth, never by error. As to other religions, the Church . . . will require . . . that they shall not be allowed to propagate false doctrine. Consequently, in a state where the majority of people are Catholic, the Church will require that legal existence be denied to error. . . . In some countries Catholics will be obliged to ask full religious freedom for all. . . . But in doing this the Church does not renounce her thesis [i.e., theory] . . . but merely adapts herself to *de facto* conditions [i.e., the "hypothesis"] which must be taken into account in practical affairs.[16]

This, declares POAU, "is the official policy" of the Catholic Church. Contrary to POAU, however, Catholics are not "bound" by the statement in *Civilta Cattolica* or any other similar statement. The ideas contained in that passage are those of its author and are not to be ascribed as "official policy" of the Catholic Church.

The late Very Rev. Franz Xavier Wernz, S.J., former head of the Jesuit Order and renowned canonist, declared before a gathering of canon law specialists:

> . . . American Catholics, preferring to rely upon the freedom granted by law equally to all and upon their efforts, have not the slightest desire to substitute for these advantages that "protection" by the State which in Europe has so often meant the oppression of the Church.[17]

Father Dunne, a prominent American Jesuit, said that the above statement by the Very Reverend Franz Wernz is one in which the latter "implicitly approves" of the American attitude of freedom granted by law equally to all. The former Jesuit head "speaks with incomparably greater authority than the author of the perfervid statement which appeared in *Civilta Cattolica.*"[18]

Father Dunne asserts that

> . . . God places so high a value upon this freedom with which He has endowed us and which defines our nature that He will not forcibly interfere with it even to save men from their own folly.

---

[16] POAU, *Truth Series No. 8,* p. 2.

[17] Cited by G. H. Dunne, *Religion and American Democracy* (New York: The American Press, 1949), p. 43.

[18] *Ibid.*

All of the arguments that are advanced to justify the suppression of religious error by the use of force fall to the ground in the light of Christ's example. . . . Millions of people [in His day] were being led astray. . . . He could, had He chosen, have silenced the teachers of error and suppressed the dissemination of their doctrines. He did not do so. All American Catholics need ask is the entire freedom [which they now have] to announce "the sweet yoke and burden of Christ" without hindrance.[19]

In addition to Father Dunne's rejection of the *Civilta Cattolica* opinion, your authors would draw attention to two facets of that publication's statement.

First, there is the reference to the "right . . . possessed by truth, never by error," and "legal existence be denied to error." As the Rev. John Courtney Murray, S.J., correctly observes:

Nothing is more unhelpful than an abstract starting point. Such, for instance, is the position of the generality, "error has no rights." As it stands the statement is meaningless; for rights are predicated only of persons (or of institutions).[20]

Therefore, we are talking about rights of *people* in error, not rights as abstract entities. Should the State grant freedom to people who are considered in religious error? If the State follows Christ's example, the answer must be affirmative, as Father Dunne has indicated.

The Catholic Church believes that she is in possession of religious truth. Obviously, she must consider those who hold doctrines contradictory to be in error. Logic leaves no other choice. But this unrelenting position of the Church merely applies to the abstract sphere of knowledge and therefore cannot transgress the rights of any person. The granting of religious freedom does not protect error. Reverend Max Pribilla cogently affirms

. . . that freedom of religion does not mean the protection of error . . . but protection of the erring man, who should not be hindered from serving God according to his conscience. Even an erroneous conscience imposes duties and confers corresponding rights. The protection granted to a man in error in the exercise of his duty *is something good*.[21] [Emphasis added.]

[19] *Ibid.,* p. 45.

[20] J. C. Murray, *Governmental Repression of Heresy.* Cited by J. M. O'Neill, *Catholicism and American Freedom* (New York: Harper and Brothers, 1952), p. 89.

[21] Cited by J. M. O'Neill, *Catholicism and American Freedom* (New York: Harper

The second aspect of the POAU-quoted *Civilta Cattolica* article which is worthy of additional comment is the "thesis"-"hypothesis" reference. The article describes the Church's thesis, or theory, as repressing "false doctrine" and religious freedom wherever there is a nation in which "the majority of the people are Catholic." The "hypothesis" (although not referred to as such) represents the Church's policy in certain circumstances. In such circumstances, the Church grants liberty and "merely adapts herself to *de facto* conditions which must be taken into account in practical affairs."

This thesis-hypothesis opportunism is truly obnoxious. As indicated by Father Murray, such repression possesses no dogmatic value:[22]

> The asserted right of a "Catholic government" to repress heresy rests on, and derives from a concept of the power of the Church in temporal matters that is indefensible today. . . .
>
> It [the asserted "right" to repress] will not return, *and should not return to the world even if, by the grace of God, religious unity should return to the world*. Consequently, the right to suppress heresy . . . enjoys *no absolute and permanent status in virtue of Catholic principle as such*. [Emphasis added.]

Obviously, if there were any such "thesis" of repression in Catholic doctrine, neither Father Murray nor any of the distinguished clergy who were quoted earlier in the chapter could have made the remarks that they did.

Regarding the theory that whenever possible mankind must absolutely repress those who are considered in moral and religious error, Pope Pius XII declared:

> Moreover, God has not given even to human authority such an absolute and universal command in matters of faith and morality. Such a command [to impede those in error when possible] is unknown to the common convictions of men, to the Christian conscience, to the sources of revelation and to the practice of the Church. Therefore, the duty to repress moral and religious deviations cannot be an ultimate norm of action.[23]

---

and Brothers, 1952), p. 84. Of course, protection of the erring man is subject to the restrictions that a State feels is necessary to engender the common good and maintain public order. Our courts have said as much in People *vs*. Pearson, 176 N.Y. 201 (1903), Reynolds *vs*. U.S. (98 U.S. 145, 1878).

[22] Cited by J. M. O'Neill, *Religion and Education Under the Constitution* (New York: Harper and Brothers, 1949), p. 40.

[23] *The Pope Speaks* (First Quarter, 1954), p. 68. From an address in December, 1953.

POAU has cited many statements from the encyclicals of Pope Leo XIII in an attempt to make people think that his teachings require Catholics to effect Catholicism as the State Church. We say simply that no teaching of Pope Leo XIII requires Catholics to work for a State Church under any conditions. And in construing the late Pope Pius XII's encyclicals otherwise, POAU is in error as usual.

Immortale Dei is one encyclical of Pope Leo XIII which has much to say about Church-State relations. In March, 1955, Vice-President Nixon asserted that "no nation in the world is more tolerant of those who differ in religious belief than Eire, which is overwhelmingly Catholic [about 93 per cent]."[24] What is the connection between *Immortale Dei* and Eire? The point is that Eire's religious freedom statutes are reconcilable with the above papal document.[25]

Article 44 of the Eire Constitution guarantees freedom of conscience and the free profession and practice of religion. Although the Catholic Church is recognized as the one professed by the great majority of citizens, Eire does not endow any religion nor does the country show a preference for the Catholic Church in civil life and education. Non-Catholic religions are specifically recognized, "and the State shall not impose any disabilities or make any discrimination on the ground of religious profession, belief or status."[26]

Some Catholics may not like the freedom given to religious minorities in Catholic Eire just as some Protestants may not like the freedom Catholic minorities receive in some predominantly Protestant lands. The point is, however, that nothing in Catholic doctrine requires Eire or any other country to give legal preference to the Catholic Church to the detriment of non-Catholic minorities. Countries such as Spain do restrict religious minorities, but not because of any "must" in Catholic doctrine. We believe that most Catholics would like to see every country adopt the principles embodied in the constitutions of Eire and of the United States, provided, of course, that public order and the common good do not seriously suffer.

---

[24] "News Events of Catholic Interest," *The 1956 National Catholic Almanac* (Paterson: St. Anthony's Guild, 1956), p. 59.

[25] Sidney Z. Ehler and J. B. Morrall, *Church and State through the Centuries* (Westminster: The Newman Press, 1954), p. 595.

[26] *Ibid.*, pp. 595, 600.

CHAPTER 17

THE FIRST AMENDMENT

SO MUCH has been said in this book about the First Amendment, that some brief study should be made of it. It is impossible, of course, in one single chapter, to give detailed presentation of what the First Amendment means or does not mean. However, certain aspects of it can be touched on.

Specifically, just what is "the problem" involved here? It is to discover what the framers of the First Amendment intended when they drafted this portion of the amendment: "Congress shall make no law respecting an establishment of religion, or prohibiting the free exercise thereof. . . ." Regarding the second clause, "or prohibiting the free exercise thereof," there is little disagreement. Almost everyone agrees that those six words simply prohibit Congress from making any law whatsoever which prohibits the "free exercise" of religion (subject to public order, of course).

However, there is wide disagreement about the proper meaning of the first part of the amendment, and that disagreement essentially revolves around the question of what constitutes "an establishment of religion."

At times, POAU's position agrees with the Supreme Court's definition of "an establishment of religion" as enunciated in the majority of opinion of Everson *vs.* Board of Education (1947):

> Neither [state nor federal government] can pass laws which aid one religion, aid all religions, or prefer one religion over another. . . . *No tax in any amount, large or small, can be levied to support any religious activities or institutions, whatever they may be called, or whatever form they may adopt to teach or practice religion.*[1]

---

[1] POAU, *Church and State* (June, 1955), p. 1. Although such was in the Court's *opinion*, the *decision* declared that free bus transportation for private school pupils does not violate the "establishment of religion" clause.

232

POAU approvingly quotes a source which asserts that the "clamoring for equal, or nonpreferential, tax aid . . . constitutes the most prolific source of open or concealed violation of the Nation's law."[2]

Again, we may perceive POAU's position regarding the clause under discussion from this remark: "There is one decisive test: that is money. Any Church seeking tax money for its operations is endeavoring to breach the wall of Church-State separation."[3] The Americans United indicates further that it regards it "as an abuse for any public official to use his office to lend *moral* — as well as *financial* — support to religious groups."[4]

Contrary to this POAU position which would disallow any aid to religion even on a nonpreferential basis, many others (of all faiths) agree with Professor James M. O'Neill when he states:

> What was meant by the men of the first Congress and the ratifying states by "an establishment of religion"? The answer is easy. They must have meant what the phrase had meant for centuries to historians, theologians, and other scholars, Catholic and Protestant, lay and religious, European and American, down to, and long after, the period in which the Bill of Rights was written, adopted, and ratified. "An establishment of religion," through all this time, meant (1) an *exclusive arrangement*, (2) created by government, (3) giving a preferential status *under the government* to one favored religion, and (4) a consequent discrimination against all other religions.
>
> Neither the modern proponents of aggressive secularism nor the Supreme Court justices, in the current campaign to amend the Constitution by substituting the figurative "wall of separation between church and state" for the literal language of the First Amendment, have ever cited a *single instance* of a contrary use of the meaning of "an establishment of religion" . . . in the whole sweep of time in which this phrase has been dealt with. . . .[5]

Needless to say, Professor O'Neill's explanation of the subject concerning which Congress was forbidden to legislate is quite different from POAU's interpretation. Using Professor O'Neill's definition of "an establishment of religion" Congress may aid religion, finan-

---

[2] *Ibid.* (April, 1953), p. 4. The source was the Baptist Joint Committee on Public Affairs.

[3] C. Stanley Lowell, *Separation and Religion* (POAU, 1957), p. 13. Since almost every denomination has received "tax money," all must be violators of the Constitution.

[4] POAU, *Church and State* (January, 1952), p. 2.

[5] J. M. O'Neill, *Catholicism and American Freedom* (New York: Harper and Brothers, 1952), pp. 45–46.

cially or otherwise, so long as no religion is given a preferred status. Quite obviously, POAU disagrees.

POAU and Professor O'Neill do agree on the method by which we should begin our investigation of what the "establishment" clause of the First Amendment means. POAU declares that "Any candid examination of the historical background of the First Amendment . . . reveals with perfect plainness what was intended by Madison and Jefferson, the men chiefly responsible for its adoption."[6] Professor O'Neill: "If the First Amendment had a purpose, the men of the First Congress who wrote and adopted it had to have that purpose in their minds."[7] Both Professor O'Neill and POAU would agree to this declaration by Jefferson:

> On every question of construction [of the Constitution], carry ourselves back to the time when the Constitution was adopted, recollect the spirit manifested in the debates, and instead of trying what meaning may be squeezed out of the text, or invented against it, conform to the probable one in which it was passed.[8]

Let us "carry ourselves back" and "recollect the spirit manifested in the debates" in order to perceive the meaning of "an establishment of religion."

On 8 June, 1789, James Madison introduced this version of the First Amendment: "The civil rights of none shall be abridged on account of religious belief or worship, nor shall any *national religion* be established, nor shall the full and equal rights of conscience be in any manner or on any pretext infringed."[9] (Emphasis added.) This will be referred to as Madison Number 1.

Madison's version Number 1 was referred to a committee which changed the version to read: *"No religion shall be established by law,* nor shall the equal rights of conscience be infringed."[10] (Emphasis added.) This we will call Madison Number 2.

During the ensuing debate on Madison Number 2, the *Annals of Congress* assert that Madison himself "apprehended the meaning

---

[6] POAU, *Church and State* (May, 1950), p. 1.

[7] O'Neill, *op. cit.,* p. 44.

[8] Thomas Jefferson, a letter to William Johnson, 12 June, 1823. Cited by J. M. O'Neill, *Religion and Education Under the Constitution* (New York: Harper and Brothers, 1949), p. 72.

[9] *Annals of Congress*, Vol. I, p. 319. Cited by G. E. Reed, "The First Amendment — Historical Background," *The 1958 National Catholic Almanac* (Paterson: St. Anthony's Guild, 1957), p. 654.

[10] *Ibid.,* p. 729. Cited by Reed, *op. cit.*

of the words to be, that *Congress* should not *establish a religion and enforce the legal observance of it by law,* nor compel men to worship God in any manner contrary to their conscience."[11] (Emphasis added.)

The debate continued, and the *Annals* report that Mr. Madison

> thought, if the word "National" was inserted before religion, it would satisfy the minds of honorable gentlemen. He believed that the people feared one sect might obtain a preeminence, or two combine together, and establish a religion to which they would compel others to conform. He thought if the word "national" was introduced, it would point the amendment directly to the object it was *intended* to prevent.[12] [Emphasis added.]

However, the *Annals of Congress* state that Mr. Gerry disliked the word "national" because he feared the term would tend to indicate that we had a national rather than a federal government. Madison disagreed with Gerry but nevertheless consented to withdraw his suggestion about the word "national."[13]

Subsequently, Mr. Livermore, of New Hampshire, introduced this version: "Congress shall make no law touching upon religion."[14] However, Congress rejected what we shall designate as the Livermore version.

On 9 September, 1789, the Senate expressed its intention regarding "an establishment of religion." The Senate recommended that "Congress shall make no law establishing articles of faith or a mode of worship. . . ."[15] Finally, on 25 September, 1789, the Senate approved the final version: "Congress shall make no law respecting an establishment of religion. . . ." It surpasses the imagination that the Senate within the space of sixteen days so changed its mind that "an establishment of religion" meant something essentially other than "establishing articles of faith or a mode of worship." In the entire debate, there was not one reference that would substantiate the POAU position of no financial aid even on a basis of equality. At no time did Congress indicate a desire to prohibit itself from aiding religion on a nonpreferential basis. As

---

[11] *Ibid.,* p. 730. Cited by Reed, *op. cit.*
[12] Cited by J. M. O'Neill, *Religion and Education Under the Constitution, op. cit.,* pp. 103–104.
[13] *Ibid.,* p. 104.
[14] *Annals of Congress,* Vol. I, p. 731. Cited by Reed, *op. cit.,* p. 655.
[15] O'Neill, *Religion and Education Under the Constitution, op. cit.,* p. 135.

Madison declared, the intention of the First Amendment is that "Congress should not establish a religion and enforce the legal observance of it by law, nor compel men to worship God in any manner contrary to their conscience."

POAU distorts the true meaning of the amendment by pointing out that proposed amendments, similar to Madison 1 and 2, were rejected. Such rejections, argues POAU, make it clear that the Founding Fathers intended to ban not only a national religion to be observed by all, but any aid or comfort to religion, especially financial aid.[16] The POAU logic is specious. No one can prove what Congress meant simply by pointing to examples of what it rejected. Using POAU's logic, the contention that Congress meant to forbid any and all financial aid would be utterly discredited by the fact that Congress *rejected* Livermore's version that "Congress shall make no law touching upon religion." Certainly, a law granting money to religion is one "touching upon religion." But Congress rejected the idea not to make law "touching upon religion." Therefore, according to *POAU* thinking, Congress by that very fact rejected the idea not to give financial aid to religion. Of course, the rejection *per se* of Livermore's version proves no such thing.

Following POAU logic farther, the fact that Madison Number 1 was rejected would mean that Congress wanted to reject the idea of merely making impossible the setting up of a "national religion," and wished to include in its prohibition something more. But we have already seen that this was not the case. The reason for the rejection of Madison Number 1 was Mr. Gerry's fear that "national" might imply that we had a "national" instead of a federal government. It is obvious that the disagreements on the First Amendment among the Founding Fathers centered not on the *substance* of the amendment, but on how best to *express* that substance in words.

If we wish to know what Congress meant, we must look at what it said it meant. Madison, as quoted twice above, indicated in a positive manner what the First Amendment meant. There was no objection to his explanation, namely, "Congress should not establish a religion and enforce legal observance of it by law. . . ." We have demonstrated that the Senate, sixteen days prior to approving

---

[16] POAU, *Church and State* (December, 1952), p. 8.

the amendment's final form, concurred with the substance of Madison's remark.

It is difficult to imagine that Congress meant something else from what it said it meant in the debates preceding adoption of the First Amendment. As Professor O'Neill remarks, "The *purpose* or *intent* of any passage in the Constitution could come only from the thought of the men responsible for the passage when it was written. . . ."[17] The POAU position is invalid not only in the light of the debates of Congress, but also in view of Congressional enactments during the presidency of both Madison and Jefferson and, indeed, during all presidencies.

In 1789, President Washington sent a recommendation to Congress for the allocation of funds for religious education among the Indians. The Washington administration began spending money for that purpose, and the practice continued for over a century.[18] President Jefferson sent to Congress in 1803 a treaty which authorized the United States to give $700 to a Catholic priest working among the Indians, and $300 for the erection of a Catholic church.[19] As president, Madison continued the Jeffersonian policy of payments to religious societies for services on Indian reservations.[20] By 1896, over $500,000 was being appropriated annually in support of sectarian Indian education being carried on by religious groups.[21]

All of those expenditures would have been illegal if we admitted the POAU-Supreme Court opinion as quoted earlier in this chapter. Indeed, after that opinion was given by the Court, Congress (1948) appropriated $173,477 to religious schools for the care of Indian children. In the same year Congress authorized $500,000 for the construction of a chapel for religious worship at the Merchant Marine Academy at King's Point, New York.[22]

Under the Hill-Burton Act, well over a hundred million dollars in tax money have been spent to construct or equip sectarian hospitals. And approximately 48,000 veterans have studied for the minis-

---

[17] J. M. O'Neill, *Religion and Education Under the Constitution, op. cit.,* p. 48. At the time of the First Amendment debates, Jefferson was out of the country, and had been for some years, not returning until November, 1789.

[18] *Ibid.,* p. 116.

[19] *Ibid.,* p. 117.

[20] *Ibid.,* p. 101.

[21] *Ibid.,* p. 118.

[22] *Ibid.,* p. 120.

try under the G.I. Bill. More than $96 million in Federal funds
has been expended on this program.[23] Most of this amount has been
paid to sectarian educational institutions in the form of tuition
payments, etc. Similar figures could be cited for other government grants. The same may be said for government research
grants. Surely all those expenditures — and they are not the entire
amounts — are unconstitutional *if* the Supreme Court is correct
when it declares (Everson case): "Neither state or federal government can pass laws which aid one religion, aid all religions. . . ."

In the May, 1950, *Church and State,* POAU believes the First
Amendment "was intended to establish the absolute separation of
church and state." If so, why does POAU approve of the G.I. Bill
payments and research grants to sectarian schools. "Absolute"
means no exception. POAU maintains that the G.I. Bill gives
"special rewards" to servicemen, and that research grants are
given in the "interest of national defense."[24] Nevertheless, both payments find their way to religious institutions and therefore, "aid one
religion" or "aid all religions." POAU approves of such grants because to do otherwise would arouse public condemnation. Such
grants apply to college-level education where the private non-
Catholic outnumber the Catholic colleges.

At the present time, millions of tax dollars are being spent on
sectarian hospitals. At the present time, many states provide bus
transportation for children attending parochial and private schools.
Both practices are considered by POAU as violations of the First
Amendment.[25] POAU has recommended "to the Senators and Representatives of the United States" that both practices be discontinued[26] (1955). Yet, in 1957, the group indicated that it knows
very well that such practices are perfectly legal. At that time,
POAU asserted:

> We believe that there is one policy on which every Protestant in
> America should agree, that no *new* concessions of tax funds to sectarian
> enterprise should be made by the federal, the state or local govern-
> ments. *If we could agree on the maintenance of the present financial
> status quo, other differences might be judiciously compromised.*[27] [Em-
> phasis added.]

23 F. R. Hood, Veterans Administration, a letter, 21 January, 1959.
24 POAU, *Church and State* (January, 1957), p. 1.
25 Glenn L. Archer, *Without Fear or Favor* (POAU, 1955), pp. 16, 19.
26 *Ibid.,* p. 26.
27 POAU, *Church and State* (December, 1957), p. 2.

Both, payments to sectarian hospitals and bus rides for students of parochial and private schools are part of "the present financial status quo," and have been declared unconstitutional by POAU. But such "differences might be judiciously compromised." POAU is now ready to "judiciously" compromise about the legality of the two practices that it had previously attacked as violations of the First Amendment.

POAU believes the state practice of allowing bus transportation for parochial students aids a religious institution and is, therefore, a violation of the First Amendment. But the fact remains that the First Amendment applied only to Congress and had no application to the states. The states were left free to decide for themselves the proper relation between Church and State. This is evident from the fact that Massachusetts had an established state-supported Protestant Church until 1833, well after the adoption of the First Amendment.

Some declare that the Fourteenth Amendment (1868) now makes the First applicable to the states. If that is validly the case — which it is not — then the states are now deprived of their right to decide Church-State problems for themselves, in direct conflict with the desires and expressed intention of the Founding Fathers who adopted the First Amendment. In effect, under the present invalid interpretation of the Fourteenth Amendment, the First Amendment now contradicts the intention of those who framed it. Originally, it did not apply to the states but according to present-day juggling it does.

When the Fourteenth Amendment was debated in Congress no one *intended* or *foresaw* that fifty-seven years later the Supreme Court would "assume" the Fourteenth made part of the First applicable to the states.[28]

Professor O'Neill confirms that:

> In the years 1868 to 1911, in cases brought under the Fourteenth Amendment, the Supreme Court decisions constituted federal intervention in state affairs fifty-five times. *None of these cases involved the religion clause of the First Amendment.*[29]

Returning to the claim that the First Amendment forbids finan-

---

[28] O'Neill, *Religion and Education Under the Constitution, op. cit.*, p. 155 (New York *vs.* Gitlow, 1925). In Hamilton *vs.* University of California (1934), the First was explicitly applied to a state religion case.
[29] *Ibid.*

cial aid to religion under any circumstances, we may be surprised to find that there have been some twenty attempts to amend the Constitution in order to make it declare what POAU and Supreme Court opinions (post-1946 *only*) have asserted the First Amendment to have meant (its allegedly state applicability excluded) since its adoption! Eleven of those attempts occurred between 1870 and 1888. All have been defeated or allowed to die in Committee by Congress.[30]

The latest attempt occurred in 1947 when Congressman Bryson introduced a bill proposing "an amendment to the Constitution of the United States providing that neither Congress nor any of the several States shall aid any educational institution wholly or in part under sectarian control."[31] This *proposed amendment* embodied the very substance of the Supreme Court's opinion (also 1947) of what the First Amendment had always meant. If it had always been understood that under the terms of the First Amendment no religious institution was to receive tax aid, why had Congressman Bryson and at least nineteen others before him submitted an amendment to a Constitution which allegedly already forbade the very practice that the proposed amendments would prohibit? The answer is obvious:

Prior to 1947, neither the opinions nor the decisions of the Supreme Court defined the meaning of the First Amendment's religion clause in a fashion contradictory to the intentions of the amendment's framers. Seven years before the unique Court *opinion* in the 1947 Everson case and eight years prior to the unique *decision* in the McCollum case, the Supreme Court correctly defined "an establishment of religion." In the words of Justice Roberts, the "establishment" section of the amendment "forestalls compulsion by law of the acceptance of any creed or the practice of any form of worship."[32] As Professor O'Neill indicates, Justice Roberts' definition is almost identical with the language of the Senate's (1789) definition: "Congress shall make no law establishing articles of faith or a mode of worship."[33] And we already know that the Senate's view paralleled that of Madison, the principal author of the First Amendment. Therefore, the answer to our question —

---

[30] O'Neill, *Catholicism and American Freedom, op. cit.,* pp. 48–49.
[31] O'Neill, *Religion and Education Under the Constitution, op. cit.,* p. 45.
[32] *Ibid.,* p. 135: Cantwell *vs.* Connecticut.
[33] *Ibid.,* p. 135.

why people like Congressman Bryson, a POAU adviser, propose an amendment to prohibit financial aid to sectarian schools — is that he and the others realized that the First Amendment did not and does not prohibit Congress from disbursing funds aiding religion and religious facilities.

A former POAU president, Dr. Edwin McNeil Poteat, also recognized the true meaning of the First Amendment inasmuch as he personally desired that Congressman Bryson's bill be adopted and submitted to the states for ratification. In addition Dr. Poteat approved the idea of POAU supporting the bill.[34]

The current POAU vice-president, Bishop G. Bromley Oxnam, obviously prefers to have the Supreme Court "amend" the Constitution instead of submitting any amendments to the people for approval; with reference to the Bryson amendment, the Bishop writes:

> . . . a conference was held in Washington [most likely a POAU organizational meeting], attended by a number of religious leaders all interested in the objective [of the Bryson bill?]. They reached the conclusion that an attempt to amend the Constitution was not the way to get the results. . . . *The Supreme Court can at the present time give such interpretation* to the amendments to the Constitution that involve the separation of church and state *as to reach the same end*.[35] [Emphasis added.]

As a matter of fact, the Court in the opinion of 1947 (Everson) and in the decision and opinion of 1948 (McCollum) did virtually "reach the same end" as would have been achieved by altering the First Amendment's meaning through the process of constitutional amendment. If the Constitution is to be altered, however, the Constitution itself lays down the procedure for amendment, and in that procedure the Supreme Court has no part.

In Chapter 14, section 11, the POAU attempt to identify "an establishment of religion" with "a religious establishment" is refuted; also rebutted is the POAU confusion tactic of a "plural establishment" of religion.

But POAU has many other methods by which it seeks to confuse the public. For example, "respecting" in the phrase "respecting an establishment of religion" is defined by POAU as "leading to-

---

[34] *Ibid.,* pp. 45–46: a letter to James M. O'Neill, 1948.
[35] *Ibid.,* p. 45: a letter to James M. O'Neill, 28 January, 1948.

ward."[36] As Professor O'Neill correctly tells us, "leading toward" is a good synonym for "pointing in the direction of or tending toward" but "for the word *respecting* it is not a synonym at all."[37] As was mentioned in Chapter 14, anyone can oppose anything on the basis that it may be "leading toward" something else which is undesirable. The example was given that democracy may be opposed because it may be "leading toward" anarchy. Madison knew the meaning of "respecting." That meaning has not changed. Neither *Webster's International Dictionary* nor *Webster's Dictionary of Synonyms* substantiate the POAU definition. The common dictionary definition of "respecting" is "concerning" or "regarding." Therefore, the First Amendment prohibited Congress from enacting any law concerning or regarding "an establishment of religion." In effect, Congress was prohibited from taking any action *either for* or *against* "an establishment of religion."[38] Since there was no national "establishment of religion" in existence at the time of the First Amendment's passage, the prohibition had the effect of rendering Congressional enactment of a *national* religion legally impossible — without condemning such state establishments as were in favor in certain sections of the country and which continued until 1833.

POAU continually avoids using the precise, deliberate, and literate language of the First Amendment; instead, the phrase "separation of church and state" is substituted for the amendment's concise wording. The word "separation" admits of various meanings depending upon the context in which it is located. For example, concerning someone who has had the misfortune of being guillotined, one might refer to the "separation of head and shoulders." In this case, the "separation" is absolute. But in my own case and yours, we may still speak of "separation of head and shoulders" even though we have not been guillotined. In this instance, the separation is effected by the neck — which, of course, joins as well as separates. Obviously, "separation" has been used in two different senses in the above examples; the meaning depends on the context.

POAU derives its motto of "separation of church and state" from this letter by Jefferson to the Baptists of Danbury, Connecticut (1 January, 1802):

---

[36] *A Manifesto* (POAU, 1957), p. 5.
[37] O'Neill, *Religion and Education Under the Constitution, op. cit.*, p. 54.
[38] *Ibid.*, pp. 53–55.

Believing with you that religion is a matter which lies solely between man and his God, that he owes account to none other for his faith or his worship, that the legislative powers of government reach actions only, and not opinions, I contemplate with sovereign reverence that act of the whole American people which declared that their legislature should "make no law respecting an establishment of religion, or prohibiting the free exercise thereof," thus building a wall of separation between church and state.[39]

The Americans United declare that "Jefferson's 'wall-of-separation' metaphor, then, cannot be dismissed as a carelessly contrived figure of speech."[40] Granted; but the fact remains that it is a "metaphor" and a "figure of speech," and, therefore, must be analyzed with reference to its context. Who built the "wall of separation"? Jefferson obviously refers to Congress, the legislature "of the whole American people." How and in what sense did Congress build "a wall of separation"? Jefferson clearly indicates the answer by quoting a portion of the First Amendment: "their legislature should *make no law respecting an establishment of religion, or prohibiting the free exercise thereof.'*" (Emphasis added.) And just how does Jefferson think any construction of the Constitution should be interpreted? We already know his answer: "On every question of construction [of the Constitution], carry ourselves back to the time when the Constitution was adopted, recollect the spirit manifested in the debates. . . ."[41] Jefferson meant what the framers of the First Amendment meant, and we know what Madison *et al.* intended the amendment to mean.

It has already been mentioned that Jefferson, as president, approved financial aid to religion, a practice which POAU now declares violates the First Amendment. Eight years after the ratification of the amendment, Jefferson summed up his position by writing, "I am for freedom of religion, and against all maneuvers to bring about a legal ascendency of one sect over another."[42] Treating all religions equally under the law with regard to financial aid or anything else does not "bring about a legal ascendency of one sect over another."

Another attempt by POAU to confuse the public is again to dis-

---

39 *Ibid.*, p. 286. Also, POAU, *Church and State* (March, 1954), p. 1.

40 POAU, *Church and State* (March, 1954), p. 1.

41 O'Neill, *Religion and Education Under the Constitution, op. cit.*, p. 72.

42 *Ibid.*, p. 85.

regard the context of this fragment quoted from Jefferson: "To compel a man to furnish contributions of money for propagation of opinions which he disbelieves is sinful and tyrannical."[43] That fragment of a long sentence was lifted from Jefferson's *Bill for Establishing Religious Freedom in Virginia* which was introduced in 1779 and passed in 1786. It is obvious, therefore, first of all, that Jefferson was not giving his interpretation of the First Amendment which was not adopted by Congress until 1789. In addition, Jefferson's Virginia Bill quotation must be analyzed in light of the entire sentence from which it was extracted. Actually, the sentence refers not to forbidding nonpreferential financial aid to religion — something Jefferson neither believed in nor practiced — but rather to "the impious presumption of legislature and ruler" who "have assumed dominion over the faith of others," and who endeavor to "impose" their own opinions on others, and who "hath established and maintained false religions"; Jefferson referred to "temporal punishments" and "civil incapacitations."[44] In short, Jefferson was opposing what is and was known as "an establishment of religion" wherein all are compelled by the State to support financially the religion of the government's choice to the obvious detriment of all other religions. That Jefferson did not oppose treating all religions on an impartial basis regarding financial support is evident from his endorsement of the First Amendment and from his actions as president.

POAU must "prove" that Madison condemned all types of government aid to religion by telling its audience that Madison's *Memorial and Remonstrance* was a declaration "against all forms of government aid, whether extended to one or many sects."[45] That statement is completely false. As Professor O'Neill so aptly writes:

> As anyone can see who will take the trouble to read the *Memorial* . . . Madison was remonstrating simply against making the Christian religion the established religion of the State of Virginia. He cited fifteen numbered reasons "against the said bill." [See note 45.] Not one of the

---

[43] POAU, *Church and State* (July, 1949), p. 1.

[44] Jefferson's *Bill for Establishing Religious Freedom in Virginia*. Cited in full by O'Neill, *Religion and Education Under the Constitution, op. cit.,* p. 275.

[45] POAU, *Church and State* (June, 1953), p. 7. The *Memorial* was directed against a "Bill Establishing a Provision for Teachers of the Christian Religion." By "Teachers" is meant "Preachers." In the *Memorial,* Madison refers to the "flocks" (congregations) on which the "Teachers of Christianity" depend.

fifteen is phrased in terms of public support of religion as such or in opposition to religion in education.

. . . Madison was arguing against "an establishment of religion" in the exact literal sense in which he consistently used the phrase. This is the consistent use by Jefferson also and other writers on established religion or established churches for some centuries. This illuminating passage [from the *Memorial*] is as follows:

"Who does not see that the same authority which can establish *Christianity, in exclusion of all other Religions,* may *establish with the same ease any particular sect of Christians, in exclusion of all other Sects.* That the same authority which can force a citizen to contribute three pence only of his property for the support of *any one establishment,* may force him to conform to *any other establishment* in all cases whatsoever?"[46] [Italics O'Neill's.]

It should be obvious that Madison was not "against all forms of government aid, whether extended to one or many sects." Clearly, Madison was opposing the *particular, selective, and exclusive* government support of the *Christian* religion; i.e., he was opposing "an establishment of religion."[47] He was only opposed to the fact that all religions would not be equal under the law.

Many other POAU errors in the area of the Constitution could be described. However, it should be quite clear by now that POAU shows no inclination to clarify the First Amendment; simply to confuse. Should the reader come across some POAU statement concerning the Constitution and desire clarification on a particular point, no better source could be relied upon than Professor O'Neill's *Religion and Education Under the Constitution.* This book, upon which much of this chapter is based, has received the acclaim of leaders of all faiths. As the *American Bar Association Journal* affirmed: "For his research and his marshalling of the historical evidence to establish this accurate meaning of the phrase 'an establishment of religion,' we are all indebted to Professor O'Neill."[48]

Religious doctrines, of course, have absolutely no relevance in determining the proper meaning of the First Amendment. As demonstrated in this chapter, an accurate interpretation of the First Amendment depends on three norms which POAU has not validly applied: history, logic, and law.

---

[46] J. M. O'Neill, *Religion and Education Under the Constitution, op. cit.,* p. 89.

[47] *Ibid.,* p. 90.

[48] Cited by "O'Neill Lecture Brochure," Alma Savage Lecture Service, New York City.

This and the preceding two chapters have endeavored to indicate the utter falsity of three basic assumptions continually harped upon by POAU: (1) that the Catholic Church is essentially opposed to democracy; (2) that Catholic doctrine requires that Catholicism be effected as the State Church with subsequent restrictions on non-Catholic faiths whenever Catholics form a controlling majority; (3) that the First Amendment prohibits Federal and state governments from giving nonpreferential aid — financial or otherwise — to religion. It is hoped, although not expected, that those three false assumptions will no longer be foisted upon the public by POAU and similar organizations whose real purpose for being is to arouse and confuse by presenting to the public highly charged and fictitious "issues" about Catholicism which are sometimes cleverly, but always speciously, clothed as reality.

POAU may change its name or its leadership, but a common trait will nonetheless prevail: grossly erroneous attacks against Catholicism as Catholicism. Those attacks may be clumsily masked by a professed patriotic goal such as POAU's "single and only purpose," the defense of the First Amendment; however, the real target will continue to be the Catholic Church. POAU has not been unique in history, nor will there be a lack of future POAU's after the present version comes to its eventual and certain end. Inasmuch as the current "issues" will be seen by the public as pure fabrications not corresponding to reality, future POAU's will have to choose new "issues."

Thus, by exposing the errors of current controversies the ultimate goal of this volume will be accomplished; namely, to reduce greatly the choice of issues upon which future POAU's will be able profitably to seize. Of course, the immediate goal of this books has been to demonstrate the true nature of current controversies and to document the fact that POAU, prime instigator of attacks on Catholicism, is an organization whose tactics are to be condemned, and whose leaders are to be pitied and repudiated.

APPENDIX

THE following is the full text of a POAU pamphlet written by C. Stanley Lowell, associate director of the organization. Mr. Lowell's article should be read prior to Part III of this book.

RISING TEMPO OF ROME'S DEMANDS

The year 1948 marked the beginning of a new epoch in the American history of the Roman Catholic Church and the beginning of a new epoch in American history itself. In November of that year the leaders of this powerful church undertook a drastic reorientation of their attitude toward the United States government. It was a change not of conviction but of strategy, not of direction but of pace; yet the new strategy and the new pace were so striking as to constitute in themselves a major change. The statement of the Bishops issued at that time will repay thoughtful reading by every American. These men serve notice that the vast power of their organization will henceforth be devoted to destroying the principle of Church-State separation.

When the Bishops sound the call to action, their language is clear. They say plainly that "Separation of Church and State has become the shibboleth of doctrinaire secularism." They pledge themselves to "work peacefully, patiently and perseveringly" for its destruction. Thus, with a bold announcement supported by the cleverest of propaganda, this powerful church has set out to destroy the free position of the American churches.

THEN AND NOW

This change in Roman Catholic strategy is expressed in the church's attitude toward education. During much of the nineteenth century, its hierarchy was concerned to [sic] eliminate from the public schools every reference to God, the Bible and religion and to make the schools strictly secular institutions. Roman Catholics brought more than one hundred cases before the courts to achieve these objectives. I cite here but one of the hundred — that of *People ex rel. Ring v. Board of Education in Illinois*. In this case Roman Catholics sought to eliminate Bible reading and devotional exercises from the public-school program. The court agreed with their contention that these practices did violate Church-State separation as expressed in the Constitution and ordered them discontinued.

Roman Catholics undertook to drive religion out of the schools not because they were atheistic or secularistic people, but because they were not powerful enough to determine the kind of religion to be taught. They preferred no religious teaching at all if they could not have Roman Catholic dogma. The provincial council of the Roman Catholic Church in Baltimore, 1840, imposed on priests the responsibility of seeing to it that Catholic children attending public schools did not participate in any religious exercises there. They were also to use their influence to prevent any such practices in the public schools.

The "secular public school" was in substantial part the achievement of the Roman Catholic Church. Today, however, this church has about-faced. Today it denounces the secular public school as "godless" and argues loudly for the return of religion to education. Today movements for the teaching of "moral and spiritual values" in the public schools, like the recent one in New York City, find the hierarchy in hearty endorsement. The change of front is due to one simple fact — the Roman hierarchy now feels strong enough to permeate any public-school moral and spiritual teaching with its own dogma, or to secure public funds for its own private, sectarian schools.

TOWARD A NEW ERA

The 1948 pronouncement of the Roman Catholic Bishops pointed the way to a new era in American Church-State relations. As far as Rome was concerned, this pronouncement marked the end of the line for Church-State separation. The principle that had received grudging recognition from this group as long as it was a weak, ineffectual minority was now to be replaced by one more in keeping with the main line of Romanist tradition.

The resources of this powerful church were quickly marshaled for action. The Roman Church claims a membership of 33 million in the United States, which has become in the hands of the hierarchy a gigantic battering ram to breach the wall of separation. The adults in this membership comprise the "Catholic vote" of which we hear so much. There are, comparatively, not many Catholics holding high public office. This is actually a source of strength to the hierarchy since it is able to keep in perpetual intimidation the Protestant officeholders who fear nothing more than that the "Catholic vote" might be turned against them.

This political power is skillfully wielded to secure preferential treatment for the Roman Church. A good example is the nearly $1 million voted by the Eighty-fourth Congress to refurbish the Pope's summer palace. The payment was for damages allegedly inflicted by American bombs upon a neutral power in World War II. The summer palace was not located in Vatican City, however, and the damage, according to impartial observers, was negligible. This subsidy to the Pope went through as a high-level, nonpartisan item. No one would have thought of voting against it. To do so might have offended the "Catholic vote."

A far more serious matter was House Bill 6568 [*sic*], which was smuggled through the Senate in the confusion before adjournment of the Eighty-fourth Congress. This provides another $8 million plus for Roman Catholic activities in the Philippines. After the war, American lobbyists visited the Philippines and alerted Roman Catholic officials to the rich potential in "war services" and "war damages." The church collected for services allegedly suffered to its installations. The Bishop of Zamboanga, the Archbishop of Jaro, the Daughters of Charity of St. Vincent de Paul and the Knights of Columbus were among the Roman Catholic groups receiving generous grants. How many millions were paid is difficult for an outsider to determine.

The above mentioned act merely amended the law so that Archbishop Santos of Manila, whose "claims" had been rejected by the Commission, could get his millions along with the millions that had gone to his colleagues. Although the sum was "only $8 million," it should be recalled that the Archbishop's claims originally ran to $30 million. All of these claims will no doubt be revived, while others from the innumerable church orders will be added. All will be paid in time. Oh yes, there is a chance that the Protestants may qualify for about $30,000 under H. R. 6586.

The public schools of the Philippines received not one cent. Nor will they, because they lack a high-powered lobby and the unveiled threat of reprisal at the polls.

SECTARIAN SUBSIDIES UNLIMITED

There have been other government subsidies to the Roman Church. The Hill-Burton Act, which authorized Federal grants to sectarian hospitals, has been a bonanza to this church. Under it the Roman Catholics have collected $112,039,000 for their institutions. Protestant institutions have received $23,118,000. Even the disparity of these figures does not tell the story. Close observers have noted the large proportion of the grants that have gone to Roman Catholic hospitals in the South. In Alabama alone, for example, this church has obtained $6 million for its hospitals. Baptist churches with a total adult membership about equal to the Roman Catholic have a conscientious objection to taking Federal funds. Only a pittance, therefore, has gone to this group. What is worse, businessmen have begun to refuse to contribute to Baptist hospital campaigns, asking, "Why don't you get your money from the government the way the Catholics do?"

The Roman Church has found the Hill-Burton Act a marvelous means for penetrating the hitherto impervious Protestantism of the South. Handsome healing centers built with Federal funds serve as a strong means for the propagation of this faith.

The campaign to shift the cost of Roman Catholic sectarian schools to the American taxpayer bids fair to be as successful as the hospital program. The campaign began easily as fringe benefits were sought from the government — bus transportation, textbooks, health benefits, lunches and the like. More recently, as for example in the Bishop's [*sic*] statement issued in November 1955, there is insistence upon the "full right to be considered and dealt with as components of the American educational system." This statement also claims for parochial-school pupils the same government aid that goes to public-school pupils.

A useful gimmick in softening the public for sectarian subsidies is the so-called "study" of education. Proposals for a "study" were slipped through the Connecticut legislature as a "noncontroversial" item. No sooner had the commission begun its work when there began a spate of press releases about how many children were in parochial schools, the proportion of the educational load being carried by the Roman Catholic Church, the "saving" thus effected to the taxpayer. Presently Roman Catholic leaders throughout the state joined in a well-directed chorus appealing for state subsidies. The demands were based on the commission's "scientific study."

During the past year the drive for tax support has developed yet a new twist. This is a demand that tuition payments to parochial schools be allowable income tax deductions. The fiftieth annual convention of the Knights of St. John meeting in Dayton, Ohio, and the Central Catholic Verein meeting in Wichita, Kansas, are among the many Roman Catholic groups that have appealed to Congress for this kind of "relief." Thus a back-door assault on the public treasury keeps pace with the front-door demand.

In many communities where they are in the majority, Roman Catholics have simply taken over the public schools. They have staffed them with nuns and priests whose salaries, paid from state funds, go directly to their superior, without deductions. It took long and expensive litigations to clear up situations of this kind in Missouri, New Mexico and Kentucky. There are still numerous "trouble spots" all around the country. Last year in Indiana, for example, more than $2 million in tax funds went to "public schools" that were in effect parochial schools of the Roman Church. There are 152 garbed nuns teaching in the public schools of Kansas with their salaries going to their church.

A MAJOR DECISION

In simple justice it must be said that the Roman Catholic hierarchy is now within sight of its goal. Success has come even faster than its leaders dreamed. Many activities of this church are already receiving tax support. Hospitals, schools, orphanages and other "welfare programs" are in this category. Other activities receive sizable grants from community chests. The measure of this support is being constantly increased. The time is in sight when all the so-called "social service" activities of the Roman Church will be supported by tax funds collected by compulsion from citizens of all faiths.

The Protestants, if they are realistic, will see but two alternatives before them. One, they must accept the principle of government subsidies to churches — that is, the principle of plural establishment — and get into the scramble to get all they can for their own denomination. Or, two, they must stop kidding themselves with the false tolerance that plays into Rome's hands, and battle to hold the line for Church-State separation.

The first of these alternatives — plural establishment — would have definite advantages over the "don't look now" policy being presently followed by the Protestants. If the Protestants were to go all-out for government subsidies, they would probably be able to rectify the absurd inequities of the Hill-Burton grants. They must recognize, however, that in changing from the principle of voluntarism to the principle of official compulsion, they are taking a drastic step, which will have the most far-reaching consequences. Also, and this is a more practical matter, they are moving into competition with old hands at this business of obtaining political favors. It is a kind of competition that, because of their own predilections, the Protestants stand to lose.

Westerly, Rhode Island, is a tiny community that offers a good sample of the sort of thing we might expect under plural establishment. The Roman Catholics of Westerly, having developed their own schools to the point where certain public school buildings were no longer needed, proceeded to take them over for their own use. The town council voted them to the Roman Church at a purchase price of $1. The Methodists of Westerly were resentful as they saw these valuable properties falling to the Roman Catholics, one by one. They decided to get one for themselves. After working some wheels within wheels and getting help from Catholic citizens who believed in "fair play" — they were able to get one of the buildings for $1. Since their success, however, there has been a rash of such giveaways in Rhode Island. The recipient has been, in every instance, the Roman Catholic Church. Now that the principle has been accepted and "the Methodists are doing it too," there is no restraint.

The worst feature of plural establishment, however, would be the extremity of its pluralism. Our culture would be hopelessly enclaved as 250 religious establishments or more threw themselves into the wild scramble for tax funds. The principle beneficiary would be the church that is prepared for an operation of this kind, a church that has, in fact, lived on state subsidies for many centuries.

THE ALTERNATIVE

The alternative is clear. Protestants must face this challenge frankly at the political level. As the Roman Church moves toward state financing and toward those favors which are the precursor of establishment, Protestants must stand in resolute opposition. They must do this in good humor and brotherliness, but with unbending firmness. The Roman Catholic propaganda that softens the nation for official favors must be dispassionately exposed. Protestants must recognize that they are not promoting secularism when they insist that the Roman Catholic Church shall raise its funds the way other churches do, or when they insist that there shall be no official favors or preferments for any church.

Roman Catholicism in the United States has come a long way in a century and a half. At first, as a feeble minority it accepted Church-State separation. The principle seemed best in the circumstances. Now, as a powerful minority — united in the midst of a divided majority — it calls for the end of Church-State separation. It intimidates Congress, censors and silences opposition, collects vast sums from the public treasury and drives toward official recognition and establishment. If the Protestants do not unite in determined opposition to this drive, another decade will see the end of Church-State separation here. We shall have, to all practical effect, a religious establishment in a country whose Constitution forbids it. That establishment will be pluralistic — or otherwise.

INDEX

Action Committee for Freedom of Religious Expression, 102

Adams, J. Q., 135

Alabama, Catholic hospitals, 189 f; ministers support POAU, 2

Allegiance, Catholic civil, 106, 112 ff, 119 f; oath of, to Vatican, 105 f

Alter, Archbishop Karl, on ambassador to Vatican, 126; on Church-State separation, 120, 226 f

Ambassador to Vatican, 108, 116 f, 124 ff; question on, 114

America, on POAU, 18

American Association of School Administrators, on private-public school relations, 79

American Bar Association, *Journal* of, on First Amendment, 165 f; on O'Neill's book, 245

ACLU, on boycott, 94; on Martin Luther film, 102; on POAU, 20

American Council of Christian Churches, and Catholic candidates for presidency, 18

American Council of Christian Laymen, on POAU, 2

American Freedom and Catholic Power, New York Times review of, 15

American Jewish Committee, on Dr. Herberg, 142

American Medical Association, on Catholic medical practices, 57 ff; on POAU, 69; on staffing of hospitals, 58 f

APA, American Council of Christian Laymen, reference to, 2; anti-Catholic, 24; and Bible in public schools, 168

American Protestant Defense League (APDL), 25

American Protestant Hospital Association, on hospitals in Alabama, 189 f

Anti-Catholic groups, APA, 24; APDL, 25 f; Blanshard definition of, 40; Council of Christian Churches, 26; Know-Nothings, 23; Order of United Americans, 22

Anti-Catholicism, POAU and, 26

Archer, G. L., biography of, 15; Catholic control of public schools, 75 f; on Catholic marriage, 135 f; on Catholic medicine, 58; Catholic president, 119; and Catholics suing priests, 134; communism and Catholicism, 28; democracy and Catholicism, 47; on Hildy McCoy, 129; on *imprimatur,* 5 f; on Martin Luther film, 97; on religious test, 116 f; reply to criticism by T. G. Sanders, 138 f; on Stanley Lichtenstein, 123, 144 ff

Atlantic Monthly, and Alfred E. Smith, 112

Baltimore, Council of (1840), on education, 171 f

Baptist Joint Conference Committee, on POAU, 11

Baptists, and Hill-Burton aid, 188 f; Jefferson letter to, 242 f; support POAU, 13, 17 f

Bellandi, Mauro, 132 ff

Bible, King James, 167 f; in public schools, 166 ff

Bigotry, Catholic, toward public schools, 70

Bill for Establishing Religious Freedom in Virginia, 244

Billington, Ray A., *The Protestant Crusade,* on Bible in public schools, 167 ff

Birth control, 62 ff Blanshard on, 64; definition of, 63; legislation against, 63

Blaine, J. G., presidential candidate, 117 f

Blanshard, Paul, *American Freedom and Catholic Power,* birth control, 64; anti-Catholic, 19; on "Augustinian conception," of sex, 67; biography of, 15; on birth control, 66; Catholic civil alle-